THE BODY MERCHANT

EARL CARROLL
**The most notorious connoisseur of female flesh
in the history of show business**

THE BODY MERCHANT

THE STORY OF EARL CARROLL

BY KEN MURRAY

WARD RITCHIE PRESS PASADENA, CALIFORNIA

FIRST EDITION

LIBRARY OF CONGRESS CATALOG CARD NUMBER: 75-41820
ISBN: 0378-05685-9

Gratitude is expressed to the following for permission to use previously copyrighted materials:

Robert Lewis Taylor
For extracts from *W. C. Fields, His Follies and Fortunes.* Doubleday & Co., 1949.

Frederick Fell Publishers
For extracts from *I'll Cry Tomorrow* (1954), by Lillian Roth.

Harry Grogin
Who originated the composographs for the New York *Evening Graphic.*

Front photo section/p. 7: top and bottom, *left;* top, *right.*

Wide World Photos, Inc.

Front photo section/p. 7: bottom, *right* (Earl Carroll and wife)
p. 10: bottom, *left* (Hollywood Theatre Restaurant, exterior).

United Press International

Front photo section/ p. 2: top, *left* (Earl Carroll at piano, 1917)
p. 3: top, *right* (Earl Carroll with telephone)
p. 3: bottom, *half* (Peggy Hopkins Joyce with car)
p. 5: bottom, *half* (Kathryn Ray and Earl Carroll)
p. 6: bottom, *half* (Courtroom scene)
Back photo section/ p. 2: bottom, *right* (Girl wrapped in fur).

The remainder of the photographs in this book are from the author's private collection.

PRINTED IN THE UNITED STATES OF AMERICA

FOR JIM CARROLL   *Earl never had a*
                    more devoted brother
                    and I never had
                    a better friend

IN APPRECIATION

The compilation of a book of this nature presents some unimaginable difficulties and cannot be accomplished single-handedly. It involves a lot of people-bothering, and the cooperation and generosity of many individuals and institutions were necessary from the commencement to the completion.

The author gratefully acknowledges the assistance of: Jack Holland, Beverly Carroll Newman, Milton Berle, Lillian Roth, Rudy Vallée, Connie Krebs, Bob Thomas, Harry Grogin, LeRoy Prinz, Teet Carle, Milt Larson, Gene Lester, John Reed, Art Linkletter, Walter Wagner, Beverly Thompson, David Cohn, Margaret Miller, Beryl Wallace's niece Billee Udko, film historian Kirk Crivello, and officials at the Atlanta State Penitentiary.

Special and permanent reference is also due here to my editor-publisher William S. Chleboun, members of his staff—Ann Harris, Neysa Moss, and Ruth Hoover, and my wife Bette Lou, whose untiring counsel and help made this whole project possible.

To all of the above I am their debtor for help that I could not only never repay, but don't even know how to give thanks.

Ken Murray
Beverly Hills

Girls are a commodity the same as bananas, pork chops, or a lot in a suburban development. They are the most fundamental of all commodities. Girls like to admire beautiful girls, and men unquestionably do, and they will all pay for this pleasure. Of course, this leads to my making money, thus satisfying my material as well as artistic desire.

From Earl Carroll's
unfinished autobiography
Through Those Portals Passed

Prologue

Will Rogers once said he never met a man he didn't like. Evidently, he never met Earl Carroll—the most notorious connoisseur of female flesh in the history of show business.

Quiet and soft-spoken, Earl Carroll was a tall, thin, almost gaunt man with a handsome physical delicacy that reminded one of a cameo. His sensitive face had high cheek bones, penetrating eyes, and a jaw like a western hero, but his hair, worn long in the back, recalled more the image of a country parson, and his ministerial demeanor belied the tough, offensive, dominating man who ran roughshod through life. Perhaps, it was these seemingly incompatible attributes that gave him an undeniable appeal to women. W. C. Fields nicknamed him, "Preacher with an erection."

Best remembered for his lavish girlie reviews—Earl Carroll's *Vanities* ("Through These Portals Pass the Most Beautiful Girls in the World"), patterned after the very successful Ziegfeld *Follies*—it is safe to say that Earl Carroll became Florenz Ziegfeld's closest rival during the peak of the Broadway Beauty Trust, and while no one will deny that Ziegfeld was the pioneer of musical extravaganzas in America, few will dispute the claim that Earl Carroll was the *greatest showman* of modern times.

He was a master publicist, had a natural flair for selling things in all media, and his large, flamboyant shows lent themselves to exploitation.

True, his methods left something to be desired, and, combined with a sanctimonious facade, there was often something cheap, tawdry, and sleazy about his publicity-conscious stunts.

This was to cause him numerous brushes with the law in the ensuing years, and to lead to a prison term in a federal penitentiary.

So, it's very doubtful that "old Will" could have ever "cottoned up" to this bizarre young producer who liked to believe that he could charm the pants off anyone and went around proving it by persuading all the pretty young hopefuls who sought to be a "Carroll Beauty" to audition for him completely in the *nude*.

Will Rogers was, of course, no stranger to girlie shows. He starred for more than 10 years in the *Follies* for Florenz Ziegfeld. Having witnessed "The Great Glorifier" try out his aspiring applicants in bathing suits (the standard procedure for all Broadway producers), it's almost a certainty that the old cowboy philosopher, with his homespun respect for "women folk," would have been offended, if not horrified, by the well-founded rumors of Carroll's outrageous procedure of sitting in the front row of a darkened theatre, wearing a black tam and a pale blue artist's smock, while an endless line of *naked* nymphs paraded past him on the fully lighted stage.

Carroll then would have all the girls line up in rows of twenty—the tall ones together and the short ones together. At the command "Now, face front!" the girls would march down to the footlights as he cast an understandably appreciative eye over them. With the next order, "About face!" they would march to the rear as Broadway's champion flesh peddler checked the most important requisite of a Carroll Beauty—undulating hips. All his life, Earl Carroll seemed obsessed by the exploitation of sex, and he had a perverted fascination for the intimacies of the female form.

Carroll spent most of his life surrounded and pursued by beautiful women, yet after one ill-fated matrimonial venture he never married again—though there were two women who were destined to play important roles in his life.

The first was an attractive, rich widow, a nonprofessional, Mrs. Jessie Schuyler—tall, well-bred, stunning, slightly older than Carroll.

The other was a voluptuous, raven-haired beauty, Beryl Wallace.

They were both in that church at Forest Lawn Memorial Park on that bright California day of June 28, 1948.

End of the Beginning

Earl Carroll's body lay in a casket draped with flowers on the altar of the Church of the Recessional.

The organ music droned on softly, lending an air of hushed solemnity. The heavy scent of flowers permeated the church—65 varieties of roses from Mr. Carroll's own garden, and, on either side of the altar, two floral pieces shaped like life-sized, costumed showgirls, sent by faithful beauties he had glorified.

And they were all there—those chorus girls, those delectable exponents of the "form divine." Some who were crying dabbed handkerchiefs gently at mascaraed eyes; others seemed to show no emotion at all. They were joined by a score of friends, some mourning for one reason, some for another.

I suddenly found myself looking at the show people who were there, among them Al Jolson, Lillian Roth, William Powell, Vincent Minnelli, and Robert Young.

I watched Jack Benny and Milton Berle enter the church. I knew why *they* were there. For the same reason I was. To pay respects to the man, Earl Carroll, who had the faith to give us our first shot in a Broadway show.

The strains of "Ah! Sweet Mystery of Life," played on the violin by Felix Slatkin, faded out as the minister approached the pulpit.

The Reverend A. J. Soldan, pastor of the Village Church of Westwood, who some years later was to conduct services for another member of his parish—Marilyn Monroe—began his eulogy:

"We are here today to pay our last respects to a man whose name is etched in the annals of the theatre...."

I didn't listen too much to the sermon. It glorified Earl. It made him more than he was, but most funeral services do. They are so often garish, insincere, even hypocritical. The truth a man leaves behind him often is obscured by the fiction that is dreamed up. Wasn't it enough that Earl Carroll made lights a little brighter on Broadway, especially in those dark Depression days, and to the end of his life was still bringing joy and happiness, in the splashy way Carroll made so famous, to millions of GIs who passed through Hollywood on their way to the Pacific war zone?

Tolerant of all religions, an early champion of civil rights—he was the first to produce a play on Broadway in which a white man married a beautiful black girl *(White Cargo)*—however self-serving he conducted a lifelong fight against what he considered the injustices of censorship.

He was a man of strange contrasts. You might have hated his guts at times, but you had to admit that he was a man you couldn't help liking. A man you could not forget.

As Reverend Soldan finished his sermon in solemn, resonant tones, muffled sobs could be heard from the beautiful showgirls. To them, this was the death of "Daddy" Carroll. It also marked the end of an era, the end of the brassiness, the superficial, the glitter, the glamour, the sex, the complete production of praise to the beauty of the female body, and, in a way, the final salute to the commercialization of that sexual appeal. Final, at least, in the Carroll style.

Others would follow who would use that same appeal, like Hugh Hefner and his titillating *Playboy* and Russ Meyer with his explicit porno flicks. But *unlike* Hefner and Meyer, who sell their wares with still pictures and celluloid, Earl Carroll persistently tried to share with his public the real thing. A mental nudist, he brought to the American theatre a fundamental sense of realism, stark, revealing, intense in its bareness.

If there were one big impediment to the Carroll chronicle, it was that he was born too early—or died too soon. If ever a man belonged to this present day and age of excessive permissiveness in show business, it was the "Earl of Pittsburgh," as he was affectionately known to his fellow townspeople in later years.

As the mourners prepared to leave the church, I recognized the distinguished middle-aged woman sitting alone in the first pew. It was the attractive Mrs. Jessie Schuyler, her face seemingly expressionless, her eyes ever so often looking longingly at the casket.

Less than 10 feet away was the younger girl, Beryl Wallace—lying in another casket beside the mangled remains of the man they both loved.

The church was empty now. The music had stopped. I took one look back at the two caskets draped in flowers. I couldn't help thinking how much Earl would have approved of the service—and, as he had to die some day, of leaving this world in the dramatic, shattering way he did, in an accident that has no equal in aviation history.

As two attendants closed the portals of the church, I thought of the irony of fate. If *only* that flip of the coin had gone the other way, Earl Carroll and Beryl Wallace might still be here today.

But that is another story—an unbelievable story.

THE BODY MERCHANT

EARL CARROLL LOST HIS VIRGINITY at the tender age of thirteen. His seductress was a chorus girl, and it happened in a dressing room of a theatre in Pittsburgh.

Young Earl was tall and gangling, with shoulders that were oddly too large for his body. Every day he would pedal his bicycle to Allegheny High School. Academic work failed to interest him; the Gaiety Theatre, which he passed twice a day, stimulated him much more than his studies ever could.

The lobby was always filled with big colored pictures of funny-faced men and of ladies in fancy dresses. He was especially intrigued by the ladies wearing fancy dresses.

Some of the ladies didn't wear dresses at all.

Of course, he thought about sex a lot. He heard bits and pieces from the older boys at school, but he really didn't understand it.

For weeks, Earl yearned to discover what wonderful world lay beyond the entranceway. All those women in their flashy costumes—what exactly did they do? Standing outside the theatre, he would stare at the blazing lights and listen to the hubbub that to him almost enshrined the building. He would gape longingly at the crowds entering the theatre. He had an overwhelming curiosity to see what was going on inside.

One afternoon, Earl summoned up enough courage to march into the lobby and point-blank ask the manager for a job. To his complete amazement, he was hired on the spot as a program boy, and was soon getting a glimpse of the world he was to spend his life in.

He was transported into a fantastic realm of music and color and laughter, where women in gay costumes sang and danced, and funny men said and did things that made everyone laugh. He had never seen anything so wonderful before, and he kept clapping long after everybody else had stopped.

After that, he practically lived in the theatre. He neglected his books, played hooky from school, and arrived at the theatre hours before the curtain went up. Backstage was a wonderland of surprise, and he hung around after each performance until the last stagehand was gone. The actors had to chase him from their dressing rooms and he pestered the stage crew with questions.

His only disappointment was the chorus girls. When they took off their long golden curls, pretty dresses, and high heels, most of them turned out to be tired, unglamorous women whose long, flat breasts hung down like a pair of cocker spaniel's ears, and who swore more glibly than any of the stagehands.

That is, all except Trixie. She was the youngest of the troupe, although several years older than Earl. She had flaming red hair, big brown eyes, and an hourglass figure that rivaled Lillian Russell's. To him she epitomized what was considered great beauty at that time, and he had a terrific boyhood crush on this flashy lady.

He would gaze at her in silent and wistful homage as she applied makeup before performances. While she was singing and dancing on the stage, Earl, at every opportunity, would watch spellbound from the wings, mentally noting her every move, her every nuance, and his heart would beat faster.

The ladies in the company—and the men, too—noticed Earl's calf-like looks whenever he saw Trixie and were amused.

But he was still the only virgin in the theatre. Not from any moral compunction, but because he was too young, too naive, and too scared. Every public toilet ominously proclaimed the danger of venereal disease, and every growing boy knew that masturbation caused softening of the brain and, if indulged in too frequently, would cause hair to grow in the palm of the hand.

His celibacy made him the butt of jibes on stage as well as off. The comics especially made him the target of asides that the audience sometimes understood and roared at, and even the chorus girls kidded and taunted him. But not for long.

Came a night when he was leaving the theatre very late and passed the open door of a dressing room where Trixie and two other girls were removing their makeup. When they saw him they started to giggle uncontrollably.

Trixie called to him and said sweetly, "Earl, I wonder if you'd be a nice boy and run down and get us some beer?"

Delighted at the opportunity to do Trixie a favor, and thrilled by the touch of her hand as she gave him the money, Earl quickly left the room; as he left he heard the girls cackling even louder.

When he returned, Trixie was alone in the room. The others, she said, had suddenly been called out on a date. Now she was wearing only a sheer dressing gown.

Thirteen years old—he began to feel he was growing up fast. As his eyes searched through the transparent material that hung over her body, he could see the outlines of her breasts. He looked excitedly at the nipples that peeped through the material. Then his eyes traveled downward to her thighs, and then to a strange-looking patch of dark hair between her legs. It was the first time he had ever seen a woman like this. He thought his heart would leap out of his chest, and he was confused by the feelings, bewildered but excited.

Earl turned to leave, even though he wanted to stay.

"Don't you want to kiss me goodnight?" Trixie asked coyly.

Earl looked at her shyly. He didn't know what to do. Trixie sat down on the dressing room cot, her negligee falling open, and said, "Come here, honey." She leaned over and kissed him on the mouth. But it was a strange kiss. He felt her tongue moving between his lips, between his teeth. It was exploring his mouth like a snake ready to strike. He didn't know what he was supposed to do, so he just let her kiss him—and tried to kiss her back.

She then unbuckled the belt of his knickers and with busy hands started exploring, causing Earl's insides to tingle and to swell and tighten with desire. He felt he was going to explode. He felt helpless, frantic, exhilarated, full of expectancy—and then the fire began to burn.

Within moments, they were lying on the cold cement floor, writhing and panting. Earl's mind went blank except for that one animalistic desire that was screaming and tearing inside of him. His heart raced faster than he ever dreamed possible. His head was beating, his limbs were swelling, his breathing became dying gasps. And then it was over.

He was completely exhausted, and while he was hurriedly and nervously adjusting his clothes, the closet door opened and out burst the other two girls.

"You win!" they laughingly exclaimed and handed his seductress the two quarters she had won on the wager.

Filled with humiliation, he turned his eyes pleadingly to Trixie. She was laughing the loudest. He was hurt, confused. He didn't know people could be like that.

He merely stood there dumbfounded and stared at the laughing girls. They kept laughing and laughing. Their laughter built to a terrible crescendo.

What effect this traumatic experience had on Earl Carroll's future relationships with women can only be imagined.

He was glad when the troupe moved on that week, as the comedians all but announced the event from the stage while the rest of the company giggled over his discomfiture.

On the last night of their engagement, in his role as the company's errand boy, he was to experience another trauma, but under vastly different circumstances.

He was sent on an unsavory mission by a musician who was a feature attraction in the olio. Though born in Brooklyn, he was billed as "Ramon—the Gypsy Violinist." With black hair and a dark complexion, he was a picturesque figure in the spotlight, and played with such fire and skill that he held even the roughnecks in the audience spellbound with classic compositions. Musicians in the pit invariably joined in the applause and commented that he could have been a great concert soloist. Unfortunately, the violinist was a drug addict. Opium was his habit, and he carried with him a hop-head's complete layout. He had a frayed memorandum book on a page of which were inked some Chinese characters. He would give Earl this book and a quarter, and instruct him to go into any Chinese laundry and, by showing the Chinese inscription, obtain the familiar little black gob of opium.

Late one night he called Earl into his dressing room. He was stretched out on the cot. His sunken eyes lit up when he saw the boy.

"Please, kid," he pleaded, "see if you can get it for me someplace, will you?" His hands shook like twigs in a windstorm as he handed Earl the book and a quarter.

Earl roamed the dark, deserted streets of Pittsburgh until he discovered a Chinese laundry where a small light was burning in the back of the store. In answer to his persistent banging, a small, tired Chinaman finally came to the door.

"What your problem, Charley? It middle of night. Go home. Come again tomorrow."

"Please! I've got to talk to you!"

"Nothing tonight, Charley. Go blow."

Earl pressed the book of inscriptions against the glass in the door. The Chinaman smiled and hurriedly opened the door.

"Why you not say so in first place, Charley? Wait here." The Chinaman ran into the back, softly giggling to himself. He returned quickly with a playing card into which the opium was folded. Still giggling, he handed it to Earl.

"Maybe you become regular customer, Charley? Good and cheap!"

Earl thanked him and left.

When he returned to the theatre, he discovered a nude woman's figure perched drowsily on the gypsy's cot in the dressing room. He had never seen her before—outside "talent," probably someone Ramon had picked up. She was obviously interested in the Brooklyn gypsy, but he was more interested in the opium.

"I thought you'd never get back," Ramon growled. "Give it to me. Hurry, dammit!"

Ramon grabbed the yen hock, cooked the pill, and filled a long-stemmed pipe. As he blissfully sucked in the soothing fumes, his taut face relaxed and his hands stopped trembling. Earl was relieved. He was almost afraid of Ramon when he didn't have his opium. Earl liked him much better this way. Ramon smiled at him more.

Hospitably he passed the pipe around and invited Earl to share it. As a further demonstration of his recently acquired manhood, Earl took a few draws. He had witnessed others smoking the pipe. Especially the gypsy violinist. It was simple. You just draw in the smoke—

For a few moments, Earl was the happiest person in Pittsburgh. And then—bam! It hit! Whatever it was, Earl felt like he had just been run over by a cement truck. His stomach started quivering and his head seemed to twist from his body and start to do somersaults around the room. He barely managed to stand.

"Whassa matter, kid? Ya want some more?"

"No, I gotta leave—"

"Aw c'mon, kid. Stay a little while longer."

"No, really, I—really gotta go—"

Somehow, Earl found the stage door of the theatre, and stumbled out into the brisk night air. His head still involved in exhaustive acrobatics, his legs still desperately trying to keep up with the rest of his body, Earl staggered to his home. At least he thought it was his home. All the houses quizzically looked alike. It didn't matter—it was a house. And all he wanted to do was fall on a bed and pass out. Any bed.

He soon discovered that he was in his own home, and he reeled into the bedroom he shared with his older brother Jim.

"Earl, where the hell have you been? Do you know what time it is? What do you *do* in that damn theatre?"

Earl stood in the total darkness beside his brother's bed, searching for the face that accompanied the voice. Finally, Jim switched on the night light and gasped at the limp figure by his bedpost.

"Earl, for God's sake, what happened? What's the matter?"

Bursting into tears, Earl threw his arms around his brother's neck and cried, "Oh, Jim—I'm a hophead—*I'm a hophead!*"

"That was Earl's first and last experience as an opium smoker," Jim recalled years later as we sat in my dressing room at the Winter Garden on Broadway.

Jim Carroll was a big, likeable, robust man, a typical hard-working product of the turn of the century. He began his career working as a motorman on the Pittsburgh trolleys, and from the time his young brother was born, Jim took Earl under his wing, guided him through his formative years. Earl adored him. He became Earl's closest friend and confidant, and through the turbulent years of Earl's theatrical career, it was the 240-pounder, Jim, who was always beside his brother when Earl needed him.

I got to know this lovable redhead well, when I was working for Earl in *Sketch Book of 1935*. Jim was kindness itself, a man I totally admired. As I remember, he told me that their father, James Carroll, and mother, Elizabeth Wills, both came from County Cork, Ireland, and became naturalized citizens of the United States in 1891. They ran a small hotel in Pittsburgh at 224 Henderson Street, on the north side, where Earl was born September 21, 1892.

There are, as one turns back to the dear, dim period of Earl's panty days, no heartaches, no privation, nothing to indicate, in the sweet story of his childhood, that our little Fauntleroy was to become the Bacchante of Broadway.

I was surprised to learn from Jim that as a kid, Earl's first love was not show business—it was aviation.

"It probably all started on the night of December 18, 1903," Jim recalled as the love of remembrance lit up his face.

"Earl was eleven years old when the whole family was sitting around the kitchen table and Pop read from the front page of the Pittsburgh *Press* about the Wright brothers making their first flight in that contraption of muslin and wire.

"Pop said: 'Imagine! Bicycle makers flying like birds!' "

"Practical Mama just shook her head and with a wave of her hand immediately dismissed the subject: 'Haven't they got anything better to do? Only a maniac would risk his life trying to fly.' "

But Jim said he could see that the news impressed Earl deeply, and from that time on he was hooked—he read everything he could about that new invention, the aeroplane.

He marveled at Louis Bleriot flying the English Channel ("Imagine, at the tremendous speed of 48 miles per hour!"); and at Teddy Roosevelt putting on goggles and taking his first flight in the new "Wright Flyer" (he waved to the people below and thought flying was "bully"). Earl was fascinated and amused when the Wright brothers took up their first woman passenger—Mrs. Hart O. Berg (there was much nervous laughter on the field when Orville had to tie down her skirts lest they blow into the pilot's face).

The first time young Earl ever saw a kite-like craft in the sky with a man in it, he stood transfixed, Jim recalled. "He actually had tears in his eyes. It was at a county fair I took him to near Mt. Carmel, Pennsylvania. He watched Lincoln Beachey, the famous loop-the-loop artist, perform, and when he saw Bill Otis, one of the first barnstorming pilots, taking up daredevil sightseers at $2 a crack, he persuaded me to let him take his first flight."

Jim went on to say that from that day on, Earl never lost his love for aviation and said many times he was so deeply impressed by that experience that whenever he saw an aeroplane in flight, he had a feeling of awe and reverence.

As Earl Carroll approached his seventeenth birthday, he was far ahead of his years on the road to maturity. He had graduated from Allegheny High, and, having achieved his theatrical ambitions in his home town (he was now supervising the distribution of programs in all the Pittsburgh theatres), he became restless and decided to see the world.

Against the horrified objections of his mother and father, but with the financial help of his brother Jim, he got to New York where he signed up as a cabin boy on a ship bound for the Orient. He arrived in the Philippine Islands, and years later (December 14, 1924), the New York *Times* recorded in a biographical story, "Pittsburgh Producer," that he was "probably the youngest white boy to land in Manila alone."

From there, he soon found himself in Hong Kong as assistant editor of one of the few English newspapers, called the *Typhoon*. His journalistic venture lasted but two weeks, when the publication collapsed for lack of funds.

Out of a job again, but undaunted and undismayed, the future Broadway producer joined a group of missionaries and became a *Bible salesman*. His route took him into the interior of China, where he tramped with the armies of various warlords. Those were the days in the early part of the century when a series of revolutions went off all over the great land of China as if on a giant string of firecrackers, the first and most Fourth-of-July of which was the Freedom Revolution of Sun Yat Sen.

It was this experience in China that provided the inspiration for the first play Earl Carroll wrote—*The Lady of the Lamp*, a romantic fantasy about a young American who visits Chinatown and there is introduced to his first pipe of opium. (Sound familiar?) He is transformed, Aladdin-like, into a warlord in ancient China, and fights for the beautiful princess against the wicked Manchus. Upon awakening, he discovers that the worshipped princess exists as an American girl. He sent copies of the play to most of the leading producers in New York City, including David Belasco, A. H. Woods, and Charles Frohman, but even with including the Chinese invention of gunpowder, for melodramatic complication, he received no response.

Having "spread the gospel" in China, he decided to try his fortune in Japan. Among other things, he organized, managed, and pitched for a baseball team composed of eight Japanese and himself. Flushed with the success of his team, Earl Carroll entered into negotiations with the New York Giants and Yankees to come to Japan and play the leading native teams, but nothing came of this project. And so, tired of his Japanese sojourn, the young wanderer made trips to Port Said, Indochina, and stopped for a breathing spell in Palestine. Here his travels were cut short when he received a cablegram from Jim notifying him of their father's death and urging him to come home.

Earl returned to Pittsburgh and for a time accepted a job as treasurer of the Nixon Theatre. But his heart wasn't in the front of the theatre, it was in the back, on the stage. Still determined to get his play, *The Lady of the Lamp*, produced, after trying unsuccessfully to interest the management in presenting it, he felt he must tackle Broadway. He managed somehow to reach New York and took up living on the east side, practically penniless.

The closest Earl got to the Great White Way was when he secured a job pasting clippings in a scrapbook in the publishing offices of Leo Feist Music Company, where in three months he was given complete charge of the professional department. It was in this atmosphere that Carroll started to write songs, initially under the name of Carl Earl. His lyrics soon won him recognition in Tin Pan Alley.

Always the opportunist, when he learned that Enrico Caruso was composing music and was casting about for a young poet to write some English lyrics for him, Earl snagged the great tenor into becoming a glorified songsmith. He wrote Caruso that he was certain he was the one to assist him, and Caruso was so taken with the youth's brashness and confidence that he sent several copies of his music for Earl to supply the words.

Out of the association came a fairly popular song, "Dreams of Long Ago," published by Feist and recorded by Caruso on the Victor label. A number of their other songs failed completely.

However, Caruso's admiration for Carroll led him to introduce the young man to Elbert Hubbard, the famous author of *Message to Garcia*, and the three collaborated on an operetta, but Hubbard's untimely death on the *Lusitania* left their work unfinished.

Advertising himself now as "Caruso's Collaborator," Carroll gained considerable reputation as a composer and lyric writer. The famous producer Oliver Morosco engaged him to write the music and lyrics for a new musical comedy, *The Pretty Mrs. Smith*, starring songbird

Fritzi Scheff. His next work for Morosco was one of his greatest successes, *So Long Letty*, starring the great comedienne Charlotte Greenwood. This show ran for five years with ten touring companies. *Canary Cottage, Florabelle*, and *The Love Mill* were his final efforts for Morosco.

Then he wrote the romantic song "Isle d'Amour," and sold it to, of all people, his future competitor, The Great Glorifier, Florenz Ziegfeld, for his current *Follies*.

World War I interrupted his career when Carroll quickly enlisted in the infantry as a private in 1917. He was assigned to the 77th Division, but he immediately requested a transfer to the Air Service Signal Corps. At the time of his enlistment, America had only 35 pilots and 55 second-rate training planes that had seen service along the Mexican border.

After ground school at Austin, Texas, Carroll completed his elementary flying in a couple of months with the Royal Flying Corps, at Benbrook Field, Fort Worth, Texas. He became a lieutenant in 1918, was assigned to the First Provisional Wing at Hazelhurst, Long Island, and was made an instructor of stunt flying before being sent overseas.

For the rest of his life, one of his proudest possessions was a copy of the book *Who's Who in American Aeronautics*, which listed him as the two hundred sixth pilot in the world to receive a Federation Aeronautique International pilot rating.

Up until World War I, the aeroplane did not seem a very useful invention. It was thought romantic—the less people knew about it, the more romantic it seemed. But by the time the sensitive young man got to the front in the early part of 1918, he found that the military had finally found a practical use for the aeroplane: *destruction*. At first, they used the planes only for observation and to direct artillery fire; and then it was only a step to bombing and aerial combat.

His disillusionment was much in evidence in his letters to Jim:

Somewhere at the front

I've just arrived in France. Everything here is a little sad.

The fighting has been terribly fierce and the country around the firing line is just one mass of holes and rubble. From the air, it looks like a very old piece of Stilton cheese.

I've had a rotten day ... had a terrible experience this morning. For my first assignment, I was ordered to take 24 pictures of the enemy's trenches. Now, picture taking is a job most disagreeable and dreaded by every flyer and therefore always given to the men upon their arrival at the front to test their nerve and prepare them for the worst. With their pinpoint requirements, the pictures themselves would be difficult enough to get even under the calmest and most ordinary circumstances, but the pilots are required to fly so low that they're in range of the antiaircraft guns all the time.

On my way back I got an awful fright. I had my aeroplane hit three times with pieces of shell and the concussion you get makes you think the machine is blown in half. It shot away a large part of my rudder, making it terribly hard for me to steer, but I still managed to keep a little control, and by the grace of God, got down just behind our second-line trenches. There is hardly anything left of the aeroplane; as it came down, it hit some barbed wire, turned upside down, and landed on its back. I was strapped in tight, and except for a cut on the nose and a bruise or two, am unhurt.

I don't mind telling you that I was sick with fright and glad to get back, only to find the damned cameraman had put the plates in wrong and I'll have to go up tomorrow and take them all over again.

The whole thing only takes about an hour, but boy, being under fire from those archies, you're a wreck. But, Jim, I love flying—I sure feel sorry for those guys in the trenches. . . .

A later letter read:

Paris

Have I got a couple of surprises for you! The first one is, I'm in Paris and it's the most exciting city in the world. I was sent here to pick up a new aeroplane, which I am to fly back, but *"fortunately"* the weather has been so bad it's been impossible to leave. I've been grounded for almost ten days and am *loving* every minute of it.

But the big news is, I met the most wonderful girl, fell in love, and was *married* last night in the Sacre Coeur (Church of the Sacred Heart) in Montmartre. Her name is Marcelle Hontabat and she works at the *Folies Bergère*. And Jim, you'll love her. She's adorable, with big brown eyes that crinkle when she laughs, long shapely legs that give her a coltish air, and the bubbling enthusiasm so typical of French girls.

But I guess I'd better begin at the beginning and tell you how it all happened.

The first night I was here I went to see the *Folies Bergère*, and Jim, it's the most luxurious and important music hall of Paris—it belongs to another world. The show itself is spectacular—just the kind I'd like to do someday. The entire theatre is drenched with lights and girls, girls, girls, draped and undraped, and all the ravishing stage effects—feathers cascading over the footlights, swirling montages, and electric rainbows—are created to exploit them. *Now* I know where Ziegfeld got the idea for his *Follies*. This place has been going strong since 1869.

The two stars are Mistinquett of the beautiful legs (and they really are!) and a charming young personality singer named Maurice Chevalier. (If he could speak English he'd be great in America.)

But the star of the evening for *me* was a lovely singer, with a haunting beauty and a warm voice with a catch in it. One moment she stirred you with songs of love and the next she had you laughing over some vulgar ditty of the streets. She was gifted from her pretty ankles right to the top of her ashen hair. It was Marcelle.

After the show some of the other aviators and I were invited to a fabulous party given by the richest man in Paris—Henri Letellier. Champagne flowed, and the apartment was jammed with English and French soldiers on leave and pretty girls from the *Folies Bergère* in low-cut dresses, displaying their charms. An American jazz band played and everyone was in a feverish sweat trying to have a good time.

Marcelle was one of the last to arrive and from the moment I met her there didn't seem to be anybody else in the room. We sat out on the balcony overlooking the dimmed-out city of Paris with only blue lights to illuminate its beauty.

In her altogether delightful broken English, she told me that she was an only child, born in Alsace Lorraine, and her parents had fled to Paris to escape the German occupation in 1914. She had started her career as a showgirl, then became a singer, and is now the sole support of her mother and father.

Our only distraction was when the sirens signalled a German bombing raid. The bombs didn't get anywhere near us, but the peculiar whistling noise they made as they were coming down provided us with a few anxious moments. It's so hard to figure out where they're going to hit.

Later, back at my apartment, Marcelle was in my arms and I knew that love was coming into my life. I could feel this girl was to be important to me. This was no casual romance. It was a joy we were going to share forever.

Marcelle sends her love to her new brother-in-law. . . .

But less than four months later, their love died as swiftly as it began:

Le Havre

Well, the war is over and I'm sailing for home tomorrow on the *Leviathan*. I'm just finishing my leave here in Paris and it's been the most miserable two weeks I've ever spent.

I'm sorry to say, it's all over with Marcelle and me. . . .

For one thing, she's now making unbelievable sums of money and spends it all on an orgy of night life in Montmartre. She's now singing at Fishers' on the Rue de la Chaussee d'Antin from midnight to two in the morning. Then begins a round of the nightclubs of Montmartre where she is always in demand. Rich, drunken revelers offer her enormous sums for the pleasure of seeing and hearing her.

Jim, she's been exposed to so much vice and so much money at so early an age that it's easy to understand why she's completely lost her head.

I've tried to let myself be lulled into this way of life, but I can't handle it. For a while I accompanied her on these nightly excursions, but I felt so uncomfortable and embarrassed that I soon gave it up. Her friends were beginning to gossip. In their eyes I was a gigolo. Someone even made a crack that I was accepting money from her.

For the last few days I just saw her at dinner at the club. Then I'd go to her apartment and wait for her. After the show she'd show up about dawn—last night she didn't show up at all.

Jim, I've come to the conclusion that marriage is an artificial state for women. They don't want to make love within the convention of the law. They want to be taken, ruled, and raped.

I've learned my lesson—I'll *never* marry again. . . .

And he never did.

Whether it was his first humiliating experience at the age of thirteen or the searing disillusionment of his first love with Marcelle, one fact is certain: from then on it seemed as if Earl Carroll had a mad on against respectable human institutions and an uncontrollable urge to break them down.

AFTER WORLD WAR I DUTY AS A FLYER, Carroll returned to the United States in 1919 still determined to continue his climb on the Great White Way. For Earl Carroll, there was only one life worth living—being a part of Broadway.

His first effort was a dramatic production, *The Lady of the Lamp*, but after finally getting on stage his celestial love story of ancient China, it was a complete disaster. The critics 'no likee.'

When he was preparing the show, for which he also wrote the words and music and designed the scenery, his ambitions exceeded his bankroll—he had only $200 to his name—and he sought out financial backers by placing an ad in a New York daily. Incredible as it may sound, a Texas oil millionaire, handsome Colonel William R. Edrington ("Colonel" through the courtesy of the State of Kentucky), a cultured and conservative man, responded and provided the wherewithal for the production, which opened at the Republic Theatre on 42nd Street.

Carroll, undaunted when the show garnered bad reviews and miserable business, showed the first signs of the premiere exploiter he was to become, by taking large space in the newspapers to advertise "My last $25,000"—in other words, "I'm down to my last nickel and your money back if you don't like my show." The public didn't—but neither did they ask for refunds. Instead, upon leaving they stopped and shook hands with the young producer. This bit of ballyhoo whimsey intrigued millionaire Edrington, and through the years he became Carroll's closest associate and continued to invest in many of Carroll's other successes—and failures, the last of which was to plunge him into bankruptcy.

The Lady of the Lamp was followed by a trio of long-forgotten pieces of fluff—*Daddy Dumplins, Jim's Girl*, and a Russian melodrama called *Bavu.* The latter ran all of three weeks, notable only for introducing to the Broadway stage a talented young actor called William Powell, later to achieve fame in the movies as *The Thin Man.*

But finally, the persistent young producer really hit the jackpot, setting the shock pattern for all that was to follow by producing, with the help of his "angel," Edrington, the most daring and controversial show up to that time, *White Cargo*, the South Seas sizzler that had a native vamp, Tondeleyo, driving the hero to drink.

It was the very provocative scene that came at the end of the first act that caused the uproar. This beautiful, dark-skinned, sultry, native girl, wearing the briefest of sarongs, slunk into the leading man's grass hut in the dead of night. Leaning back against one side of the doorway, breast heaving and pelvis protruding, she murmured, in the sexiest voice heard on any stage, those memorable words: *"Me, Tondeleyo."* On opening night, at that point, the noted critic George Jean Nathan quickly got up and said, "Me, George Jean Nathan. Me go home," and walked out of the theatre.

The subsequent physically amorous performance of the two principals (Betty Pierce and Richard Stevenson) writhing on the floor of the dimly lit stage aroused the anger of the clergy and the press, and the show was banned by the police.

By promising to tone it down—which he never did—Carroll managed to have the charges quickly dropped, and *White Cargo* went on to become an enormous success: it played 864 Broadway performances. With this theatrical sensation he accumulated the first of many fortunes, which he dissipated. *White Cargo* ended up having nine road companies taking it to all of the 48 states.

Because of this production, Earl Carroll suddenly vaulted into spectacular prominence. He quickly became recognized as one of the most handsome, rich, and eligible bachelors on the Main Stem. With his accustomed flourish, he was the first man to build a penthouse in New York, where he had a star-swept bungalow constructed on top of the office building at Seventh Avenue and 49th Street—and rumors about the scandalous goings-on at the colorful showman's apartment were the talk of the town.

It was there, at a gala party celebrating the first anniversary of the successful run of *White Cargo*, that Broadway's new Boy Wonder was enthusiastically expounding to his guests about a new show he was planning. It was to be a big musical called the *Vanities*. In spite of his current success he was sure that the public wanted more than just dramatic plots or straight comedies.

"Look at Flo Ziegfeld!" Carroll expostulated. "The tremendous success he's had in presenting beautiful girls bedecked in jewels and furs. Let Flo spend money dressing them. My plan is to *undress* them, and display them in more expensive settings than Ziegfeld ever imagined. Everything will be bigger! If Ziggy uses 50 girls, I'll use 100! And some day I'll have a big theatre of my own. You can't stage good shows unless you have your own theatre. It will be a wonderful structure, not a barn like some of these New York theatres."

That same night he was to meet a girl who was to become one of his great loves, Dorothy Knapp. Her face and figure conformed to all requirements of rare beauty. Large eyes, regular nose, lovely lips, exquisite form.

Born in Dallas, Texas, she had come to New York for a visit and was persuaded by the celebrated artist G. Maillard Kesslere to do some modeling. Her breathtakingly beautiful face started to appear on the covers of many of the leading magazines of the day.

When Kesslere introduced her to Carroll, the attractive young producer was immediately captivated. Like everyone else who read the periodicals, he had seen her name and pictures countless times, but not until that moment did he realize why the artist had selected her from among all the models in New York for elevation to pictorial stardom.

He turned to his guests and said, "Folks, I've just found one of the stars of my new show. I want you to meet the most beautiful girl in the world! Dorothy Knapp."

As the crowd merrily laughed and applauded, he pulled her over and sat her up on the piano. He then played and sang the score he had written for the new show, completely captivating all the women in the room, particularly Dorothy. She sat rapturously listening like a lovesick kid.

Long after the other guests had departed, as they lay contentedly together in his ornate baroque bed, dawn beginning to break over the skyline of Manhattan, she intently listened to the grandiose schemes of the sensual impresario. His mercurial mind moved so fast, had so many ideas, that it was hard for her to know where one started and the other ended.

But one thing she did know—she was in love.

Through the years, that love was to bring her not only ecstatic joy but much sorrow.

The twenties were the peak years for the revue, and the girlie fanfare was in the air. There were three great revue cycles on Broadway. Florenz Ziegfeld's *Follies*, which started in 1907; George White's *Scandals* in 1919; and Earl Carroll's *Vanities*, the only one born in the twenties.

As Earl Carroll was of the war-hardened generation of "dancing daughters" and gin-toting "sheiks," he sensed, better than Ziegfeld or White, the moral, philosophical, and esthetic anarchy of the post-war era.

The show he had in mind was neither burlesque nor peep show. It was simply an artful catering to the spirit of the times.

And what times they were! I know—I lived through them. It was an era of crackpots, show-offs, floozies, illicit speakeasies, murderous hoodlums, and exciting murder trials.

The young generation, which had made the world safe for democracy, thumbed their noses in rebellion at the old codgers who sent them into the trenches and then fouled up the victory. They cut loose in a hot frolic that has been labeled the Jazz Age and that hasn't cooled off yet. They jazzed up everything—music, plays, books, clothes, and, most of all, sex, which got the biggest billing since the Garden of Eden. It began to be spelled with a capital S.

It was against this hotsie-totsie backdrop, of the Jazz Age in full swing, that Carroll produced his first *Vanities* in 1923. Matching the show to the pattern of the times, he put the accent on jazz and sex.

For his initial venture, Carroll planned to assemble as beautiful a chorus as Broadway had ever seen. Equally beautiful would be the costumes and scenery. But he needed the brilliance and power of a well-known name. Someone not necessarily endowed with talent, but more like the attractions that the wily showman Willie Hammerstein used to present in his great variety theatre, the Victoria, on 42nd Street.

Willie was the son of Oscar the first, the cigar maker who became an opera impresario, and father of Oscar the second, in whom the family talent for showmanship reached its highest manifestation (in *Oklahoma, South Pacific,* and others).

As Willie Hammerstein was perhaps the most skillful manipulator of publicity the theatre has ever known, he had always been Earl Carroll's idol. The headliners on his billboards reflected the headlines in the press. Anyone who achieved sensational newspaper notoriety promptly received an offer of an engagement at Hammerstein's. No sooner were a couple of showgirls acquitted of the shooting of a millionaire than they were headlined at Willie's theatre, and when Jack Johnson won the heavyweight title, Willie lost no time in exhibiting the new pugilistic king to the public on his stage.

Emulating Hammerstein's policy, Carroll scanned the field for an eligible prospect and decided to make a try for the notorious Peggy Hopkins Joyce, whose blonde charms and financially astute matrimonial ventures had brought her international renown. Although she had had roles in several stage productions (*It Pays To Flirt, Sleepless Night*—she was discovered by Ziegfeld in 1917), she won wider audience notice through the publicity given to her numerous trips to the altar.

At the time Carroll was considering her, Peggy Joyce had just emerged from a sensational and messy divorce from her third husband, millionaire Stanley Joyce. (She was to rack up six before she hung up the cue.) In addition, she was linked romantically—not only between marriages but during—to members of the English and French aristocracy, financiers and industrialists, and other men of substance—Charlie Chaplin, Jack Dempsey, Irving Thalberg.

Stories dealing with her gowns, jewelry, and romantic escapades filled hundreds of columns here and abroad. Peggy's image was immortalized by Anita Loos with the character of Lorelei in her perennial *Gentlemen Prefer Blondes:* Carol Channing on the stage and Marilyn Monroe on the screen singing "Diamonds Are a Girl's Best Friend."

Even as late as the fifties, when *Life* magazine published its midcentury edition (January 2, 1950), Peggy Hopkins Joyce was included in the list of the most important women of the first fifty years of this century, along with Maude Adams, Carrie Nation, and Ethel Barrymore, though she had never played *Peter Pan*, nor swung an axe, nor was known to have uttered those famous words, "That's all there is, there isn't any more." Peggy Joyce achieved recognition the hard way. Her best performances were for a horizontal audience of one.

Sex to her wasn't a word—it was a way of life.

It was this esoteric courtesan that Earl Carroll sought for the starring role in the first *Vanities of 1923*. Learning that she was on the high seas coming back from Europe aboard the *Aquitania*, he sent her a cable.

3

PEGGY HOPKINS JOYCE is worthy of more than a moment's digression in the story of anyone whose path was crossed by this celebrated gold digger.

Born Margaret Upton in Norfolk, Virginia, into a Victorian family of moderate circumstances (her father was a barber), Peggy was an extremely beautiful young girl—luminous blue eyes, porcelain skin, long blonde curls, and a figure that caught the eye of all the boys.

Typical of the period, she wore bloomers, middy blouses, and a big bow in her hair, rode a bicycle, and, like most schoolgirls of that period, kept a diary. Excerpts from the diary through the years reveal the narcissistic transition from her innocent past to her more sophisticated future.

> *As this is my Diary and I am going to tell everything in it I guess I should start at the Beginning. . . . On second thoughts I don't think I shall write everything in this Diary because there are so many things a girl wants to forget, but I am going to write nearly everything and no Living Soul will ever see what I write because I shall probably say lots of things that I only want myself to know. . . .*

Peggy was to have a change of mind in the late twenties when she was persuaded by her most ardent suitor, Henri Letellier (one of the few she didn't marry), to allow him to serialize her intimate memoirs in his Parisian newspaper, *Le Journal.* They were subsequently translated in a number of languages, raising eyebrows across the continent.

O my Diary I wonder what wonderful things are going to be written in your Virgin pages? Because I am not going to have a Dull and Dreary life, I am going to have a thrilling and exciting life full of Ginger and Glory. . . .

And she certainly did. Running away from home at 15, she joined the vaudeville act of Jack Huertin, "The World's Greatest Cyclist." Dressed in tights, she became his female stooge.

Now I am on a train traveling away from my Dull and Dreary Past to my Glorious Future. . . . I know I shall be a Great Actress one of these days and Mr. Huertin says he thinks so too because I am so pretty, but he says I must work hard and learn some tricks. . . .

And she did. It was while playing the Orpheum Theatre in Denver on the same bill with the great Sarah Bernhardt, whom she watched avidly from the wings every performance, picking up a few acting pointers (The Divine Sarah, 73, with one leg, still playing Camille), that Peggy met her first husband, Everett Archer.

Thursday
I have met a man who is too goodlooking for words, he is very tall more than six feet and has thick wavy hair and is awfully well-dressed. . . .

He is one of these Big Rugged strong men and he is very Rich because his father is the Borax King of America and owns all the Borax mines which is the mineral they put in washing soap. . . .

I met him backstage after the show and he asked if he could take me home. When we got to my boarding house he kissed me passionately and said Peggy Darling I love you, I want you to marry me, I fell in love with you when I saw you on the stage tonight.... Of course I replied, Why Mr. Archer don't be silly we've just met. So he said What difference does it make how long you have known me when we love each other? Which of course was perfectly true.... We cuddled on the seat of his buggy. His hands went under my dress and all over me. I shouldn't have let him I suppose but it felt so wonderful.

Friday

I have married Everett Archer and my name is no longer Miss Margaret Upton it is Mrs. Everett Archer, wife of the Borax King's son and I am so excited and thrilled. . . .

But the thrill was gone after Peggy's introduction to sex on her nuptial night:

Saturday

My heart is broken. It is all over. Oh God God God why wasn't I told marriage was like this? My heart is broken. I am bruised and sick and I hope I shall die soon so I shall never have to remember this horrible night....

I hate HATE Everett Archer.

My life is ruined.

I hate men, hate them, hate them, they are nothing but animals....
After all I am only fifteen—nobody told me it would be like this.

Love is not beautiful and romantic but horrible and disgusting. . . .

In two days she was brought back home to Norfolk. The marriage was annulled.

After this distressing incident, her family decided to send her to a girl's finishing school. Though of modest means, the Uptons seemingly were possessed of influential friends (there was an Upton on the staff of the second governor of Virginia), and they somehow managed to enroll her in one of the most important and select girls' schools in Washington, D.C. It was there that Peggy met her next husband.

Washington, D.C.

The girls here at school hate me because I am so pretty. They all laugh at me among themselves and sometimes I care terribly, but other times I do not care at all because I have my secret. Poor kids they have no secrets in their lives. . . . The only one who is nice to me is my roommate Judy. She has a brother in the French Army, she has his picture in an awfully smart Uniform on her dresser and I think she likes me because I said he was goodlooking. . . .

Gee I wish I had a brother in the War. I would not care if he was with the Germans as long as he was good-looking and had a smart Uniform. But I have not got a brother and anyway if I had I don't suppose he would be in the War. Only Rich boys can go to War, the Steamer fare is so expensive. . . .

Monday morning

I feel terrible today. I think Judy is mad at me. I don't think she appreciates it, but last night I saved her from an awful experience. . . . She's been going with a very tall, handsome young man. His name is Sherbourne Philbrick Hopkins Jr. and he is very social and Rich. His eyes are sensuous—very dark brown—and the minute I saw him I was attracted to him and I felt he liked me. Every time he came to pick up Judy I would catch him watching me as a cat watches a bowl of cream. . . .

Judy says he's very much in love with her. I told her You're mistaken, He's in love with me. I can tell. I told her she must not marry him until we found out who he really loved. I told her to invite him over and I'd meet him alone and she should go across the street and if she sees the light turn off come back right away. When he came in and found that Judy wasn't there he walked over to me. He didn't say much, but he didn't have to. He took me in his arms and whispered Peggy I'm crazy about you. He was wonderful—very loving and gentle. As I turned off the light we laid down on the sofa. I knew what he was up to but I had to go all the way because then I could prove to Judy he loved me. . . .

Tuesday

Today "Sherby" took me shopping and bought me some beautiful clothes—two morning dresses, three tea frocks and three Evening gowns—SIX PAIRS of shoes—and simply piles and PILES of the most wonderful LINGERIE. EVERYTHING WAS SILK. . . .

And a BIG DIAMOND RING. . . .

We're eloping tomorrow. . . .

In any case, I've saved my girl friend a terrible life. . . .

From then on, as Mrs. Sherbourne Hopkins, Peggy had everything she could ask for. But after awhile her role as a society matron palled and she became restless because "I'm afraid I will never be a great actress now but just a rich man's wife like thousands in New York and Washington."

On a pretense of visiting her friend, Fanny Brice, whom she'd entertained when the Ziegfeld *Follies* played Washington, she prevailed upon "Sherby" to allow her to visit New York. Fanny's boss, Flo Ziegfeld, struck by her beauty, offered her a job as a showgirl in his current *Follies*. She accepted, and despite Sherby's repeated entreaties she never returned to Washington.

In my dressing room

Here I am in the Ziegfeld Follies playing at the New Amsterdam Theatre, and I'm the happiest girl in New York. They have given me a scene with Bert Williams, it is only one line but that is more than most of the other girls have and I am very happy. Mr. Williams is so nice and kind to me. He has a great big heart and everyone adores him in the theatre. He is one of the big stars, the other is Fannie Brice. . . .

She has been wonderful to me and last night I was talking to her about life and how strange it is and how you can start out for one thing and find yourself in quite another without knowing how or why. Here I am becoming quite a well-known actress in New York when only a little while ago I was a Society woman in Washington and the wife of a prominent millionaire and before that a traveling vaudeville artist. Now I am a Celebrity. My pictures are in the papers every day nearly. And I still can't see how it all happened. One paper I think it was the journal, said I was one of the most photographed girls in New York, which is quite a compliment as of course I do not pay for my photographs. . . .

I love Fannie. She's so sweet and so funny. She's got a great philosophy about men. She says Don't stop a man from making promises but see that he keeps them. Nine out of ten men will welch in the morning on a promise made at night. Lots of men with bad reputations have good hearts but a good heart is no good if the man cashes a bad check. And give them the air when they tell about the wife who doesn't understand them. . . .

Then she asked me, What sort of men do you go out with. And I said I had met hardly any men yet. So Fannie said, Well you've been married so I don't have to tell you anything, but if you will take a tip from me you will not make a fool of yourself over any man unless he can help your career. . . . And remember, Don't accept presents from a man unless you love him—or they are valuable presents. . . .

Peggy must have had Fanny's advice in mind a few months later when the *Follies* went on tour to Chicago and she was introduced to millionaire lumberman J. Stanley Joyce.

He met, fell in love with, and ardently wooed and pursued Peggy Hopkins all over the country, lavishing her with expensive gifts. (Actual figures produced later at their divorce trial showed that Joyce spent $1,400,000 in one week buying baubles for the blonde fortune seeker, including $65,000 for a diamond tiara.)

It was obviously this display of generosity—certainly not love—that prompted Peggy finally to accept his proposal of marriage. Even after he had arranged and paid for her divorce from her previous husband. Peggy's only comment was, "I suppose Stanley will want to be married right away. Well, he has been wonderful to me and I hope *he* will be happy."

Her subsequent shameful treatment of that small, unpresuming, generous man was Peggy Hopkins's most disgraceful behaviour.

Charlie Chaplin said Peggy told him that on their bridal night she had locked herself in her bedroom and would not let her husband in unless he put a $500,000 check under the door.

"And did he?" Chaplin had asked her.

"Yes," she replied petulantly and not without humor, "and I cashed it the first thing in the morning before he was awake. But he was a fool and drank a lot. Once I hit him over the head with a bottle of champagne and sent him to the hospital."

"And that's how you parted?"

"No." She laughed. "He seemed to like it, and was even more crazy about me."

At their divorce proceedings, Joyce named the Parisian playboy, Henri Letellier, as correspondent, and charged that even when the newlyweds were honeymooning in Paris, Peggy openly flaunted a love affair with Letellier and had spent a weekend at Deauville with her new-found love. This while still a bride of only two weeks.

On board the Ile de France

We dock tomorrow and a wireless has just come from Earl Carroll, the theatrical producer. He says he wants to engage me as the star in the Earl Carroll Vanities and he will meet me at the pier....

I think I would like to go on the stage again. It means hard work and that is just what I need the most to take my mind off other things....

I have received a wireless from Henri Letellier every day and he wants me to return on the first boat and marry him. I am a little bit frightened at becoming the wife of a Frenchman.

Frenchmen understand women too well. A girl should never marry a man who understands women.

The difference between French men and American men is that while an American is shaking cocktails for you a Frenchman is kissing your finger tips and calling you "exquise," and "charmante," "bellem," "Jolie" and "epatante."

A Frenchman's every other word is a caress and he treats "l'amour" as he calls it like a friend. When you are shocked at what he says he opens his eyes and shrugs his shoulders and asks, "Mais, pourquoi? C'est la nature!" With an American, love is an act caused by sexual emotions he does not understand, but with a Frenchman it is an art and the principal business of life.

Henri is perhaps the most wonderful man I have ever met, but he is jealous and self-centered, and I cannot afford ever to go through again with a man what I went through with Stanley Joyce.

I can go back and marry Henri and have another millionaire husband or I can go to work on the stage again and also be independent.

I think I would rather work than be married again just now, but I will not tell Henri that, I will keep him guessing. I'm glad Mr. Carroll's show is a musical. I've had my fill of dramatic plays like my last one. That was a nightmare.

Peggy was referring to a little Thanksgiving offering called *It Pays to Flirt,* which opened and closed in one night. Of course, Peggy laid all the blame on other members of the cast.

I hate my leading man, Norman Trevor. I do not think he is even a good actor and he had the audacity to tell Mr. Shubert the other day that he would not go on with the play if I stayed in it.

And all because of a perfectly ordinary and simple incident on opening night which really might have happened to anyone. In one scene, I am supposed to come galloping up looking for my sweetheart, you hear the horse's hoofs offstage and then I come rushing on as if I had just got off the horse.

Well, the opening night I was very nervous because it was the biggest part I had ever had and I ran on the stage a few seconds before my cue, so there was I standing on the stage speaking my lines with the horse's hoofs still galloping off stage.

Of course everyone laughed and I cried and Norman was furious. Later during our big love scene on a couch he pushed me so hard that it hurt terribly and all the time I had to pretend I was loving him to death when I was hating him.

And he was supposed to be saying "I love you, I love you, you are my dearest lover," and instead he was saying under his breath, "Whoever gave you the idea you can act, you spoil every scene

I have," and I was nearly hysterical I was so mad I pulled his toupee off his head on the stage and the audience laughed, hissed and hooted until the curtain had to be brought down in the middle of the play. . . .

But my producer Lee Shubert is wonderful. He came backstage and said don't worry, stars aren't born, they are made and some day I'll be a big star if I don't pay any attention to the critics.

There is a horrible critic [George Jean Nathan] *I do not know him personally but he is hateful, he writes terrible things about me. I think all Dramatic critics are terrible and I do not see why they let them in the theatres when all they say is bad things about the stars and keep the people away. In fact they all write terrible things about me. . . .*

When the *Ile de France* docked in New York the next morning, there was the usual hubbub that always attended the arrival of Peggy Hopkins Joyce. Earl Carroll had come out in a tender to meet her and had arranged a reception for newspapermen. Champagne and liquor flowed. Everyone was taking advantage of being on board ship where there was no Prohibition.

The photographers arrived like an assault battery. The cameras clicked endlessly. They snapped her from all angles. There were continual smiles and handshakes as Carroll welcomed her to New York. Peggy was seated on the railing and had to pull up her skirt. The photographers kept shouting, "Come on, Peggy, show us those pretty gams!" This went on for at least an hour.

Then she had to face the interviewers. Dozens of newspapermen kept asking her questions. Her flip, casual responses, her frankness always provided good copy. Standing beside her was Earl Carroll.

"Miss Joyce," said one reporter, "now that your last marriage from a millionaire has, shall we say, dissolved, what are your plans? Are you going to get married again?"

"Oh, I suppose so. You get used to being married and you feel kind of undressed single."

"I hear you got a bundle out of that last divorce. How much did Joyce give you?"

Peggy smiled softly and said, "Why, you make me sound like an absolute conniving woman." After a pause, she added, "I haven't had any financial breakdown as yet. But I don't want you to think I'm only after money. Obviously, I have to have some kind of financial settlement. After all, I have been conditioned to a certain kind of living and you wouldn't expect me to give it all up, would you?"

Then she added, petulantly, "I have earned that money, you know. I may be expensive, but I do deliver the goods."

"Now that you might work for Mr. Carroll, any chance of Earl being your next husband?" asked an eager beaver.

Peggy and Earl exchanged looks, somewhat on the coy and amused side.

"I would at this point," replied Peggy, "say no to that. I'm not sure we'd be the ideal husband and wife." She smiled. "It's an interesting thought, anyway."

Seeing she was becoming exhausted, Carroll said, "That's all, boys."

As they started to leave, one reporter shouted, "Miss Joyce, you've been married three times. Now that you're single again, does that mean you are completely cut off from sex?"

"My dear boy," she tossed over her shoulder, "just because you don't live near a bakery doesn't mean you must go without cheesecake!"

Carroll rushed her to a car through the swarming crowds on the dock and sped to the Waldorf Astoria where he had reserved a luxurious suite for her.

Waldorf Astoria, Saturday
Well I have seen Earl Carroll and really his offer is quite flattering, it is a percentage with a guarantee and if the show is a success I shall make about $5,000 per week which is more than Henri would give me, so why should I marry when I can make more myself than any man can give me?

I have told Earl I will consider the offer because it is always best to keep these theatrical managers guessing, like husbands, but I have decided to accept but I will ask for more money. . . .

Monday
Earl Carroll called me this morning and I went over to his office and signed the contract. . . .

Earl has given me one percent more than the original offer, so it didn't do any harm asking.

It never does any harm to ask for what you want and sometimes it is a good policy to ask even if you do not want a thing because it is always better to have a thing than not to have it.

Anyway a woman can only get out of life what she asks of it and the same goes for a husband.

Earl has a beautiful office. It's all so elegant—so Chinesey—bright red carpet you sink into—a big statue of Buddha—and behind the desk he sits in an antique Chinese throne.

He has the cutest phone. Carved on the back of the gold receiver is the figure of a beautiful nude girl. Tres sexy!

With his star attraction signed and a new theatre nearing completion, thanks to his angel, Will Edrington, Carroll plunged into production and took quite seriously the matter of selecting the beauties for his new show. Paying more than any theatrical producer had ever paid for showgirls, he managed to gain the pets and prides of another celebrated producer, but he studiously avoided the cold, stylized, stage automaton types.

"The Ziegfeld clotheshorse is passé," Carroll declared to reporters. "It's not enough for a girl to be beautiful and dumb. Today vivacity must be a girl's outstanding characteristic, for vivacity means youth and the speed of modernity. And the girl must be intelligent."

He was determined that only fresh, animated faces, with the pristine bloom of youth and typical of the wholesome, clean-cut American girl, would smile across the footlights, and he planned to display them like goodies, temptingly laid out in a show window—meant to be looked at, not touched—except, of course, by Carroll's personal barber, who had the enviable job of shaving all the hair off the girls' bodies, not excluding the most private places. When you consider that Carroll interviewed between 1,000 and 2,000 prospective beauties for his new show—that's a helluva lot of lather!

Then came strenuous days of rehearsal. Carroll tirelessly pacing up and down the aisle with a telephone apparatus on his head. Through this he gave instructions backstage, under the stage, and in the electrician's booth plastered on the back wall of the balcony. To his left was a little table. His secretary sat there and took his memos. He filled two steno books at every rehearsal. During all this, he was continually drinking Poland mineral water.

His first thoughts were to find new and novel ways to present his beauties. He rehearsed days on a flower number in which girls dressed to represent various flowers sprang up through a trapdoor in the floor of the stage. When the opalescent curtain of beads that formed the backdrop was lifted, the figures of two young Venuses were seen in what seemed to be two huge iridescent soap bubbles; in one, the star, Peggy Hopkins Joyce, in the other, the breathtaking Dorothy Knapp. He was sure another scenic effect, in which fully dressed girls were transformed into nude marble statues, would bring audible gasps from the opening night audience.

And then more nights of rehearsal while more curtains rolled up, drew back, or just hung there with the girls in all kinds of sexy positions, like the living curtains he had seen at the *Folies Bergère* in Paris.

Sunday

I was too tired to write in my Diary yesterday but there is no rehearsal today so I have a few minutes. . . .

I am sure I am going to love the show. We have got our costumes. They are glorious and I have five changes and they make me look wonderful. . . .

There is one number—"Furs"—where I come out just dripping in Chinchilla. . . .

Joe Cook is in the show and has the male lead, he is a marvelous comedian and Mr. Carroll says that with me and Cook he is sure of a big success. . . .

Everyone is wonderful but there is one girl in the show who hates me—Dorothy Knapp. I think she's jealous because Mr. Carroll bought me a new crystal radio set for my dressing room. . . .

They say she's sleeping with Mr. Carroll. I don't think it's right to have an affair with the producer you're working for, but if another actress wants to go places on her back, it's okay with me. . . .

Although not completely reconciled to combining low comedy with his tapestries and his blazing cycloramas, the astute producer realized that in a revue it was as important to tickle the ear with the stuff that laughs are made of as it was to dazzle the eye with splendor. Notoriously humorless, he still wrote five of the comedy sketches and never had an easier time finding ideas.

Postwar America had become a caricature of itself, and all he had to do was put on the stage what was going on around him. There is nothing at which an audience will laugh louder than its own foibles—it's always the other fellow who is being laughed at—and Mr. and Mrs. America and their offspring were never such animated cartoons as they were in those crazy days. Prohibition, the traffic jam in the boudoir, movies, current dramas, business, and politics practically wrote their own comedy scenes. The result was a dish served slightly raw, but even the matinee audiences, made up largely of the fair sex, giggled and shrieked at jokes and gags that a few years before would have brought blushes of embarrassment. Spice was what the public wanted, and they got it.

To expedite this plethora of humor, he had hired the versatile Joe Cook, who assumed none of the wiles of make-up and impersonated no one but himself. Likeable, by reason of his personality, he played the absurd scenes in a monotonous voice, unaffectedly, and hilariously recreated the sequences that Carroll prescribed for civilized life.

As the opening date drew near, the Broadway wiseacres wagged their heads ominously when they learned that the rash Mr. Carroll was intending to open his revue on Broadway *cold*, without benefit of out-of-town tryouts in Boston, Philadelphia, or New Haven, which had been a tradition with all veteran producers. Carroll's answer was that the new *Vanities* was made on Broadway *for* Broadway with no bucolic taint of provincial tryout. He added, "It is a show for the people who know what's what and are used to the best there is."

On a hot humid night in June 1923, the first Earl Carroll *Vanities* opened. The born showman exhibited his promotional ability by staging the biggest premiere in the history of the Great White Way.

Long before the hour set for the formal opening, an imposing throng gathered in front of the Earl Carroll Theatre on Seventh Avenue and 49th Street. They were eager to see notables from the

Broadway stage, Hollywood and members of society whom they had read were scheduled to attend.

The night brought to it a picturesque scene of splendor and opulence. Liveried coachmen leaped down from their seats to open doors of horse-drawn carriages for white-haired dowagers in trailing silks and for their silk-hatted escorts. Others drove to the theatre in black Pierce Arrows of an ancient vintage, which rolled disdainfully by the new, flashy cars of the parvenus. Fifth Avenue society was crumbling before the invasion of the new millionaires, who wore soft-collar shirts with dinner jackets, but there was still a remnant of the Four Hundred to whom theatre attendance was a ceremonial with inviolable formalities.

Banker Otto Kahn stepped out of his limousine, regally handed out instructions to his chauffeur, and then, with his Inverness cape draped around his shoulders, strode into the theatre, doffing his silk topper to the new impresario, Earl Carroll, who was welcoming guests in the lobby.

Millionaire Jules Brulatour and his glamorous bride, Hope Hampton, aglitter with gems and sporting a new fur piece, entered, followed by "Merchant Prince" Hiram Bloomingdale.

The legendary syndicated columnist, O. O. McIntyre, affecting a high stiff collar, entered with his charming wife and effusively wished Carroll, his old friend, good luck.

Then came other members of the press—Brooks Atkinson, Robert Benchley—followed by a cigarette in a long holder, held by the most fearsome critic of all, George Jean Nathan, who deigned to accord recognition to Carroll as an equal as he swept past the producer.

The street became so crowded with a milling jumble of men, women, and children that finally no one could either get through the street or reach the entrance of the theatre.

Reserves were sent for from the West 47th Street Station, until finally there were 125 policemen on duty. Even so, the police had much trouble forming lines and directing them to the entrance in orderly fashion.

No tickets were sold at the box office and no speculators were in evidence. The tickets for the opening had been distributed to a select list well in advance, and most of those outside who vainly tried to get in had no chance whatever of doing so, but they kept on trying.

For the most part, the crowd had to content itself with staring at the people who descended from limousines and taxicabs, trying to identify the celebrities among them.

"There's John Barrymore!" some one cried. "And his sister, Ethel!" "Look at Irving Berlin." "Isn't that Mayor Hylan?" "There's Texas Guinan. Hello, Tex!"

Then a tremendous buzz went up when the crowd recognized Gloria Swanson and her new husband, and other visitors from the then booming Hollywood, among them Harold Lloyd, Eric Von Stroheim, Charles Ray, Jesse Lasky, and Will Hayes. The crowd went wild when they saw Charlie Chaplin enter the theatre.

When there were no prominent persons to watch, they had to satisfy themselves with gaping at the mammoth building with the name of Earl Carroll carved in granite, which was brilliantly illuminated by a 2,000,000-candle-power spotlight mounted on a truck.

That opening night audience witnessed a production that was perhaps the most elaborate and daring thing of its kind ever to reach the Broadway stage.

The program left no doubt as to whose show it was. Carroll's picture adorned the cover and his name appeared inside six times. Besides being the producer, he wrote the music and the lyrics for the complete score, staged the show, designed the scenery, and supervised the lighting and costumes. As Texas Guinan quipped in the lobby during intermission, "Well, at least Earl wasn't his own wardrobe mistress."

During the show, the audience was startled at the audacity of the new entrepreneur presenting a vast acreage of pretty pink epidermis in varying degrees of exposure.

The few scattered "pallbearers" who had somehow managed to get into the theatre—agents, actors, and Broadway hangers-on curious to see for themselves what they predicted, and probably hoped, was a dead-sure flop—read in the paper the next day:

Those Paris revues with their living curtains can't walk away with all the orchids being thrown this season. A great big bouquet goes to Earl Carroll and his new opulently eye-filling *Vanities*, which makes a strong bid for the distinction of the gaudiest, spiciest, and most lavish entertainment on view. The lovely, young, and shapely Carroll beauties match anything Paris, or for that matter, Flo Ziegfeld has to offer.

Word had gone down the Main Stem that Carroll had a hit.

The speculators, who had been apathetic about buying tickets in advance, came to make deals for blocks of seats. To the box office came letters and telegrams for reservations that bore signatures of society notables and Wall Street millionaires.

It was a great night for Earl Carroll: he had hit the jackpot. At the finish of the show he was forced to come out on the stage and make a speech of thanks to the distinguished audience.

And it was a great night for Peggy Hopkins Joyce.

> *The notices were splendid and George Jean Nathan who never praises anyone except a few was very lovely to me. He said Had nature endowed Peggy Hopkins Joyce with even a little talent in addition to her beauty it would have been manifestly unfair to the rest of the female sex. I think he is one of the greatest critics in the world, but he has no sex appeal.*

Peggy had another interesting entry in her diary about opening night, but this concerned somebody *with* sex appeal.

> *I had a very exciting thing happen opening night. I suppose I shouldn't put it down in print in case someone ever reads this, God forbid. But after all, I'm sure no one will ever see this but me. . . .*
>
> *I had just dismissed my maid, Yvette, and had taken off all my clothes to relax, when there was a knock on the door and I heard Earl's voice say Peggy open the door. There's somebody who's come all the way from Paris to see you. I hurriedly slipped on my pink chiffon dressing gown and opened the door expecting to see Henri Letellier. Instead Earl was standing there holding the hand of a cute monkey. Earl laughed and said Henri couldn't make it tonight so he sent BoBo in his place. The monkey was so adorable. He had a long furry tail and a little narrow face with great big brown eyes and pursed lips. He let go of Earl's hand and marched right into my room as if he owned the place.*
>
> *He immediately jumped up on my dressing table, which was buried under all sorts of flowers and corsages, cards and messages, and fruit baskets. BoBo was a little shy at first but I handed*

him a banana and we began to be friends. As a matter of fact, he quickly jumped over and put his arms around my neck so enthusiastically that he pulled my negligee open and I was very embarrassed. Oh, perhaps not embarrassed but intrigued. I'd never had a monkey undress me before. Well, Earl finally untangled me and put BoBo back on the dressing table. Then Earl turned to me, his eyes casually undressing me further. He moved closer and said something about how wonderful I was tonight, but I wasn't as interested in what he was saying as in what he was doing so expertly. He took me in his arms and hugged me tightly. A hug with just my flimsy robe—bodies pressing together—was quite intimate. He seemed to vibrate a readiness for love that excited me. Then he kissed me passionately nibbling at my underlip. I think he said something like Peggy, you're so delicious and cuddly. And then his hands went under my robe and began to move insistently over me. His touch was so thrilling I just let him do what he wanted to do. It felt so good and I didn't say anything. His fingers scratched the upper part of my backside near the cleavage. I gasped and he whispered Relax Peggy, it's good for you. He looked so handsome I couldn't resist him. Smiling as if it were the most normal thing in the world he took my robe off and dropped it to the floor. He started to push me onto the couch. I admit I was excited, but I didn't want him to have the satisfaction of seeing me yield. For a moment, I tried to resist him, but I couldn't. Then I whispered For God's sake, Earl, not now—Dorothy's out there waiting for you. I was still standing and he began deliberately kissing me all over, starting at my breasts and working down across my stomach. At my first moan which was involuntary he picked me up and carried me over to the couch. I was too tired to resist. I just let him make love to me right there. Oh God it was wonderful.

Suddenly I heard an unearthly scream. It was BoBo. The ring-tail monkey was going crazy. He started to tear up everything in sight. He deliberately broke all my bottles and pushed a flower pot off the dressing table. My corsages and flowers were hurled into the air like confetti. He emptied the fruit basket, throwing the fruit against the wall and all the time shrieking madly. One orange just missed Earl's head. It splat against the wall.

The room was dark but light enough for me to see its juices pouring down Earl's face. He was in a state of ecstatic oblivion, totally unaware that he was being attacked by a perverted monkey. You wouldn't believe what that ape did to the room. Every inch of the floor was covered with debris. Then BoBo gave out one last shrill screech as he turned on the water faucet and started spraying us with ice water. Still screaming he started to do a flying trapeze act swinging on the hanging lamp by his tail. As the lamp broke loose from the socket BoBo made a flying leap landing heavily on the lower part of Earl's back. O God it was wonderful. Suddenly there was a terrific pounding on the door. It was the stage manager shouting Miss Joyce is everything all right? As BoBo sat defiantly pulling the stuffings out of my silk pillows and covering us with feathers, all I could do was murmur softly Yes, everything is just wonderful. . . .

During the run of the show the affair continued, but because of Earl's liaison with Dorothy Knapp and Peggy's with Henri Letellier, who had joined her in New York, it had to be conducted in secrecy.

It became a kind of hit-and-run affair. The results were like an old Mack Sennett comedy—speed but no finesse. "Jousting with Joyce" had to be impromptu—on the spur of the moment. For devious reasons they got together in various locations as chance afforded—in dark hallways, freight elevators, bumpy taxicabs, and even high in the flies of the emptied theatre.

It was all so thrilling. The secret made it more exciting. There was nothing sentimental about it. They just lusted for each other.

I know this is terribly personal but Earl loves me because I have frequent orgasms. It makes him know he is thrilling to me. It makes him a man. What he doesn't know is during love affairs with all men I have frequent orgasms. . . .

Even when the show closed, this bizarre relationship continued— not even interrupted a few weeks later by the marriage of Peggy to her fourth husband, Count Morner. That marriage lasted only six weeks.

Incredible as it may seem, Earl was still crazy about Dorothy Knapp. He had given her a slave bracelet for *her* performance on opening night, inscribed "Forever Yours," which she wore constantly on her ankle. Earl, thinking he was successfully maintaining a delicate balance between the two women—there was never a hint about it in the columns—and believing Dorothy was unaware of his affair with Peggy, was considerably stunned when, after the show closed, Flo Ziegfeld, irritated and annoyed by this successful young upstart, Earl Carroll, simply offered Dorothy more money and, much to Earl's surprise and dismay, she left Carroll and Ziegfeld put her in his own glorified garden.

I N THE NEXT EDITION, Miss Knapp was quickly replaced on and off the stage by a new Carroll paramour. Luscious blonde Kathryn Ray was a 19-year-old Florida sun-kissed beauty who had been in New York only a short while. Carroll had spotted her in the chorus line at Texas Guinan's nightclub, and she was to become the number one beauty in the 1924 version of Earl Carroll's *Vanities*.

But he needed some publicity stunt for her if she were to replace the popular Dorothy Knapp, and the opportunity presented itself when he learned that the New York *Evening Graphic* was sponsoring a beauty contest.

The decade's most fantastic newspaper was the brainchild of Bernarr Macfadden, one of the oddest of the oddball twenties. He was the original health nut. He used to walk *barefoot* to his office from his home on Riverside Drive every morning. He had become the "Father of Physical Culture" and the multimillionaire owner of *Physical Culture* magazine and *True Story* magazine. A farm boy from the Ozarks, with almost no education, Macfadden was convinced that a daily newspaper aimed at the same audience that bought his magazines would quickly elevate him to national prominence and eventually the presidency of the United States.

At the preliminary beauty showing at Coney Island, Carroll surreptitiously managed to become one of the judges, and, with the help of some private entertaining of his fellow beauty experts, had no trouble arranging for Kathryn Ray to be the winner, making her eligible to go to Atlantic City and compete for the Miss America title.

When Bernarr Macfadden saw the picture of the girl who was to represent the *Graphic* in Atlantic city, though the 5-foot 6½-inch beauteous Miss Ray's measurements were a perfect 36-21-35, the publisher expressed his dissatisfaction to his managing editor, Emil Gauvreau.

"Why must they all be so thin! This one looks anaemic!" roared Macfadden, who had been raised on a diet of the Lillian Russell, hourglass style of pulchritude. "It's a bad omen for the future mothers of the nation!" he complained.

Gauvreau, after a little investigation, went down to Atlantic City to cover the beauty contest, which had started out as a publicity gimmick for the seaside resort three years before. The *Graphic* certainly gave the contest plenty of publicity. Two days later it carried the headline: "BEAUTY CONTEST EXPOSED. FRAME-UP IN ATLANTIC CITY."

After observing the devious tactics of Carroll wining and dining the officials of the pageant and a number of other irregularities in the competition, the story went on to disclose the dishonesty in beauty contests. It kept hammering away at Miss Ray's ineligibility to compete, as the contest was for amateurs only. Her Texas Guinan stint had made her a pro, the story claimed, and the paper had the satisfaction of seeing her withdraw from the contest.

Next, the president of the Atlantic City Chamber of Commerce, who had been the annual sponsor, resigned, and this heaven of beauty was closed up for a few years.

Questionable tactics in the picking of Miss Americas eventually were abandoned, and the pageant was reformed to become the simon-pure institution it is today.

When the *Graphic* indicated that Earl Carroll had tried to fix the contest, he called Gauvreau and told him he was suing the paper for damages of $500,000. Gauvreau facetiously informed him he would pay no attention to the threat unless he raised the sum to $1,000,000. Which Carroll did.

Earl Carroll was to regret that phone call for the rest of his life.

But, the wily producer had achieved at least part of his objective: certainly many more people were aware of the name Kathryn Ray. So after the *Graphic* hoopla and the praise and publicity the girls of the 1923 *Vanities* garnered, hundreds of beauty aspirants flocked to audition for Carroll's next show, and if a lucky girl was called back by the producer, her heart and mode of living leaped. She had been selected to become a Carroll Beauty. Suddenly she was earning the extravagant salary of $100 a week and was on the threshold of a round of late-night supper dates with millionaires and frequent mentions in the gossip columns.

There was a feeling of pride, a feeling of being guided—"Daddy" Carroll would take care of them. A mighty rare and beautiful thought in those unenlightened times.

In contrast, Flo Ziegfeld, acknowledged at the time as the nation's arbiter of feminine beauty, was affable, courteous, and respectful to his statuesque beauties, but he was demanding, going to infinite lengths to display his girls properly, and, if they were slow to learn, Ziggy could become, as one girl remarked, "Mr. Icewater."

In view of this, it's little wonder that these lovely creatures fought, actually *fought*, to become a Carroll Girl. And in one instance, was ready to *die*, as noted in the New York *Times*, November 1, 1924.

CHORUS GIRL TRIES TO DIE
DRINKS LYSOL IN TAXI
WAS TRYING TO GET HER JOB BACK

Miss Florence Allen, 22 years old, rehearsing to regain her place as chorus girl in Earl Carroll's *Vanities of 1924*, attempted suicide early yesterday by drinking Lysol in a taxicab at Seventh Avenue and 55th Street. She was reported improved last night at Roosevelt Hospital.

Thomas Vaughan, operator of the taxicab, said Miss Allen entered his machine in front of the Club Richmond, 157 West 56th Street, and evidently took the poison at once. Vaughan sped to the hospital where the prompt use of a stomach pump probably saved the girl's life.

When Carroll was informed of this near tragedy, he became terribly upset and saw to it that all her hospital bills were taken care of and assured her that her job would be waiting for her when she recovered. This was one of the many acts of unpublicized compassion in the Carroll chronicle.

For his *Vanities of 1924*, Earl Carroll assembled as beautiful a chorus as ever seen on the Broadway stage. Having received unanimous acclamation from the press and public for his first effort, Carroll came to the full realization that in his revues, scantily clad feminine beauty and charm *must* be paramount, and he went about selecting the beauties for his new show with a ceremony almost as elaborate as the coronation of a foreign potentate—much more exacting than any other beauty pageant in the world.

His eyes would sparkle and his enthusiasm warm when he saw a new female specimen nearer to perfection, just as does the lapidary or precious stone collector when he discovers a new gem.

As a setting for his jewels, Carroll conceived a big, dazzling spectacular number called "Blue Paradise," that he was certain would make audiences gasp at the first *full view* of his *Vanities* girls, and express wonder at how and where he found all the perfect feminine bodies.

It was a very sensuous "peacock dance," in which each girl was to carry a huge fan and, to the strains of the music, wave it provocatively, intermittently revealing glimpses of her totally nude body.

During rehearsals his startled associates reminded him that the law of the land *banned* total nudity on any stage in America.

"But, gentlemen, you don't understand," Carroll remonstrated. "What I am trying to create here is a *Biblical scene*. The story of King Solomon."

Since Carroll had become aware of him during his old Bible-selling days on the Nanking Road in China, Solomon had always been his favorite Biblical character. Any guy who could handle 700 wives, princesses and 300 concubines, was Carroll's kind of man.

The spectacular producer's enthusiasm was boundless as he exclaimed, "Can't you see it, boys? We'll open the scene with King Solomon rising from his golden throne in the palace welcoming the Queen of Sheba, who has brought him gifts of gold, ivory, precious stones, and hundreds of wild peacocks from India. That's where our beautiful girls will come out as peacocks. And the esthetic art of the number," Carroll insisted, "demands that the girls be in the absolute buff this time, not even G-strings."

Determined to be the first to find a way to circumvent the age-old obscenity law, this notorious peddler of flesh designed, and was the first to use, what he humorously described to the girls as "pasties."

They were little round cut-outs of skin-color tape pasted on the nipples of the breasts of all the nude beauties. And finally, under the supervision of the boss, a long narrow strip was pasted over the most strategic area of each girl's anatomy. Jealous wags of the period nicknamed this contraption "Carroll's Chastity Belt."

When some of the more puritanical damsels protested, Carroll quickly placated their queasiness with the explanation that he was just trying to protect them from the searching eyes behind the long binoculars that were used by so many of Carroll's male clientele.

Opening night of the new Earl Carroll's *Vanities of 1924* was another glittering affair, as the first-nighters poured into the theatre excitedly anticipating the much-discussed salacious peacock number. Rumors had filtered down the Great White Way—probably initiated by Carroll himself—concerning the intimate details of the scandalous "Pastie Parade."

It came at the close of the first act. As the big orchestra, under the direction of Ray Kavanaugh, burst forth with the exotic musical strains of Ravel's "Bolero," the curtains parted, revealing a stage bathed in rainbow lights and a shimmering Biblical tableaux, followed by 108 luscious creatures strutting and gyrating around the stage, each carrying a big fan made entirely of peacock feathers and wearing a replica of the proud bird as a headdress—and *nothing else*. It was a sensation.

Everyone loved it except the two uninvited plainclothesmen who had slipped through the famous portals and witnessed the very provocative "peacock dance." Even without benefit of binoculars, they didn't approve of what they saw, and rushed back to give a detailed report to the chief of the Vice Squad.

The next morning, District Attorney Banton's office called Carroll and said a complaint had been made about the costumes, or lack of them, in his *Vanities* show.

Carroll's answer was, "I refuse absolutely to make any changes. The present exhibition is not immoral and indecent. It is merely a display of beautiful figures."

Banton then warned him that he had been ordered by Police Commissioner Enright to keep a close watch from then on and would take the necessary steps "if any proprieties are violated."

When that evening's performance began, the superintendent of the Vice Squad stationed a patrolman in the wings of the Earl Carroll

Theatre, one Tom O'Leary, who was ready to leap lightly onto the stage and throw a blanket over any female who flaunted the law.

He didn't have long to wait. In the opening number, when Kathryn Ray appeared au naturel swinging upside down on a large pendulum, Patrolman O'Leary, seeing his duty to protect the morals of his audience, sprang into action. He rushed out on the stage, pulled the surprised (to say the least) Miss Ray off the huge clock, and proceeded to try, unsuccessfully, to wrap the startled Kathryn in his blanket.

The audience, at first bewildered by the sudden intrusion, gradually became amused, and then broke into loud laughter when the panic-stricken Miss Ray, after grappling with the determined O'Leary, broke away from her would-be abductor and started to run around the stage, closely chased by what appeared to be a Keystone Cop fresh out of a Mack Sennett comedy. As the uniforms of New York's finest and the outfits of Sennett's crazy police force at that time were identical—bowler hats and all—the audience just naturally came to the conclusion that the innovative Mr. Carroll had injected a touch of "flicker magic" in his new show. And they howled.

Amid an entangled mass of bruised and skinned arms and legs, ensnared by the now shredded blanket, the "comedy team" of O'Leary and Ray were finally yanked off the stage by a number of burly stagehands. The theatre was in an hilarious uproar.

However, they soon quieted down when Earl Carroll appeared on stage, apologizing and explaining the unexpected interruption. He told them of the difficulties he was having with the Vice Squad, and announced to the audience that he wished to serve them and therefore would abide by their wishes as to what kind of a show they wanted. He asked whether they wanted to see the show in its original form. The audience assented with tremendous applause. Then Mr. Carroll asked whether they wanted to see the show as the Board of Censors had ordered it. This request was greeted with boos and cat-calls. As he finished by asking those present to stand behind him when recommendations were made to the mayor to close the show, he signalled for the orchestra leader to strike up the introduction for the provocative "peacock" number.

What thoughts went through Patrolman O'Leary's mind as he stood in the wings and watched the 108 nude girls seductively slither on the stage will never be known. Whether it was stage fright, reluctance to face the hostility of the audience, or the realization of his helplessness, he suddenly left the theatre, dragging his blanket behind him.

The next day Earl Carroll was arrested on the charge of indecent exposure, *not* for the performance on the stage but for impairing the morals of youth and others by exhibiting nude pictures in the *lobby* of his theatre. Evidently Patrolman O'Leary's abortive attempt to deliver physical evidence the night before prompted Police Commissioner Enright to subscribe to the popular saying of the day, "There's more than one way to skin a cat." He had ordered another policemen, one Patrick Meehan of the Special Service Squad, to be stationed in the lobby of Carroll's theatre the next morning to discourage patrons from buying tickets to this immoral show.

Officer Meehan had reported that while he was standing there, he noticed the indecent paintings outside the theatre and the groups of persons attracted to them. As he testified later at the trial, "The pictures had a bad effect on a bunch of kids in the lobby as I was standing there." He called his sergeant and together they went up to Mr. Carroll's office. Sergeant Maloney asked the producer whether he was responsible for the pictures. He said he was. The sergeant demanded that he take them inside and said that if he didn't there would have to be an arrest. Mr. Carroll said he was willing to stand for the arrest, adding "I will not remove a single picture from the lobby. I'm sick of this harrassment! If the commissioner wants to go to bat, I'm ready. I would like to see the matter tried by a jury. I deny that there is any offense to the law or to public taste in nudity that is artistically presented."

Carroll was subsequently hauled down to court, where he issued a statement. "This is ridiculous—there must be some other motive back of my arrest, which I have not been able to solve," he said, "and why should our show be picked upon? There are pictures in the lobbies of some other theatres in this town that I wouldn't allow in the front of my theatre. The beautiful paintings of our girls are by a famous artist, G. Maillard Kesslere, whose position as an artist is above reproach."

Magistrate Moses R. Ryttenberg, who presided over the preliminary hearing, declined to permit artists and connoisseurs to give their opinions as to the effect of the paintings on the morals of spectators.

The only art criticism came during the cross-examination of Policeman Meehan, who had arrested Carroll:

"Have you ever been in a museum of art?" asked James A. Timony, the producer's lawyer.

"No, sir," replied Meehan.

"Then how do you know how to judge a painting?"

"All I know," said Meehan, "is that the pictures had a bad effect on a bunch of kids in the lobby as I was standing there."

Their comments and snickering at the pictures was proof of their immoral tendencies, according to the policeman.

George Maillard Kesslere, who painted the pictures, admitted that they were not exact representations of what took place in the theatre.

"I painted them from inspiration," said Kesslere.

"I don't care whether you did or not," said the magistrate. "What I want to know is whether you painted those pictures from actual scenes and subjects in the show."

"I painted them from photographs and sketches," was the reply. "I saw the performance and was inspired by it."

"That's enough," said the magistrate.

Hamilton D. Bouvier, a celebrated artist (uncle of Jacqueline Kennedy), was then called to the stand to give his opinion on the morality of the paintings, but Assistant District Attorney Charles A. White objected, saying the Court of Appeals had declared that expert testimony was worthless on the question of the morals of a work of art and that the matter was wholly one for the layman. Magistrate Ryttenberg agreed with this and ordered the artist from the stand.

"Have you any other witnesses?" he asked.

"None except artists," replied Carroll's lawyer.

"We have barred them."

"Then we rest."

Carroll, who had brought into court enough artists to fill several benches, hurried to his lawyer and argued excitedly for a moment or two, but no further effort was made to use experts.

"The prosecution also rests," said the prosecutor. "All I want to show is two things. First, that these pictures are immoral, and second, that they do not truly portray the performance. They're a hoax, and the public has been duped."

The question of guilt or innocence thus was made to rest wholly on the view that the court took of the pictures.

Magistrate Ryttenberg then announced his decision to hold Carroll for trial in Special Sessions, and said: "There is no doubt an artist in his studio looking at the nude model before him, the figure of a perfectly formed woman, may be so much under the influence of the esthetic principles of his profession and so absorbed in reproducing the perfect figure before him as not to have one obscene, indecent, or impure thought or the slightest sexual desire, but it by no means follows that, if he should open wide the doors of his studio and fill it full of persons from the crowds on the street, they would be moved by the same lofty feelings; and in passing on the question of whether there has been a violation of Section 1151-A of the Penal Law, a jury would not be justified in considering *only* the feelings of the artist, but rather the feelings and passions of a merely animal nature that would be aroused in any spectator. After careful consideration of this case, the evidence is sufficient and clear and I do hereby hold this defendant for the action of the Court of Special Sessions."

The next morning, October 18, 1924, even the dignified New York *Times* came to Earl Carroll's defense on its editorial pages with the headline.

EXPERTS AGAIN REJECTED

It does seem absurd that in a matter involving a question of art, a testimony of artists and persons rather vaguely described as "connoisseurs" should be excluded. The Court of Appeals, however, has decided that when the morality of a work claimed to be of art is put in doubt, what experts say about it cannot be considered. Therefore, Magistrate Ryttenberg, before whom has been brought the momentous case of the pictures of chorus girls displayed in the lobby of a theatre, refused to hear anybody except a policeman, and apparently that course was the one prescribed by the law as it stands interpreted.

Magistrate Ryttenberg set Carroll's bail at $300. It was immediately refused by the defendant, who then announced his determination to stay in a cell in the Tombs until the case was disposed of.

"I'm going to jail *not* for publicity," Mr. Carroll assured the reporters as he prepared to leave for the Tombs, "but to focus attention on these self-appointed censors. If I gave the bail of $300 set by the judge, this case would be merely one of many. I want it to stand out so the real people of New York, who are against fanatical censorship, will see what is being done. It is all a very serious affair to me, for conviction could mean the end of my career."

Soon after, handcuffed to an attendant and carrying under his other arm a paper-covered novel, *Le Jaloux*, by Prince Bibesco, the Rumanian minister to this country, with whom he had lunch at the Hotel Ambassador earlier in the day, Earl Carroll was led to a motor prison van and placed in it with four other prisoners who had been handcuffed in pairs—a drunk, two cokies, and a big, likeable colored fellow named "Yellow Charleston," who on the trip down Carroll was astonished to learn was a convicted murderer.

As Warden John Hanley received Mr. Carroll at the Tombs, Carroll quipped: "You know, warden, a funny thing happened on the way down here to the Tombs. When the van was nearing the Tombs, one of the cokies leaned over and took a watch from the drunk. I don't believe he gave it back, either." And then, stroking a flower in the lapel of his light overcoat, he added with a laugh, "Well, I'm ready to retire. I hope I don't get any fleas while I'm in here."

But Warden Hanley brought his merriment to a halt when he said, "Not unless you've brought them with you," and summarily called a guard to escort Carroll to cell #118 on the second tier.

The next morning, the last tap of six o'clock found Earl Carroll the first up among the 500 prisoners in the Tombs. He told about it later when reporters talked to him. His thin, white hands grasping the bars of the interview room, his face framed in smiles and a grille of the Sing Sing Renaissance period, the youthful producer said the first thing he thought about when he awoke was food.

He heard one of the prisoners down the line calling for bread, so he called also. That was a social blunder, said Carroll, because as one of the prisoners pointed out afterwards, it is not etiquette to eat the regular Tombs' fare.

"Not that it isn't fine, mind you," said Carroll with a laugh, "but it is simply a question of prestige. They told me that only the lowest among them failed to send out for food. A confident order for a dish of ham and eggs from outside puts the newcomer in his proper niche at once, it seems. 'Yellow Charleston,' who has a cell near me, was broke this morning but he managed to maintain his dignity with $2 which I sent to him. You get a curious slant on things when you're sitting on your prison cot in a ghastly cell lighted by a swaying bulb. For instance, there isn't a single man here, so far as I can find out, who isn't certain he is going to be liberated 'in the morning.' It appears everybody was put here by mistake. Even Charleston, who is facing death in the chair, is confident his appeal will set things right. Incidentally, Charleston asked me to put on a benefit to provide money for his appeal. I told him I would put one on at the Lafayette Theatre up in Harlem, perhaps. Charleston said he didn't think that would fill the bill 'cause they'll shoot me up there.'"

("Yellow Charleston" had killed Barron Wilkins, also a Negro, a cabaret owner in the Little Africa section of Harlem, when Wilkins refused to give him money to flee the city ten minutes after Charleston had shot and killed another Negro in a quarrel over a crap game in a nearby tenement.)

Carroll went on to say: "There are a number of other Negroes in the cells near me, and last night, when they learned in some mysterious fashion I was among them, they began to call 'Carroll, Carroll.' I let them go on for awhile and then one said, 'Mr. Carroll.' Just for a laugh, I said 'Yes,' and they began to ask me about my show. They even sang for me. One in particular—a bathroom tenor—has a fine voice. He sang *I Wish I Had Died in My Cradle Before I Grew Up To Fall in Love With You.*" It was touching, here in the Tombs. They rattled their tin cups for accompaniment, just as in the cabarets. One of the boys said to me, 'What are you-all in here for?' I told him I was in for art. He didn't get that at all."

Carroll praised Warden Hanley as an "ideal host" and added that even though he was forbidden to have visitors the next day, he was certain he would be entertained over the weekend with another song fest in the cell block. But Carroll reiterated he was determined to stay right there until the court decided whether the paintings displayed in connection with his revue, *Vanities*, were art, or something else. His trial, he said, might come up on Monday.

On Tuesday, November 14, 1924, fed up with jail after four days of voluntary incarceration in the Tombs, Earl Carroll gained his freedom. His bail of $300 was paid by his brother Jim.

The first indication that he would rather be free came in the morning, when his case was called in Part One of Special Sessions. Then his attorney, Jim Timony, asked that his client be placed in his custody pending trial.

Earl Carroll was glum when he spoke of his imprisonment and announced he had had enough of cells and bars. "All those who have seen the pictures in question know there are no grounds for this attack," he said. "I beg those who have not seen them to hold their judgment until the judges themselves have rendered their decision. And please remember that it is the pictures and not the stage production, *Vanities*, which are under discussion."

His imprisonment had, however, one ennobling effect upon him, he said. He attended chapel on Sunday in the Tombs, and realized, more than he ever had before, the significance of a church service.

On Thursday morning of the same week, when the case came up in the Court of Special Sessions before Justices Moses Herrman, Daniel Murphy, and Henry W. Edwards, Mr. Timony pleaded "not guilty" for his client. Assistant District Attorney Daniel Direnzo thereupon requested an adjournment of 48 hours to give him time to prepare the prosecution.

"Why can't we try it today?" inquired Justice Herrman.

The prosecutor said he was not ready, as he had to "look up the law" and in other ways prepare for the presentation of the evidence.

"I don't see what law you have to look up," Justice Murphy stated. "The only question here, as I understand it, is whether or not the pictures come within the prohibitions of the statute."

After a little more wrangling, the justices marked the case "Ready."

There was but one witness—Patrolman Patrick Meehan, who had made the arrest.

Under cross-examination by Carroll's attorney, the officer expressed no personal opinion about the merit of the pictures; he said only that he saw they were having "a bad effect" on "a bunch of kids" who were in the lobby looking at them.

Mr. Timony argued for a dismissal, which was denied, and then, in a surprise move, asked leave of the court to permit his client to read a prepared statement in his own defense. Although the request was unusual, the court granted it and Carroll rose with a sheaf of papers in his hand that he scarcely glanced at.

Standing erect before the three judges, he began, "I feel a great injustice has been done to me. I have always staked my name, my reputation, and when I had it, my money, on the conception of what people wanted to see. Sometimes I won—frequently I lost. But I assure you, at no time did I ever intend to corrupt the morals of anyone."

He went on to say that he had listened with great interest to Officer Meehan's testimony when he stated that the pictures of beautiful girls painted by a great artist, in the lobby of his theatre, were corrupting the morals of a bunch of kids who were viewing them. "Possibly this was not the worst of basis for judgment," he said, "but Your Honors, I'd like to point out it would be alarming if this censorship had been extended to all art museums and galleries and to the public and private libraries of the city and of the world and the bad effects that might have been produced through the ages."

As the three judges listened intently, he continued, "A vast amount of words have been spoken and written on the subject of censorship, most of it, on both sides, in bitterness. I have nothing to say against the censor individually, but I will point out clearly, I hope, and without rancor, how reactionary and out of date the Board of Censors is. It is a commonplace to everyone who has given any attention to the origin and history of ethics, that what is prohibited in one age is apt to be orthodox and quite correct in the next."

"It was once shocking," Carroll continued, "for a woman without stockings and flowing skirt to be seen on a bathing beach. But, today, in this year of 1924, men and women and our young people in their unafraid companionship preach and practice a freedom formerly unknown.

"This freedom, both of action and utterance, is finding abundant expression in the dramatic field. Then along comes the censor with frown and formula out of a forgotten age, and applies the cloture. And the evil thing about this is that cloture is not only drastic and effective, but puts lasting fear into the hearts of the owners of theatrical property.

"Take the case of *What Price Glory*, a play that has received public praise and award as the outstanding work of dramatic excellence of the year. It depicts the stark realism of war with the attendant profanity of its lusty Marine participants. Yet part of the dialogue of this play was expurgated last week by the censors after Commissioner of Licenses William F. Quigley had appealed to the Army, the Navy, the Department of Justice, the police commissioner, and the Corporation Council to assist him in suppressing profanity in Broadway shows.

"Only two nights ago, to investigate the complaints made to Admiral Charles P. Plunkett and transmitted by him to the mayor, a party of police inspectors and others entered the Plymouth Theatre. They forced Arthur Hopkins, the producer, to cut some of the realistic oaths ('Sonofabitch' . . . 'God damn' . . . 'Go to hell' . . . 'You dirty bastard') of the fighting Marines."

At this point, Prosecutor Direnzo jumped up and registered a strong objection on the ground that the argument was going outside the record.

Judge Hermann disagreed and denied the motion. He said, "The issue here is one of freedom of speech, and that takes in all forms of speech—not only art but literature and drama," and Carroll was permitted to proceed.

"I have no objection to what is called 'stark realism,'" he continued. "In his time Shakespeare, no doubt, would have been called a stark realist. Shakespeare lives for all time, appealing to humanity not because he transcended morals or defied the censor but because he made the thought and emotion of the world articulate.

"Under the present law, however, the office of censorship cannot adjust itself to change. It is under the old compulsions, the old dominations. In the days of the early Italian astronomers, a dramatist who produced a play with a plot based on the shape of the earth and the possibility of the hero circumnavigating it, would have been in danger of the rack or the stake.

"The censor stands equally in the way of progress now. The only light he gets is the feeble glimmer from the past. Infinitely better than concentrating the power of censorship in one individual's hands, even when that individual is supported by policemen or other witnesses, is my sincere belief that such standards can be safely left to the *people*. Only then can we have regulation without strangulation. I have always been impressed by the verdict the public places upon a work of art. I thank you."

As Carroll sat down, there was an argument between counsel and a five-minute conference between the justices before they announced their decision. They studied the pictures in chambers, having decided previously that the whole matter was a question of facts and not of law.

"We have examined the exhibits that are specimens of nudity and find they are not sufficient to hold the defendant," Justice Herrman announced. "We find that the defendant should be acquitted."

On the same day, November 11, 1924, that the New York *Times* carried the headline, "EARL CARROLL FREED ON PICTURE CHARGE," there was another news item on the same page:

NEGRO MURDERER TO DIE

"Yellow Charleston," a Negro, who was convicted of killing Barron Wilkins, a cabaret owner in the Little Africa section of Harlem, was sentenced yesterday by Judge McIntyre in General Sessions to die in the electric chair in the week of December 22nd.

The slayer, whose right name is Julius Miller, was poorly attired all during the trial, but when he appeared before Judge McIntyre for sentencing, he wore a blue suit, which, it developed, had been given to him by Earl Carroll, the theatrical producer, when Carroll was a fellow prisoner in the Tombs awaiting trial for displaying nude pictures in a theatre lobby.

5

I T WAS AN IRONIC TWIST. Earl Carroll had just built a strong case against censorship in his impassioned remarks in court. Then, not long after that, he was almost directly responsible for bringing censorship to a fledgling new medium, radio, and creating the Federal Communications Commission, an organization dedicated to the noble idea of protecting the morals of the public.

The trouble came when he decided to use this fertile new field to advertise for chorus girls, and in his most intimate manner he brazenly invited any girl who felt she was beautiful enough to be on the stage to meet him at the theatre.

He walked right into a hornet's nest—and also into the life of a 13-year-old girl named Beryl Heischuber.

Radio had made its appearance and was starting to make its dent on the American public. Advertisers seized on this new invention as an exciting new medium for their wares. Of course, the network stations got the cream of the new revenue, and small-time radio, the independents, were forced to pick up the crumbs.

One station, WHN, atop the Loew State Building on Broadway, in an effort to drum up business, introduced the first late-night talk show on the ether waves. It was hosted by Nils T. Granlund, a sort of frustrated actor-producer who turned to radio to sell himself and to launch a new kind of career.

Anyone with a pitch and a little fee for N.T.G., as he was called, was welcome. He turned over air time to phony salesmen, furniture peddlers, and even bootleggers. The latter fact was discovered when broadcasts giving price quotations for "white stuff" (gin)—plus a telephone number—were heard after midnight.

With a set-up like that, it didn't take Earl Carroll long to get into the act. The program gave him a chance to send his appeal to prospective showgirls. His pitch was not unique for him. He appealed to them in the most persuasive, intimate tones to come down to his theater so he could check their measurements, possibilities, and other attributes that might qualify them to be one of his beauties.

Little Beryl Heischuber, over in Brighton Beach, Brooklyn, heard his broadcast and was utterly fascinated by Mr. Carroll's voice on the radio. She felt a response, a warmth, even a closeness to him. She even allowed herself the fantasies of dreaming of being an "Earl Carroll Girl."

A few days later, she was absolutely incensed when she read in the paper that the nice Mr. Carroll was in trouble over that broadcast.

Stephen L. Coles, a radio editor, had written a letter to Secretary Herbert Hoover directing his attention to the quality of the matter broadcast by WHN. According to an official of the radio station, the appeal for chorus girls had been suspended. The incident was referred to as unfortunate, and it was also said that this appeal was made without the knowledge or authority of the station, which had claimed that Carroll had obtained permission to use its broadcasting facilities only to tell something about his forthcoming new stage production.

Nevertheless, the American Radio Association launched a protest against station WHN and against Earl Carroll's tactics in advertising, and it asked Congress to pass legislation regulating broadcasting. For all intents and purposes it labeled Carroll a seducer of young American girls.

Beryl's ear was close to the speaker the night Carroll was forced to reply to the charges:

It is a rather ridiculous attitude to take, on the part of the American Radio Association or a few unidentified mothers, that I am invading the home in search of chorus girls. There is no attempt on my part to lure any girls from their homes or firesides, as one writer put it.

I am inviting these girls to meet me on the stage of my theatre as a purely business proposition. The usual procedure of inexperienced girls is to call at a theatrical agent's, and he derives a fee if he is successful in obtaining an engagement for the girl. With my offer, there is no middleman's profit. The girls pay no fee and they receive the greatest and most courteous consideration.

Beryl couldn't quite comprehend what the controversy was all about, but she felt he must be right. To her young, impressionable mind, the voice of Earl Carroll was warm and persuasive, and it struck a responsive chord within her.

She wondered what the man with the wonderful voice looked like. She didn't have long to wait.

Unknowingly, Beryl's father, Harry Heischuber, fostered his young daughter's future involvement with Earl Carroll, and thereby changed the destiny of the entire Heischuber family.

He, as well as Beryl's mother, Fanny, had immigrated from Austria at the turn of the century with their homeland's innate, strong love of independence, and settled happily in the land of their dreams to raise a family of nine—four sons: Roy, Morty, Allie, and Mickey; and five daughters: Pearl, Mari, Millie, Rosalind, and Beryl, who was the oldest. Of all the children, she seemed to have inherited the imaginative and artistic traits of her Austrian ancestors.

She was an unusually beautiful child, with large expressive brown eyes and naturally wavy brunette hair that cascaded over her shoulders in thick curls. Her warm personality and flashing smile made her very popular with her schoolmates, and as her generously proportioned teenage figure, which she never consciously flaunted, began to develop into what promised to be a very voluptuous young lady, the boys took particular notice.

A fair scholar, she was more interested in the singing and dancing courses than the academic studies, and secretly nurtured dreams of becoming a star on the stage like Marilyn Miller or Ann Pennington. With the little money she earned by baby-sitting, she attended every local stage show or movie she could wheedle her family into letting her go to, filled scrapbooks with pictures of her favorite movie stars, and was an avid listener to all the entertaining programs on radio.

God bless Papa for buying that new Crosley 5-tube radio. She had known it would be a drain on the family bank account when she persuaded him to buy it at the Abraham and Straus Department Store. Fourteen dollars and fifty cents was a big indebtedness for a waiter with 11 mouths to feed. But Papa had assured her that he could manage the $1 down and $1 a week, especially as it was a treat the whole family could enjoy.

Beryl hugged and kissed him for being such a wonderful Papa, and was even happier about their new acquisition when she realized how much pleasure he would derive from it. Though a very bright man, her father had never had the time to learn to read or write English; he had been so busy working as a waiter to support his family. He became so proficient that his employer wanted to finance him in his own restaurant establishment, but the language barrier prevented this small miracle from happening.

One night Papa Heischuber, knowing of his daughter's infatuation for her invisible radio hero, brought her a copy of the Brooklyn *Eagle*. As he walked into the kitchen, he tossed the paper on her lap and said laughingly, "Here's a picture of your dream man—Earl Carroll."

Beryl grabbed it eagerly and exclaimed, "Mama, look. Isn't he handsome?"

Mama Heischuber shoved the roast back in the oven and wiped her hands on her apron. She seemed surprised as she looked at the picture of a handsome young man in a spic and span *aviator's uniform* sitting on the steps of City Hall. His puttees gleamed and his buttons were polished to a fare-thee-well. She nodded approvingly but commented—"Yes, he's a good-looking boy. But what's with this flying business? I thought you said he was a show producer."

Beryl had no answer. She was a little puzzled, too, as she started to read the story.

First Lieutenant Earl Carroll, of the Reserve Corps of the Army Air Service, stood on City Hall steps for one hour and three quarters yesterday morning all dressed up in a brand new aviator's outfit waiting for Mayor Hylan to come to the steps and hand him a letter. Lieutenant Carroll, who was a pilot in the first World War and who is now serving his required time to retain his proficiency, had orders that he was to obtain a letter from Mayor Hylan and fly with it to Mayor Frank X. Schwab at Buffalo where a new aviation field was to be officially dedicated.

The lieutenant's orders distinctly said that he was to obtain the letter from Mayor Hylan, and at nine o'clock yesterday morning he was at City Hall ready to receive the letter from His Honor. The letter arrived, but not in the hands of the mayor, and then and there, Lieutenant Carroll decided that it would not be carrying out his orders to take the letter, so he refused it.

He politely but firmly explained to Augustin Kelly, executive secretary to the mayor, who had the letter in his hand, that he could not accept it even from an executive secretary. He further reminded him that in the army there is no deviation from commands. They must be carried out just as they were given, and the person to whom the command is given is not allowed to place his own interpretation on his orders. That has been done for him.

"From the mayor or not at all," was Lieutenant Carroll's ultimatum as he sat down on the steps of City Hall to await the appearance of the city's chief executive. Perhaps the presence of a half a dozen moving picture cameramen and a dozen photographers from newspapers and photographic agencies, all ready to snap a picture of the mayor handing the letter to the lieutenant, may have had something to do with Carroll's decision.

"The mayor is in conference," Secretary Kelly pleaded. "He simply cannot come out to you." "This treatment is not courteous," Lieutenant Carroll countered. "I cannot take the message under such circumstances. Unless Mayor Hylan comes out personally, I refuse to start on the trip."

Beryl giggled at the audacity of her Prince Charming, and she avidly continued to read:

Executives were seen flying in and out of the mayor's office. What transpired may never be known, but the result was that a few minutes later, Mayor Hylan emerged and jovially remarked: "Well, well, what's this all about?"

Explanations followed; the mayor took up the letter and walked to the steps of City Hall. Spotting the many cameras doing their duty, he put his arm around Lieutenant Carroll, expressed his apologies for being delayed, and told the crowd that this young man was taking a very important letter from the people of New York to the mayor of the great city of Buffalo.

His Honor then handed the letter to the impatient Lieutenant Carroll, who tucked it safely, in approved manner, under his Sam Browne belt, and sped back to Mitchel Field. Army mechanics had warmed up a fast pursuit plane and he took off for Buffalo about noon.

Later in the afternoon, word was received at the Operations' Office at Mitchel Field that the flyer had arrived safely at Buffalo at 4:15 P.M. It took four hours and ten minutes flying time for the 450-mile trip from New York.

Beryl cut the picture out of the paper and placed it in her scrapbook alongside that of Rudolph Valentino, and she dreamed all night that she was flying in an airplane with her shining knight. She had seen a picture of his face and had heard his voice. She was to see him in person in a strange way as the result of another of Carroll's passionate pitches.

The third edition of Earl Carroll's *Vanities*, in 1925, was a huge success. The reviews were glowing.

The critic in the New York *World* said:

The girls, like the eye-popping backgrounds, are quite a tantalizing lot. And as is generally the case when the Carroll cunning is rampant, they conceal no assets and are as numerous as job-hunters around the headquarters of the political "ins."

Though slightly sobered by his brush with the law—he had replaced the pasties with G-strings—Carroll couldn't resist at least tweaking the tiger's tail when planning this new extravaganza.

As a novelty he sought to introduce a nightclub note into legit. He planned to have his cuties dance with patrons, and to have a row of eight tables of $11-customers who would be rewarded by having his beautiful showgirls sit with them. It was an old burlesque bit, started years before by "Beef Trust" Billy Watson, who would have the customers come onstage to terp with the choristers.

Under existing regulations in New York, "mixing" by the chorus with patrons was taboo, particularly in the niteries, as a defense against the notorious clip joints. But Carroll managed to get around this law, much to the chagrin of the two plainclothesmen sitting in the back, simply by having his beauties in short skirts and sheer stockings act as ushers and introduce patrons to the special "hostesses" he had hired for the out-front stuff.

Business had been brisk, but as the holidays approached, to circumvent the usual pre-Christmas doldrums at the boxoffice he came up with another publicity gimmick.

He had noticed the tremendous news coverage Mrs. William Randolph Hearst's Milk Fund had received, so he struck upon the idea of having a Santa Claus of his own give away food and toys to the poor children of New York City from the bandstand in Central Park. But Carroll had a unique twist to get his Santa there. Instead of the traditional reindeer and sleigh, he proposed to bring Santa Claus into the park in a plane that he, Carroll, would pilot. Against the horrified objections of Mayor Hylan when he tried to secure a permit—"But Mr. Carroll, no one has ever attempted to land an airplane in Central Park!"—his enthusiasm won over His Honor, who finally issued a permit allowing Earl to be the first man to attempt such a landing.

Carroll then went about the problem of securing a Santa Claus for the project, and he approached comedian Joe Cook, who was then appearing in his current *Vanities*. Cook immediately turned down the project, proclaiming that he had never been in an airplane in his life and had no intention of starting now. But Carroll finally persuaded him by pointing out what a tremendous contribution he would be making to the poor children of the city, at the same time boosting his own career. Carroll neglected to mention that it was also a helluva good publicity stunt for the *Vanities*.

Reluctantly, Cook finally agreed to go, but only if Carroll would promise to *fly low and slow*.

On the afternoon of departure, after securing permission from his commanding officer to use a military airplane, one of the aircraft from an observation squadron, Carroll climbed into the open cockpit of the DeHavilland DH9. After making sure that Santa Claus was securely fastened in the rear cockpit, he took off from Mitchel Field for the approximately 30-minute flight to Central Park.

After two dangerous forced landings en route, caused by a clogged fuel line and filthy weather, he finally arrived three hours late at his destination, where by now thousands of children had set up a clamor for the delayed Santa.

In clear weather, the venture would have been hazardous, but the sky had become overcast in the afternoon and soon Central Park was swept by an icy, howling wind. But Carroll, determined to complete the mission and land the shivering Santa Claus, after some desperate maneuverings 500 feet above the festivities finally brought the plane down between two rows of tall trees in the sheep meadows a short distance away.

As he landed, the wing of the biplane hit a branch of a big oak tree, spinning the airplane around in an exaggerated ground loop, much to the delight of the crowd of youngsters, who applauded loudly. They screamed their approval of the thrilling show Santa Claus was putting on for them.

Luckily, there were no injuries, and as the excited crowd gathered about the plane, Kris Kringle Cook, a mass of icicles, rose angrily from the cockpit in his rumpled red suit. He yanked off what was left of his white whiskers and wig and shouted:

"To hell with Santa Claus! I'll never ride in one of these God-damned things again!"

Among the children in the crowd, one was more concerned with the safety of Earl Carroll than she was with Santa Claus. Little Beryl Heischuber had managed to get over to Central Park that day, hoping to see her hero in person.

Little did this girl know how close she and Earl Carroll were to become in the years ahead. Perhaps if she had known, she might never have made her life's objective the alliance with this man with the soft, endearing voice and the persuasive ways. But, on the other hand—she probably would have walked steadily ahead with him, with no fears and no regrets.

She sighed with relief as pilot Carroll extracted himself from the wreckage. There were tears in her eyes when the Fire Department had to dismantle the plane and drag it—ignominiously—out of Central Park.

The attendant glare of sensational publicity that Carroll garnered for the stunt gave the 1925 *Vanities* an added boost. It became the hottest ticket in town. It ran longer than either of his two previous editions. It chalked up a stout 390 performances, outdistancing all the other revues on the New York boards. He swamped George White's *Scandals*, which ran only 171 performances, and had the satisfaction of beating, for the first time, Flo Ziegfeld's *Follies*, which barely reached the 200 mark.

The suave, spectacular producer-composer-writer was in his glory. He loved the limelight, but less than two months later, he took a bit more radiation from its glare than he could handle. He staged a stunt that was to cost him a stretch of his life in a federal penitentiary.

IT ALL BEGAN WITH INVITATIONS to a party on February 22, 1926, from "midnight 'til unconscious." They came from Earl Carroll, whose theatre at 49th Street and Seventh Avenue housed his famous annual *Vanities*.

He was honoring the mutual birthdates of both the father of our country and his rich angel from Texas, the same Colonel Edrington, labeled by Carroll as "the father of our theatre."

After the curtain came down on the evening performance, guests began to arrive through the stage door. To their surprise and merriment, they were handed "release forms" that they were asked to sign before being allowed to join the party:

> **Know all men by those present that Whereas I, _____, am about to participate in a certain party, entertainment, feast, or bacchanalia given by Earl Carroll in honor of his friend and patron, William R. Edrington, and whereas I am doing so entirely at my own initiative, risk, and responsibility, and am not acting upon orders or suggestion of Earl Carroll, Jim Carroll, Harry Thaw, or any of their agents; now therefore, in consideration of permission extended to me by the Earl Carroll Theatre through its stagedoor man to attend the said celebration, I do hereby for myself, my heirs, executors, administrators, and assigns, release and forever discharge the Earl Carroll *Vanities* and the beauties contained therein from any and all claims, demands, actions, or causes of actions, arising out of any injury or death, that may occur to me by reason of the said revel irrespective of how much injury or death may occur.**

At the bottom was **"Please memorize this phone number—***Trafalgar 8200.***"** Trafalgar 8200 was the number of the *Campbell Funeral Parlor*!

As the guests entered, they were greeted by the rousing melodies of Nick LaRocca and his Original Dixieland Jazz Band. They found a long buffet at the rear of the stage and two bars, one on each side of the proscenium. Three men served drinks while one man served food to the guests. There was singing and dancing.

The party sprawled throughout the entire showplace: backstage, lobby, and auditorium. A photographer's booth was in the lobby to dispense snapshots of the guests as remembrances of the occasion. Instant photography wasn't around then; the pictures were to be delivered in a few days.

Early in the festivities, the chorus girls engaged in a Charleston contest, the winner to receive a silky chemise. After an energetic match, Carroll declared them all winners and gave a chemise to each girl who would wear it for the party. So the theatre was filled with scantily clad nymphs, many having their pictures taken while seated on the knees of generally respectable leaders of society. One of the girls was a thin, wall-eyed and momentarily pie-eyed 17-year-old model named Joyce Hawley, little known that evening but destined for considerable notoriety.

The guest list was filled with the names of notables and people not so notable. Prominent from Great Britain was Vera, Countess of Cathcart, who barely made the party after battling her way past immigration authorities on Ellis Island. They were attempting to bar her from these shores as an undesirable alien, on charges of moral turpitude because of a sensational London divorce from the Earl of Cathcart. He had accused her of "shacking up" with one Lord Craven on a freighter bound for Africa. Her defense was, "adultery is not a crime in South Africa."

Also attending was the distinguished war correspondent and American humorist Irvin S. Cobb, author of the "Judge Priest" stories then appearing in the *Saturday Evening Post.* He joined merrily with the crazy, pleasure-loving crowd, which included the very popular Broadway comedy star Frank Tinney, whose career at that moment was on the skids as a result of a messy escapade in the apartment of his beautiful girl friend, Imogene Wilson. It seemed that the comedian, indulging in too much giggle-juice, allegedly *bit* the nipple off the right breast of the luscious *Follies* girl. Imogene, understandably perturbed with one teat missing, called the authorities. The lurid details of this breach of propriety, plus the fact that Tinney had a wife and family, shocked not only press and public, but he was blasted from the pulpit by one of the best-known sin-chasers in New York, the Reverend Doctor John Roach Stratton, of Calvary Baptist Church. When he denounced Tinney from the pulpit with "Anyone who strikes a blow at the sanctity of the marriage vow undermines the foundation of the nation," Tinney was barred from working in America for a while. Earl Carroll was giving him his comeback try on Broadway in the current edition of the *Vanities.*

Harry K. Thaw arrived at 2:00 A.M. He had just recently been released from an insane asylum for killing architect Stanford White in a quarrel over his wife, stage beauty Evelyn Nesbit. As he emerged from the wings, Earl Carroll shouted: "Here's Harry Thaw! Three long cheers for Harry!" Thaw grinned at the laughing, applauding crowd, many of whom were important members of the press, including Walter Winchell, Ed Sullivan, and O. O. McIntyre. The much-bejewelled Peggy Joyce was escorted by Philip Payne, managing editor of the William Randolph Hearst *Daily Mirror.*

It was dawn on Seventh Avenue when the host stepped center stage and invited all to drink to the birthday of his friend and backer. He said he had a great surprise for them and ordered his guests to the orchestra seats. They went.

Then from the wings, an old plugged-up bathtub, set on a wheeled platform, was rolled on to the stage. A chair was placed in front of it. Willing hands filled it from casks containing an amber liquid. This, despite a federal statute known loosely as the Prohibition Law, was later proved to be champagne.

The tipsy Miss Hawley, attired in a pink chemise, stumbled from behind the proscenium and mounted the chair. Carroll called for a cloak. Peggy Joyce, sitting in the front row beside the aforementioned Phil Payne, quickly volunteered and threw her sable coat up on the stage. Then Carroll, assisted by Edrington, the honored guest, held it between Miss Hawley and the revelers, hiding her alluring torso. She daintily dropped her chemise around her ankles and, still protected by the furry curtain, climbed into the tub filled with the sparkling champagne. She gingerly sank down, languishing in the bubbly.

With a flourish, Carroll swept aside Peggy's sable and produced a feminine slipper, and Miss Hawley ladled out the first toast to the guest of honor, the ebullient Mr. Edrington.

Then, at a signal from the host, "Gentlemen, the line forms on the left," 15 or 20 eager bon vivants leaped onto the stage, glasses in hand, and started to dip their goblets into the mermaid's bathtub and partake of her "Piper Heidsieck." Needless to say, there was toast after toast in rapid succession.

The level of champagne had just started to diminish when the shapely but shivering girl halted the revelry in a husky, inebriated drawl, "Hold it, everybody! Wait a minute! C'mere—C'mere."

As the playboys gathered closely around the tub, feasting their eyes on the bathing beauty radiantly awash in the vintage, Miss Hawley; her eyes half-closed, languorously stretched out in the tub on her back, totally relaxed, legs spread apart, and, with a smile of relief on her face, murmured, *"Guess what I'm doing?"*—and then passed out.

There was an immediate convulsive reaction from the "little old wine-tasters" to the body-churned beverage.

Phil Payne, sitting in the front row of the theatre taking it all in, started to scribble notes.

Peggy Joyce, sitting beside him, paid little, if any, attention, for as everyone understood, members of the Fourth Estate who were invited to these intimate soirees of Earl Carroll and other producers were sworn to relative secrecy. It was the unwritten law of newspaperdom that what is "off the record" is just that.

But Phil Payne was the maverick of the tabloids, believing that all rules were made to be broken. If hell didn't break loose when he was around, he'd raise hell until it did.

He was short of stature and stocky, his eyesight had never been good, and he wore large horn-rimmed glasses, but there was personality in his pleasant round face and warm bucolic smile that belied his force and determination.

Payne's astonishing career began in New Jersey as city editor of the *Hudson Dispatch*. His nimble mind and knack of finding angles in stories quickly brought an offer from Captain Joseph Patterson, a member of the powerful Chicago *Tribune* family, to join the city's first (and still most successful) tabloid, the New York *Daily News*. His terrific energy and accomplishments caused his rapid rise to the post of managing editor, a lofty perch for a young man in those days.

As Payne rose in the newspaper firmament, so did his pay. With money and power, he was soon considered a very important person along Broadway, and became highly susceptible to glamour and charm. It just so happened that Peggy Hopkins Joyce was between marriages. Payne couldn't have avoided her if he had tried, and he didn't. From the time they met, they were together constantly—at the races, smart cafes, theatres, and nightclubs. Those in the know were sure this was the real thing, and close friends were predicting that Phil would become number four on Peggy's charm bracelet.

But, it was not to be. Unfortunately, it was this tempestuous association with the glamorous Peggy that was to cost him his prestigious job at the *Daily News*.

It had happened just a few months after they'd met. Peggy had begged him to let her come down to the *News* office to watch a newspaper in the making. She was just like a kid, eyes bright with curiosity, following the news from typewriters to rows of noisy linotype machines. She had marveled at the huge sprawling presses like giant monsters with thousands of big and little parts, and begged him until he let her push the button that set in motion those massive pieces of iron. And then, startled and terrified at the unearthly din she had created, she clutched him in fright and screamed, "Shut it off, Phil—Please shut it off!"

The abruptness of the presses stopping brought employees from all over the building, rushing down to find out what had happened, much to the embarrassment of the managing editor.

As Phil Payne took Peggy Joyce back to his office, he was unaware that the very hand that had changed the destinies of other men's lives was now fated to smash the pattern of his own.

Payne's boss, Captain Patterson, was a man of simplicity and purpose who didn't ask much of his employees but demanded compliance. He had imposed a strict code upon his top editors. They were not to associate with judges or actresses, or drink to the point of intoxication. He learned about Peggy Hopkins Joyce, and when he was informed that she had started the presses, he called Payne into his office and summarily fired him.

It was a staggering blow from which Payne never fully recovered, though his ego was somewhat soothed when William Randolph

Hearst sent for him. The powerful publisher welcomed him with a generous contract into the fold of his new tabloid, the New York *Daily Mirror*. Hearst, unlike Patterson, built no fences around the private lives of his executives—he was more interested in production and results than deportment—so Phil and Peggy continued to be a hot item.

Then Payne, as the new managing editor of the Hearst tabloid, became restless with a consuming ambition to even the score with Captain Patterson by making the *Mirror* the greatest newspaper on earth, by outdistancing the *Daily News* so badly that it would never catch up.

He was always after that BIG story, and as he watched the bathtub with the unconscious nude girl being pushed off-stage by the riotous revelers, the thought flashed across his mind that *this* might be it. Exposing the details of this drunken orgy might be the sensational scoop, skyrocketing circulation, against the unhappy *News* and that new upstart, the *Evening Graphic*.

Excitedly, Payne turned to Peggy and said, "Come on—let's go. I've got to get back to the office."

She pouted, "Oh Phil, I don't want to go yet. The party's just getting started." Putting her arms around him lovingly, she said, "You go ahead, honey. I'll get someone to drop me off and I'll call you later."

As Phil Payne made his way up the aisle, many of the guests who had noticed his pen and notebook visibly busy, and wanting the world to know they had participated in this glamorous event, importuned him to "get my name in." Later that week, they were frantically phoning to "keep my name out." But it was too late.

Phil Payne had decided to break the unwritten law and print the story and show the world how tough he could be. He was going to scoop the town.

When he entered his office on the second floor of the *Mirror* building, located at Frankfurt and Williams Streets by the Brooklyn Bridge, he tossed his crushed Fedora hat onto the rack and sank wearily into the chair behind his desk.

Putting paper in the carriage of the typewriter, his nimble fingers started to type the words: **"The bacchanalian revels of Ancient Rome were eclipsed last night by Earl Carroll when he staged a disgusting orgy...."**

At the theatre, the party was finally coming to an end. The musicians were packing up their instruments. The last of the guests were staggering out, being carried out, or walking under their own power. The gushing "Had a lovely time, Earl," "So glad we came," and the like were tinkling with brassy hollowness through the stage. The bartenders were taking the empty bottles out to the alley, tossing down the remaining few nips on the way. And Earl was offering his perfunctory goodbyes.

He sat down on one of the cushiony seats in the front row and sighed a deep sigh. This was one night when he could honestly say he had had enough of parties. He was damned tired.

"You wouldn't like to help a lady in distress, would you?" said a feminine voice near him. He hadn't even noticed that Peggy Joyce had come down the aisle.

"Be a good Samaritan and drop a little girl at her apartment, will you, honey?" she asked softly. Then, with her hands running teasingly down his neck, she added seductively, "I might even invite you up for a nightcap."

Earl got the message. He knew the Joyce version of a nightcap. He stood up, gave her a long kiss, and, with an affectionate pat on her behind, said, "Let's go."

Peggy's apartment was a plush, lush affair with satiny chairs, a white couch, white rugs that you sank into up to your ankles. Everything was terribly feminine with sexual and sensual overtones. And everything was reeking of money and luxury.

Earl threw off his coat and lay down on the big couch.

"I'm bushed!" he exclaimed. And he was surprised to hear himself say it. The prospect of jousting with Joyce now took a momentary back seat.

Peggy leaned over him, letting her amply displayed bosom come temptingly into more complete view. She kissed him warmly on the lips and said, "Have a little nap, honey. You can go home later."

Peggy took off his shoes, loosened his collar and belt, covered him with an afghan, and went into her boudoir.

She undressed slowly, standing in front of her three-way mirror. Once the last bit of slinky lingerie had fallen to the floor, she stood naked. She gazed admiringly at her body, with all its inviting curves, the firm, beautifully shaped breasts, and the legs that had inspired many men into unabashed action. She knew this body was her ticket to fortune and fame. She had one hell of a figure. And she knew it.

Peggy got into a bubble bath, luxuriating in the soft suds. She began to feel a little drowsy and quickly got into bed—*nude* as was her custom. Before turning the lights out, she performed her nightly ritual of jotting down the events of the day in her diary.

> *Another party tonight at Earl's ... fabulous ... everyone who was anyone was there. ... The champagne, the excitement of people. Earl is such a dear. It has been a long, eventful night. It didn't quite end as I had expected but....*

The words on the page trailed off as she fell asleep. Later, the pages in "Dear Diary" told the rest of the story.

> *Suddenly, I was awakened by the thrilling sensation of someone massaging the nipples of my breasts with his tongue. The touch was unmistakably Earl's. His hands moved over my body. Each place he touched aroused me more. Suddenly our bodies became like one. ... Oh, God, it was delirious ... sheer possession ... ecstasy. Then I heard the incessant ringing of the phone—it kept ringing and ringing—and just as suddenly it stopped....*

Phil Payne hung up the phone and muttered to himself, "Poor kid, she must be knocked out. I'd better stop and see her on the way home."

He glanced at the clock on the wall. He had finished just in time to make the deadline for the early edition, the one that would hit the newsstands at 1:00 A.M. the morning of the following day.

He ripped the page out of the typewriter and gave the copy to Art Irwin, his night editor. Irwin glanced at the sheet and said incredulously, "Boss, are you *sure* you want to run this?"

"Positive," Payne snapped back. "Make it the lead story on page one and mark it 'Exclusive to the Mirror.' "

Phil Payne hailed a cab outside the *Mirror* Building and in less than ten minutes he was at 34 East 52nd Street. With the gold key Peggy had so endearingly given him, he opened the door of her apartment and walked into the bedroom.

WHEN THAT FIRST EDITION of the *Daily Mirror* with the scoop of the Carroll orgy hit the newsstands in the early morning hours of February 24, 1926, not only the *Daily News* but all the other New York papers were in a frenzy. But none took it harder than the *Evening Graphic*, the tabloid that made all other yellow journals look like Sunday school publications.

Truth and principle seldom bothered publisher Macfadden. While he spoke piously of ideals of journalism, he left not one single gutter unexplored.

He was so enraged when he read the Payne story that the old building that housed the *Graphic* on City Hall Place shook as violently as it did when all the presses were in action. But this time, it wasn't the huge machines, it was Bernarr Macfadden roaring at his managing editor, "We've got to get that sonofabitch Carroll." Emile Gauvreau, the only important newspaperman in the city who had *not* been invited to the Carroll party and still smarting over the $1,000,000 suit (still pending) that Carroll had slapped against him when the *Graphic* had exposed the phony beauty contest in Atlantic City, immediately went into action.

Having learned from an inside source that photographs of the guests at the party had been taken in the lobby of the theatre, he had his whole staff frantically phoning all over town trying to locate the photographer. But thanks, undoubtedly, to Mr. Carroll, the photog was nowhere to be found—and much to the lasting horror of

Gauvreau and the other New York editors, but to the extreme *relief* of the celebrants, those photos *never* surfaced, even to this day.

There were shrouds of gloom at the *Graphic*. The biggest orgy in the history of Broadway, and *no* pictures!

Gauvreau hurriedly called the Art Department and shouted, "Get Harry to work on a composite."

The paper's photo service was unfailing: its art director, a young man by the name of Harry Grogin, fixed it—he created (or recreated) the scenes reported in screaming headlines and their lurid descriptions by clever photomontage.

The composite picture was a *Graphic* specialty, officially called a composograph in the paper. They were not merely pictures pushed together, but rather some shocking or revealing picturizations of scenes from which photographers were barred.

It had all started the year before, when the *Graphic* came out with something sensationally new. It was a faked picture showing a girl naked except for her mid-section, standing in what was supposed to be a courtroom in White Plains, New York. It was a pictorial scene of the notorious Rhinelander case. Kip Rhinelander, a wealthy socialite, sued his bride of a month, lovely Alice Jones, on the ground that she had concealed from him the fact of her having Negro blood in her veins. In rebuttal, Alice contended he had known it all along, and bared her body down to the waist in court for the judge and all concerned to see that she was a quadroon. For decency's sake the judge had, of course, barred all cameras. But just the same, the *Graphic* carried the picture of the court scene with Alice in front, her loins skimpily covered. Harry Grogin had hastily hired a model, beautiful Agnes McLaughlin, and had her pose before an array of the *Graphic's* staff reporters, court fashion! That was the picture he took. He then simply superimposed the heads of all those present, including the *real* members of the jury reproduced from a genuine shot of the tribunal—and there was the first composograph! It was fabulous. You felt you were looking into the courtroom.

Circulation soared. It soared each time another scoop succeeded with the help of Harry's phony photos.

While the *Graphic* hailed and acclaimed composites as new trends in journalism, and a hot controversy raged over them in the trade, Grogin remained unimpressed. He could never understand the commotion his brainchild had provoked. Even in 1975, at the spry age of 83 he wryly remarked, "My fancy tells me there must have been other such composed pictures from the time the greatest photographer of all, Mr. Mathew Brady, packed his wet plates in a wagon, said 'Giddap' to his horse, and went after pictures of Mr. Lincoln and the Civil War."

Despite Grogin's modesty, *Graphic* leaders felt at the time that they were actually making newspaper history by contributing a notable and novel device for the free use of contemporaries. They regarded themselves as trailblazers in a profession that everybody thought had been all blazed up.

Enjoying the sweet smell of success, the *Graphic* next exploited the potential of its composites with vigor in its coverage of the hanging of Gerald Chapman, bad man of the times, whose notorious career had been touched by an aura of glamour that delighted the younger generation.

Graphic composites, however, reached their all-time *low* in showing the bedroom shenanigans of Daddy Browning, an 85-year-old Lothario, with his 16-year-old bride, Peaches Heenan. Wags of the period insisted that Browning's doctor had called him the day after the wedding and said, "You'd better watch out—a union like that could be fatal." And Daddy had replied, "Well, if she dies, she dies!"

But the composites reached their absolute zenith in reader interest during the furor over Carroll's "bathtub" orgy. If Phil Payne's exposé served to light the fuse, Harry Grogin's phony picture caused the explosion.

On February 25th, when the front page of the *Graphic* carried the sensational composograph showing Joyce Hawley sitting in the bathtub on the stage with wine spilling over the side, and with Earl Carroll and his guests looking on, people fought for copies and the newsstands had to be protected by the cops. Even though they knew the picture was spurious (it was so identified next to the caption), the subway readers ate it up for its essential reality and, as the phony pics pushed circulation skyward, Gauvreau and the whole staff took it with that humor and amazement that characterizes the newspaperman's reaction to the outlandish.

But the federal authorities found no humor in it when they read published reports of the all-night bacchanalian orgy on the stage of the Earl Carroll Theatre, ending with men drinking wine from a bathtub in which a nude chorus girl was immersed.

They were particularly incensed when they saw the actual picture "graphically" depicting the wine spilling over the side of the bathtub onto the floor.

Police Commissioner McLaughlin said there would be an investigation to get the facts of what happened.

District Attorney Joab H. Banton said that he would take immediate action if he received a complaint that there had been an indecent performance, but that he would leave any Prohibition violation to the federal authorities. In spite of rumors that no action was contemplated by officials because of what they feared was "a publicity stunt," reports persisted that an investigation was in progress.

Two days later, Chief Prohibition Enforcement Agent Tuttle announced that he had sent a representative to United States Attorney Emory R. Buckner to ask for a subpoena for Earl Carroll.

On February 27th, Earl Carroll spent more than an hour before a federal grand jury. He was the first witness examined.

Mr. Carroll came out of the grand jury looking decidedly annoyed. Uncharacteristically, he tried to dodge the reporters. He was joined by Chris Scaife, his bodyguard, and as they left the building on the Broadway side, Carroll tried to avoid several photographers who were maneuvering for a picture. His bodyguard, without a word, aimed a blow at one of the photographers. The other cameramen went into action in support of their comrade, and during the melee, Carroll disappeared. There were no casualties and no arrests.

Following Carroll's departure from the Federal Building, United States Attorney Buckner, who previously had intimated that he was not interested in the Carroll party, admitted that the Prohibition phase of it was under investigation.

The next day, Phil Payne was seen entering the grand jury room followed by Peggy Joyce, Harry K. Thaw, and a number of other guests at the bathtub party, including Irvin S. Cobb and Countess Cathcart. None would talk to the press.

On the last day, Joyce Hawley arrived with her attorney, Morton Abrahams. Miss Hawley, obviously nervous, entered the grand jury room alone as her attorney stayed outside and talked to reporters.

He explained to them that he had been retained by Miss Hawley to compel Mr. Carroll to live up to his alleged agreement, to pay her $1,000 for the bathtub act and to give her a part in one of his productions. He stated that after promising these things, Mr. Carroll gave her $20 and advised her to "take a drink and forget it." Mr. Abrahams said he had conferred with Mr. Carroll and that "negotiations" were under way. He intimated that Miss Hawley would not be content to receive merely $1,000 but wanted the job or something like its monetary equivalent.

After being questioned for almost an hour and a half, Miss Hawley, still distraught, came out and her nervousness overcame her. Seeing photographers, she ran down three flights of stairs to the street, closely followed by Mr. Abrahams.

Though the federal officials were reticent about saying anything of what had happened in the grand jury room during the investigations, Buckner, when pressed for an explanation of Carroll's appearance, finally admitted that he'd issued the subpoena for him in order to learn the source of any liquor that was served at the party. "If Mr. Carroll took the stuff from his home to the theatre without a permit, he might be liable to prosecution on the ground of possessing and transporting liquor. If he obtained it from a bootlegger, he will be required to *name* the bootlegger."

THE REAL POWERHOUSE from which the Jazz Age drew its energy was Prohibition. The bootlegger took his place alongside the grocer and butcher as a household tradesman. The speakeasy became a national institution, and nowhere was Prohibition flaunted so openly and nowhere was it such a joke as on the Gay White Way. Side streets became a succession of locked doors with peep holes through which guards, on the lookout for raiders, appraised all who knocked for admittance. Clubs that catered to a select clientele issued admission cards, which were highly prized by their possessors.

Typical of these bistros was one conducted by a buxom, garish blonde, the darling of the butter-and-egg man, Texas Guinan, who greeted her customers with "Hello, sucker!" The appellation was well confirmed by the checks the chumps paid—water never sold so high, even in Wall Street—and though they knew Tex was taking them for a royal ride, they loved it, and all because her raucous, husky, sexy voice and slap-on-the-back greeting made them feel important. It was no wonder she had an abundance of friends in all circles of New York life—high, low, and journalistic—and one of her closest was Earl Carroll.

Tex had always had a warm feeling for her old friend, Earl—never a romance. He was her kind of guy. He played up the sucker bit, too, but with more subtlety and gloss.

Now he was in trouble and she had great empathy for him. As the most celebrated heroine of the Prohibition Wars, she knew exactly what misery Earl was now experiencing.

Everybody was taking swipes at him. Just that morning, Ziegfeld had been quoted as saying:

This Carroll party is especially to be regretted from the angle of the entertainment world. At this time, I can imagine no one being so short-sighted as to stage such an orgy as this of Carroll's as it was described in the newspapers, even in Alaska. However, I have such an abiding faith in the fairness of public opinion that I am sure the amusement part of our daily life will not be judged by such an incident, which is surely unfortunate when one considers the tremendous good and the joy and happiness entertainment fields have brought to the entire country.

"That pompous ass!" she exploded when she finished reading the item. "No wonder Earl's become a recluse, and won't see or talk to anyone. Well, he'll talk to me," she said as she picked up the phone in her office at the club.

"Hi, Earl," she exclaimed heartily. "How's my boy friend?"

"Okay, Tex," came back the zip-less reply.

"You sure as hell don't sound like it. Don't let those Prohibition guys get you down. Look—I've been padlocked so often, I feel like a Yale man."

"No, it isn't that, Tex," Earl said.

"It's not that Ziegfeld crap, is it?" she cut in. "Who the hell is he to pass judgment and act so damned righteous?" She was really steaming now as she continued, "Somebody ought to break wide open the rough time Ziegfeld's been giving Billie Burke, screwing around with Marilyn Miller and Lillian Lorraine and the rest of those broads—let alone the hell he caused his first wife, Anna Held. Next to him, baby, you're almost—I said almost—Little Lord Fauntleroy."

She could almost hear the weak smile on his face.

Changing the subject, Tex then said, "Hey, kid, what are you doin' tonight?"

Earl explained that he was just having dinner with Dorothy Knapp, Jim, and Countess Cathcart. Tex said, "Look, after you're finished why don't you all come over here to the club and we'll have some fun. I might even take my clothes off and get into a bathtub full of wine. But, Christ, where the hell am I going to find a tub big enough to fit my ass?"

She could hear him chuckling as she hung up.

About 1:15 in the early morning of April 1, 1926, when Earl Carroll and his party arrived at Texas Guinan's club on 50th Street, between Sixth and Seventh Avenues, he found a hastily made oilcloth banner paraphrasing his famous slogan, "Through These Portals Pass the Most Beautiful Girls in the World." Carroll smiled at Guinan's version, which read "Through These Portals *Pass Out* the Most Beautiful Girls in the World!"

Being an expected guest, it wasn't necessary for Carroll to go through the intricate and mysterious rites that the average patron was subjected to before being admitted to the cellar of the old brownstone dwelling that was now a speakeasy aptly called the *Rendezvous.*

As Texas Guinan, the female Don Rickles of her era, spotted Carroll walking into the sardine-packed room, she cued the band to play "The Prisoner's Song," much to the delight of the 300 patrons, which included Peggy Joyce with her rumored but never-to-be next millionaire husband, Stanley Comstock. (One little thing—Stan had a recalcitrant wife who refused to divorce him.) They were sitting at the table next to where the Carroll party was seated, when the show started. The floor, which was the size of a barrel top, was so jammed that the dancing girls, one of whom was a pretty teenager named Ruby Keeler, had to exhibit their high kicks, wiggles, and other charms right in the customers' faces.

As Texas Guinan, whose brassy voice could penetrate even the din of her own clubs, gave her celebrated closing line to the chorus, "Come on, give the little girls a great big hand," a burly man in the audience jumped up and shouted, "How about giving the little girls a great big big pair of *handcuffs?*"

The hostess's reaction, "Oh, my God, we're pinched!" was no surprise to the crowd. She owed her fame to brushes with the Eighteenth Amendment.

That was the signal for several other men throughout the room to jump up, shouting, "Don't anyone move—this is a raid!"

The sound of a siren reverberated through the room, actually coming from the drummer on the bandstand.

As soon as Texas Guinan had scared the hell out of everyone, she yelled, "April Fool!" and ordered her phony vice squad, who turned out to be the waiters and bouncers of the club, back to work.

Everybody laughed, and even Carroll gave a weak smile.

At this point, Carroll was informed that Phil Payne had just entered the club. Immediately, Carroll and his party got up and walked out. Tex ushered them to an exit through the kitchen to escape a horde of reporters who were waiting outside the club, evidently in response to a "mysterious" tip that he was there.

But they spotted him and greeted him with shouts of "Hey, Earl, what about that orgy the other night?"

"Yeah, what about the naked broad in the bathtub?" exclaimed another.

"Where the hell did you get all the hooch?"

His face sobered noticeably as he vehemently denied that the party had been an orgy.

"There is absolutely nothing to the story," said the producer. "I gave an anniversary party, which included the cast of the *Vanities* and the stagehands of the theatre. There were about 200 guests. The party was as orderly and decorous as any affair ever given anywhere. It might have been held in a church for all the revelry there was among the guests. It was a party that any man, even a minister, might have attended with his wife."

Carroll calmly went on to say that the bathtub episode was a mere frolicsome jest, that the tub was filled with harmless fruit juice compounds, and that no young woman got into the tub. He emphatically denied that any illegal beverages had been brought into the theatre by him.

As the party was getting into a limousine, one reporter spotted Vera Cathcart and ungentlemanly quipped: "Any moral turpitude at the orgy, Countess?"

Lady Cathcart, taken aback by the audacity of the questioner (things like that just aren't done in Britain), icily retorted in a crisp British accent: "I am not certain I understand the question. If you are referring to the after-theatre party given by Mr. Carroll, let me say it was definitely not what you referred to as an orgy. Nothing occurred to which anyone could take the least exception. It was a wonderful party. I'd never seen anything like it. The people I met were, without exception, ladies and gentlemen." Then the party drove away.

Later, about 11:00 A.M. on the same morning of April 1, Earl Carroll was busily poring over the plans for his upcoming edition of the *Vanities* with his set designer, Willy Pogany.

It was to be a particularly ambitious project, as his plan was to transform the whole interior of his theatre into a Spanish castle and, as always with a new project, he was enthusiastically making revisions and adding suggestions.

Suddenly, the door burst open and his secretary, Miss Ruth, rushed in, closely followed by two burly men.

Before she could explain who they were, one said, "Mr. Carroll, we have a warrant for your arrest."

Carroll, startled by the interruption, slowly rose from his desk and with a touch of annoyance inquired, "What is this—another April Fool's joke of Guinan's?"

The two officers assured him that it definitely wasn't and handed him a subpoena. It read that he was being indicted for perjury in testifying falsely before the federal grand jury investigating his after-theatre party.

Instructing Miss Ruth to call his lawyer, he was accompanied by his brother Jim, to the Federal Building, where he was joined by his attorney, Herbert C. Smyth. There, pale and nervous, Earl Carroll was arraigned before Judge John C. Knox and pleaded "not guilty."

It had been generally accepted that the grand jury's investigation was to be confined to the question of whether the Volstead Act was violated. The perjury indictment, which carried a maximum penalty of five years imprisonment and a $2,000 fine, was an unexpected outgrowth. It was a complete surprise to Carroll, who had felt safe because under existing liquor laws, all witnesses who testify in Prohibition cases receive automatic immunity.

But United States Attorney Emory R. Buckner pointed out that the "Volstead Act specifically provides also that a witness who testifies *falsely* shall be prosecuted for perjury. It would not be fair for the government to trade immunity for evidence and get in return only false testimony," Mr. Buckner observed. "Hence, the penalty of perjury applies."

The indictment counts set forth were that Carroll perjured himself in February when he denied that liquor was served at the party, that anyone was in the bathtub, and that he had any record of the guests who attended. These same three counts were repeated with reference to his testimony before the grand jury in March.

Carroll's attorney stated that the indictment was "absurd" to mention the bathtub incident in connection with a liquor charge. "It must be obvious to everyone, that any liquid poured into a bathtub that anyone bathed in, *if* such an incident occurred, could not have been intended for beverage purposes."

He then asked for a bill of particulars from the government. He wanted to know who was in the bathtub on the stage of the theatre, according to the government's contention.

"Why, I thought everyone in New York knew who was alleged to have been in the tub. It was Joyce Hawley," said Buckner. "And I'm willing to stipulate on the record that this is the answer to that question, so the defense may not be taken by surprise when the trial begins," he added sarcastically.

Mr. Smyth then wanted to know what the government claimed was in the bathtub when Miss Hawley was alleged to have entered it.

"Wine," said Mr. Buckner.

"And whose authority for the statement that there was wine in the tub?" asked Mr. Smyth.

"Joyce Hawley," replied Mr. Buckner.

Carroll, standing next to his attorney, fidgeted nervously at the mention of the wine bath girl.

The necessity for a bill of particulars having thus been eliminated, Carroll was released on $2,500 bail.

Buckner then requested that bail be raised to $10,000, but Judge Knox, saying that the case was of "just the ordinary garden variety" to him, fixed the smaller amount when informed that Carroll had property and other interests in the city, which would make his departure out of the question.

While under bail, however, Carroll was ordered not to leave the Southern Judicial District, not even to go to Brooklyn.

PHIL PAYNE SAT AT THE DESK in his office at the *Daily Mirror,* holding two legal documents in his hand. One was a subpoena ordering him to appear in court as a witness for the prosecution in the Earl Carroll perjury case.

The other was an entirely different matter. A Mrs. Frances Stevens Hall was suing him and the *Daily Mirror* for libel, claiming that the paper had accused her falsely of murder.

The brutal slaying of her husband, the Reverend Edward Wheeler Hall, and Mrs. Eleanor Mills, choir singer and wife of the church sexton, at a lovers' tryst, had rocked the nation. That Reverend Hall and Mrs. Mills were having an affair was obvious from the passionate love letters that were strewn over their desecrated bodies. The details of the brutal slayings were so lurid, they could not be described in the newspapers. (Somebody had cut off the dead "dominie's" penis and shoved it into the choir singer's mouth.)

The great silent accusation had been that the Reverend's wife, Mrs. Frances Stevens Hall, looked cold, steely, and as able to commit murder as any other outraged wife. But the grand jury of the peaceful little community of New Brunswick, New Jersey, had refused to indict her.

For four years, every New York newspaper had wanted to spring this sensational case, still unsolved in the eyes of the law, but the *Mirror* plunged ahead.

Still pursuing that elusive BIG story that would cornerstone a monumental citadel of public service for the *Mirror,* Phil Payne decided to reopen the Hall-Mills murder case.

He quietly sent his sleuths to the scene, with pockets filled with Hearst cash. For months they sorted old evidence and sought new clues, and on the strength of their conclusions, Payne had Mrs. Hall, the pastor's widow, as well as her two brothers and a cousin, secretly indicted and arrested.

The sensational trial, in an era that liked its homicide socially prominent and sexy, had some notable ramifications—including a district attorney who seemed reluctant to prosecute; a detective who seemed to scramble and hide evidence rather than bring it forth; an expert marksman related to Mrs. Hall; and a brother of Mrs. Hall, said by the prosecution that developed four years after the murder to have Negroid features. He was the town fire buff, Willie Stevens, said to be silly in the head but, like many such characters, quite shrewd on the witness stand.

Phil Payne had broken another unwritten law. It was a mistake: you don't wade into the muddy waters of a case—perhaps deliberately muddied—four years after a murder and accuse the most prominent woman in town without sufficient evidence. The accused hired a battery of noted lawyers.

After a dramatic court battle all were exonerated, and Mrs. Hall instituted a $2,000,000 libel suit against the *Daily Mirror.* Phil Payne knew he was in deep trouble again. He grabbed the crushed Fedora from the rack and, not without relish, headed for the Carroll trial, secretly hoping that "They would send that dirty bastard up for 100 years."

On the day, May 20th, when the trial of Earl Carroll opened, all witnesses were excluded from the courtroom. Joyce Hawley, who was to be the chief witness for the government, paced the corridor outside the courtroom during a part of the day. It was said that only those having business in the room would be admitted, but the seats were practically all occupied. A double line, half a block long, stood in the corridor.

Although Carroll, through his attorney, had pleaded for an immediate trial at the time of the indictment, he now urged delay on the ground that Colonel William R. Edrington, his chief witness, in whose honor the bathtub party was given, was in England.

There was a lively argument between United States Attorney Buckner and Carroll's counsel, Smyth. Mr. Buckner sarcastically remarked that the government was willing to admit that Colonel Edrington would willingly testify that Carroll's testimony before the grand jury was true.

With that point settled, Judge Goddard marked the case "Ready," and the selection of the jury began. It was completed only after the government had exhausted all of its six peremptory challenges and the defense had used nine of a possible ten. Each juror said he was not opposed to a host serving intoxicating liquor to his guests at a private party, and that he had no affiliation with any organization actively interested in the enforcement of Prohibition.

The trial jury, members of which had said also that they were not opposed to any theatrical performances then showing in the city, and had not been invited to Carroll's party, was composed of two insurance brokers, Max Klein and Mortimer B. Rosenthal; a printer, Henry Brownstone; an importer, Ernest H. Boyschen; two salesmen, Franklin D. Pagen and Benjamin J. Brotman; a manufacturer, Max S. Weil; a realtor, Charles W. Smith; a retired cotton broker, David Mayer; two credit managers, William Retz and Jerome W. Bickart; and Roscoe Van Newland, who listed "no occupation."

Despite Carroll's attorney's valiant efforts, he was unsuccessful in having any women picked for the panel.

One prospective female juror, Mrs. Zoe Anderson, admitted that padlock proceedings were pending against one of her tenants and was excused after the defense had lost a fight for her retention. Another, a prissy, straight-laced housewife from neighboring Yonkers, said she did not "approve of serving liquor under any circumstances," and was promptly challenged by the defense.

All of Carroll's testimony before the February and March grand juries was read to the jurors and thus made public for the first time. The reading occupied about an hour. According to the transcript, he had testified, among other things, that he very seldom drank intoxicants, that he had possibly drunk one glass of champagne in his life, and that he could never tell the difference between Scotch and rye whiskey. He had also testified that liquor was neither "possessed nor furnished" at the affair by anyone, that the bathtub had contained only Canada Dry Ginger Ale and nothing stronger. He had given the grand jury only seven or eight names of guests, including Vera, the Countess of Cathcart, Irvin S. Cobb, Harry K. Thaw, Frank Tinney, Joe Cook, and Peggy Hopkins Joyce; and a number of members of the press, including Walter Winchell, O. O. McIntyre, Ed Sullivan, and Phil Payne. He added that the "release cards," which he had asked his guests to sign as a joke, had mysteriously disappeared on the night or early morning of the party. He said that the guests had been invited and paid nothing, that the party had been orderly throughout, and that there had been about as many guests there at the "finish" as at the "start." His testimony was that the bathtub had been on a raised platform and that no one stepped into, was pushed into, or had fallen into the tub at any time during the party.

Just after the noon recess had been declared, the reporters started to scurry around when a strange, attractive, well-dressed woman, in her early thirties, walked down the aisle accompanied by a court attendant. She rushed up to Carroll at the counsel table and threw her arms around his neck, exclaiming, "Mon Cheri, Mon Cheri!"

Carroll seemed surprised, if not astonished. He kissed her perfunctorily on the cheek.

Pressed for an explanation by the press, during the recess they went upstairs to the reporters' room to be photographed. Carroll put his arm around the woman's waist and said to photographers: "Let me be snapped with my *wife*. There are a lot of people who do not know I have one."

Carroll acted as though Marcelle's arrival was a matter of little significance. When questioned by the reporters why he and his wife lived apart, he glibly remarked, "Nothing unusual about that. She lives in France and spends a good deal of her time with her ailing parents." His attitude was casual, but he had a set smile and the tone in his voice was tinged with ice.

Marcelle smiled broadly at the remark, just as though she, too, believed what he had said. She was obviously enjoying the attention.

However, during the recess Carroll managed to get Marcelle out of the room. Then he exploded at both Jim and Smyth.

"What the hell's the idea, bringing her here? Christ, I didn't even know we were still married," he thundered.

"Don't look at me," Jim protested. "It was Smyth's idea."

"It was a damned lousy idea! I haven't seen her for seven years. And I had no interest in ever seeing her again!" Carroll's face was red with anger.

The attorney, not to be ruffled by his client's flare-up, remarked softly, "It was a smart thing to do, Earl. Look at it this way. You have a 'playboy' image, a man who has women falling into bed with him every ten minutes. You're a sex object. That won't set well with the judge or jury. So I thought it would be a good idea to bring over Marcelle. She sits by your side, she looks like the loving wife, and she gives you a new image."

"But I don't want a new image!" Carroll roared. "I don't need it. I can win this thing by myself!"

"I wish I could believe that," Smyth replied, "but it just isn't in the cards. Did you see this story in the paper today?"

Earl waved it away in irritation. His usual composure and self-assurance was fast disappearing.

"He's right, Earl," pressed Jim, taking the paper from Smyth. "The sin-chasers are out in full force. Listen to this: 'The Reverend John Roach Stratton, pastor of the Calvary Baptist Church on Fifth Avenue, last night in his sermon declared that the Earl Carroll "bathtub party" was an indecent, disgusting, and un-American drunken orgy....' "

" 'Un-American'!" exclaimed Carroll incredulously. It was obvious his temper was becoming frayed as Jim continued to read.

" 'I've never been so ashamed as when I heard that in this great American city, in this Christian land, such a barbarian spectacle, lower than those in Rome's worst day, could be admittedly put on. Imagine those veterans who, in three wars, gave their lives to purify and enrich the flag!' "

Carroll's face reflected the resentment and contempt he held for these self-styled moralists.

"And listen to this for a punch line," Jim went on. " 'Even though legal legerdemain frees Earl Carroll, this culprit ought to be branded before the world, and should be shut out of decent circles until there are signs of repentance.' "

"See what I mean, Earl?" said Smyth, picking up the argument. "We've got to create the ideal marriage. To that crowd there, the loving looks between man and wife are a lot more acceptable than playing leapfrog from bed to bed. Look what happened in the Fatty Arbuckle case. He was a dead duck after two trials. So his loyal wife, Minta Durfee, joins him at his side at the third and last trial, and he is acquitted. And they'd been estranged for years."

Carroll, however, was not convinced, but he reluctantly gave in with the assurance of both Jim and Smyth that Marcelle would be put up in a hotel so that he would not have to see her except in court.

In his opening address to the jury, Mr. Buckner stated that "the government would show that Carroll had unlawfully, knowingly, willfully, and contrary to his oath, stated material matter which he did not believe to be true," and that therefore Carroll had committed perjury on all counts named in the indictment.

The government's first piece of testimony, that there had been intoxicating liquor served at the party and that there had been someone in a tub of champagne about four o'clock on the morning of February 23rd, was given by witness Phil Payne.

After taking the oath, Payne testified he had arrived at the party with his "companion," Peggy Hopkins Joyce, about 2:00 A.M., and had been preparing to leave, around 4:00 A.M., when Carroll approached him and said:

"Don't go yet. I'm going to put on a wow of a stunt. Remember when Ziegfeld had Anna Held take a milk-bath? Well, tonight I'm going to go him one better. I'm going to have a beautiful girl take a bath in a tub of wine."

"May I print the story?" Payne said he asked Carroll.

"Go as far as you like," the producer replied, according to the witness.

Carroll could hardly be contained in his chair. "That's a *Goddamned lie*," he muttered in a hoarse whisper that caught the ear and reproving glance of the judge.

Carroll leaned closer to Smyth, his voice shaking with emotion.

"That sonofabitch is lying. Can you imagine me giving an exclusive to him or to anyone, with all those other newspapermen there? I'd be an idiot!"

In answer to the question from Buckner, "Was there any liquor served at the party?" Payne replied, "Yes, I drank two glasses of champagne during the evening."

Then Buckner asked, "And did you see a girl enter a bathtub of champagne?"

"I did."

"Could you describe the incident for us?"

"Well, they pulled a bathtub onto the stage and put it on a platform. Two men came out and emptied two kegs of wine into it.

Then I saw a nude woman—a woman without any clothing on at all—get into that tub. I saw her climb over the side of the tub."

"What happened next?"

"And then Mr. Carroll invited everybody up to have a drink out of the tub."

"That's all. Your witness, Mr. Smyth."

Under cross-examination, defense attorney Smyth's first question to the witness was: "Mr. Payne, would you tell the court in what capacity you attended the Carroll party on the night of February 22nd?"

"I was there as a reporter," Payne answered.

"Do you go wherever you are invited as a reporter?"

"Wherever I go, I am a reporter first of all."

"Then you are a dangerous man to invite anywhere, aren't you, Mr. Payne?"

"Not to everyone, Mr. Smyth. Perhaps to you. Most of my hosts have nothing to fear. Mr. Carroll wanted the publicity. I attended the party primarily to talk business with Lady Cathcart, who was a guest there, and Mr. Carroll asked me to stay for the bathtub scene."

Mr. Smyth stressed the point that Payne, according to his own statements, had gone as a guest of Carroll, and had then reported the story about the alleged violations of the Prohibition Law. Payne said he had testified under subpoena, and had told only the truth.

"And you consider yourself a gentleman?" asked Mr. Smyth.

"Yes. More of a gentleman for telling the truth, don't you think so?"

"Well, if you ask me what I think," said Smyth, "I will tell you I'd rather cut off my right hand than give the testimony you've just given."

Mr. Buckner objected at this point, and Judge Goddard rebuked Mr. Smyth. "It is a tradition of the profession," announced the judge, "not to take advantage of the fact that the witness cannot ask questions."

Smyth apologized to the court and then asked Payne: "Did you talk to Carroll about this publicity after the party?"

"Yes. I called him on the phone the following day, and asked him whether he was denying the story we published. He said he was forced to deny it, because it was getting him into trouble. I told him that I did not object to his denial of the story but resented his saying I had violated a confidence while I was his guest, when the truth was, I had asked him expressly about publishing it and had received his consent."

Much to Carroll's annoyance, Payne went on to testify that two nights later Carroll had talked to him in Texas Guinan's club and asked him to lay off.

"That's another lie. I never spoke a word to him that night," Carroll whispered to his attorney.

Payne was then asked by Mr. Smyth whether he had not received word from his "boss, Mr. Hearst" to stop publishing stories about the Carroll party and replied he had received no such message.

"Mr. Payne, do you not have a small interest in a theatrical production called *The Bunk of 1926?*"

The witness replied, "Yes, but I do not consider myself a competitor of Carroll as a producer." He said he would not by any means call his production an attempt to "glorify the American girl," adding that he was certainly no expert in such matters.

The next question was: "Mr. Payne, you testified earlier that you were served two glasses of champagne."

"That is correct."

"How did you know it was champagne?"

Payne said he knew it was champagne because it was effervescent, it sparkled, it was tangy, and it had a pleasant taste. He was then asked to explain what taste meant, and also the meaning of effervescence, tang, and sparkle. Lost in a maze of technicalities, Payne finally said, "Give me a glass of champagne and I can tell you quickly it's champagne."

This caused Mr. Smyth to say he was "afraid" to do so in Mr. Buckner's presence. Judge Goddard again rebuked him and Mr. Smyth again apologized.

"One more question, Mr. Payne. Did this tangy champagne that you drank come from Miss Hawley's bathtub?"

Payne, a little hesitantly, said, "No. It was poured from green bottles taken from a table nearby. But I'm certain it was champagne because I recall distinctly the peculiar name on the labels. It was Pol Roget."

"Will you tell the court how the name was spelled?" asked Mr. Smyth.

"P-o-l R-o-g-e-t," replied the witness.

"Why, don't you know," said Mr. Smyth smiling broadly, "that the *real* champagne of that name is spelled P-o-l R-o-g-e-*r*? Are you not aware that there is on the market an alleged *nonintoxicating* beverage called Pol Roget Champagne?"

Buckner jumped up and objected on the ground that "today labels mean nothing," and Judge Goddard sustained the objection.

"That's all," concluded Smyth, and the witness was excused.

A point indicating a possible line of defense developed during the testimony of Phil Payne. It became apparent the defense was centering its efforts against any attempt to prove that the bathtub contained any intoxicating beverage, as the contents of the tub were admittedly material to the grand jury's investigation.

The name of the next witness was then called, and there was a distinct murmur from the spectators in the courtroom as the back door swung open and the lady-of-the-diamonds, Peggy Hopkins Joyce, swept in, dressed in a mauve suit, cloche hat, and sable scarves. Midway down the aisle, without a flicker of recognition on either part, she passed Phil Payne.

After being sworn in, she sat jauntily in the witness chair, threw her furs off her shoulders, and crossed her beautiful legs in a pose reminiscent of countless shipboard news photos that the public was well acquainted with.

After giving her name, she was asked her occupation, and when she demurely murmured, "Housewife," it drew not only muffled giggles from the courtroom but even a smile from the sedate Judge Goddard.

Mr. Buckner began, "Miss Joyce, am I correct in saying that you accompanied Mr. Philip Payne to a party given by Earl Carroll on the morning of February 23rd?"

"Yes, you are," she replied. "We arrived there about two o'clock in the morning. We decided to have dinner and see the late show at the Palais Royal on Broadway because it's only a block or so away from Mr. Carroll's theatre on Seventh Avenue. We both are very fond of Paul Whiteman. He has a marvelous new group called the Rhythm Boys. There's one singer he's got named Bing Crosby and he's just wonderful. You should hear them sing "Mississippi Mud.""

At this point, Judge Goddard politely admonished Miss Joyce with, "It's not necessary to elaborate. Just answer the questions."

Mr. Buckner continued: "What time did you and Mr. Payne leave the party?"

"Well, Mr. Payne left first—about a quarter to five. He had to get back to his office and do some work. I left around six, and Mr. Carroll dropped me off at my apartment."

Buckner then said, "Before Mr. Payne left, did you at any time overhear Mr. Carroll give him permission to print the story about the party?"

"Definitely not!" Peggy retorted. "For one thing, Mr. Carroll never came down into the auditorium, and if Earl had said anything to Phil from the stage, not only I but many people around us would have most assuredly heard him make the statement."

Buckner then asked, "Miss Joyce, during the time from midnight to six in the morning, did you see a girl enter a bathtub?"

"Yes, I did. It was about 4:30 in the morning."

"Well, tell us about it."

"A couple of stage hands wheeled the bathtub out, put it on a platform, and filled it with ginger ale—"

Buckner tried to interrupt with, "Miss Joyce, are you cert—" but Peggy kept rattling on.

"We were seated in the front row of the orchestra when Miss Hawley came from the wings. Mr. Carroll called for a cloak, and I handed my fur coat to a friend in the orchestra who passed it up to him. I remember yelling to Earl 'Treat it gently. It cost $65,000!' "

She wriggled in the witness chair, causing her short skirt to carelessly crawl up over her knee, high enough to reveal just a glimpse of her soft, lily-white thighs. It was not totally overlooked by the all-male jury.

For the first time that day, Carroll smiled, relaxed. He seemed to be thoroughly enjoying Peggy Hopkins Joyce's performance. Here was a real woman. No mental giant, but a woman who was smart enough to know what her best selling point was—and she used it with no apologies.

"Did you see Miss Hawley in the tub?" queried Buckner.

"Yes, I did after Mr. Carroll took my coat away, but all I could see was her head and shoulders."

Peggy seemed about to add more when Judge Goddard interrupted her to adjourn the trial until 10:45 the next morning.

On the second day of the trial, Peggy Joyce was again called to the stand, to complete her testimony.

Buckner continued his questioning. "Miss Joyce, you testified yesterday that the bathtub, in which a nude girl sat, was filled with only ginger ale."

"I did."

"How can you be certain of that?"

"Well, Mr. Buckner, I've been drinking champagne for 15 years. I go to Europe every summer, and over there we drink it daily with our dinner. I'm very familiar not only with its taste, smell, and effect, but I certainly know it when I see it."

She continued, as if explaining to a small child, "And, I *tell* you that was a *brownish liquid* in the tub, unlike any champagne."

Buckner then posed the question, "Well, Miss Joyce, will you tell the court, at any time during the party did you see anyone, or participate yourself, in the consumption of any kind of alcoholic beverages?"

Peggy retorted, "Certainly not. Wine affects me more readily than most persons and two glasses would be sufficient to make me feel the effects keenly. Yet, I had two drinks at the party and did not obtain the slightest suggestion of a 'kick'—because, as *I said before*, it was ginger ale."

Buckner, resenting the tone of her voice, then went in for the kill, "Well, Miss Joyce, it may interest you to know that your escort, Mr. Payne, has just testified that *he* took two drinks at the party and his was champagne."

Miss Joyce laughingly replied, "Oh, Mr. Buckner. You don't know Phil Payne. He's no authority on wine. He very seldom drinks intoxicants. He's almost a teetotaler—he wouldn't know the difference between Scotch whiskey and rye."

Buckner, becoming exasperated, finally asked her whether she had seen all the men standing around, waiting their turn to get a drink from Miss Hawley's bathtub. When she answered in the affirmative, Judge Goddard asked one question that brought a broad smile to Mr. Buckner's face.

"Miss Joyce, is the court to understand that all these men were standing around that bathtub just to get a drink of *ginger ale?*"

"That's correct, Your Honor," she answered sweetly.

Judge Goddard stopped the laughter in the courtroom with his gavel as the witness was dismissed.

The next witness called by the government was Irvin S. Cobb. Mr. Cobb said he had known Carroll for a number of years, that they had visited each other socially, and that Carroll's reputation for "truth and veracity" was, so far as he knew, "excellent."

When questioned by Buckner regarding intoxicants served at the party, Mr. Cobb continued. "Well, I am not a drinking man because you can't be sure of what you're getting these days. Once in awhile, I drink a cocktail, when I am reasonably certain that the effect will not be immediately fatal. For that reason, I am not in a position to state whether any intoxicating liquor was served at the party. Personally, I only had a glass of Canada Dry Ginger Ale just like they serve during the show. There were boxes of it stacked up backstage, and I also saw a half-barrel of what I was told was near beer, but that is all I can tell you about that."

"Do you drink at all?"

"Not brandy or whiskey—except medicinally. I have not drunk champagne for some years. I am acquainted with a real champagne called 'Paul Roger.' "

He was reminded with a laugh from Mr. Buckner that the first name of the wine was spelled "P-o-l."

Cobb, when questioned about the girl in the bathtub, said, "No, unfortunately I left before it occurred. But, perhaps it's just as well. At my age, I don't think my blood pressure could have taken it."

Pleased with the testimony of this friendly witness, Mr. Smyth had little to add.

"I hope you will pardon the question, Mr. Cobb," he said, "but you are one of the foremost writers in the country, are you not?"

"In my own opinion, I am," replied the witness.

"And what was your opinion of Mr. Carroll's party?"

"Well, measured by the accepted standards of Broadway, the party seemed to me to be perfectly proper."

Just before he was excused, Cobb said, with a twinkle in his eye, "I don't think I've been much help around here. I suppose the only reason they subpoenaed me was my face is one not easily forgotten."

As he passed Carroll, seated at the counsel table, he extended his hand and cordially shook that of the producer.

During the trial, Smyth produced many other character witnesses for Earl Carroll, including David Belasco, the dean of the American theatre. The eminent producer said Carroll had a good reputation and the Lambs Club had found him quite acceptable. Asked by Mr. Smyth if the Lambs was a club of gentlemen, Mr. Belasco replied: "That is the understanding."

Next on the stand was one of the most distinguished and successful American dramatists, Augustus Thomas, the prolific author of, among other things, *The Copperhead*, which had made a star of Lionel Barrymore.

He had just given his name when Mr. Smyth, saying the jurors might not all know him by reputation so well, asked him to "tell us who you are."

"Well," said Mr. Thomas, "that is my right name. I am a member of several social clubs, democratic clubs, and anti-Prohibition leagues. I have been a dramatist for 50 years, and I think I've had more success than I deserve." He said he had known Carroll for several years and in his opinion, "Earl's character is excellent."

There was almost a ripple of applause from the spectators when the inimitable Al Jolson took the stand.

He testified he had "no occupation," but had been an actor for 25 years. He went on to say that he considered Carroll "one of the finest men I've ever known," and was proud to be a friend of the defendant.

When "Jolie," the greatest entertainer of his time, left the stand, he gave Carroll a warm smile and an affectionate pat on the shoulder as he jauntily walked out of the courtroom.

After the noon recess, the trial was marked by sharp clashes between government witnesses and the trial counsel for Carroll. Twice Judge Goddard, at the request of Attorney Buckner, rebuked Mr. Smyth.

Witnesses testifying for the prosecution included Robert Bruce Coleman, Jr., dramatic editor of the *Daily Mirror;* Max Lief, assistant dramatic editor; Arthur F. Irwin, night editor; and Paul F. Lubben, a cub reporter on the same tabloid.

Throughout his cross-examinations, Smyth tried to make each witness appear to be a person who accepted Carroll's hospitality and then turned against him. He openly accused several witnesses of having done exactly that, and several times Judge Goddard rebuked him for his methods of examination.

The *Mirror* men on the stand answered Mr. Smyth's charge by saying that Phil Payne had published the story because Mr. Carroll wanted him to do so, and that he later falsely accused their boss of having violated a confidence.

Mr. Smyth then scored a strong point for the defense when all members of the *Mirror* staff were forced to admit that *none* of them had actually been present when Carroll was alleged to have given Payne permission to print the story.

Smyth also endeavored to show that the witnesses who testified were not capable of recognizing the taste of wine or champagne, and challenged the 22-year-old cub reporter, Lubben, as being "too inexperienced" when Lubben said he had drunk champagne a year before Prohibition and had had 10 or 15 glasses of it thereafter.

Smyth made no attempt, however, to disprove that Miss Hawley was in the tub. On the contrary, he made it clear that the defense contended that whether a woman bathed in the nude in a tub of liquid on a stage, February 23rd, was not material to the grand jury investigation that resulted in Carroll's indictment.

When court convened the day Joyce Hawley was to take the stand, the courtroom was crowded. At the morning session, there had been a sprinkling of women, and 200 or more persons were permitted to remain standing. In the afternoon, when the taking of Miss Hawley's testimony began, no one was permitted to stand. As a result, 200 or more persons could not get in and the women in the audience had dwindled to two; one was Dorothy Knapp and the other was Earl Carroll's wife, who sat across the counsel table from her husband. There had been a dozen or more young girls, members of Carroll's *Vanities*, in court but Judge Goddard suggested they be asked to retire, as he thought they looked too young to hear the kind of testimony that might develop. The young women walked out, smiling.

Miss Hawley was then called. Although she had been told to appear at 10:30 A.M., she did not arrive until about noon. Judge Goddard declared a recess because of her absence, and said he would issue a bench warrant for her if she did not appear in 20 minutes. Upon arrival, she explained she had understood that four witnesses were to be examined before she was to be called.

On the stand, she said her real name was Teresa Daugelas, and she had attended public school and high school and spent one year in a convent. She had come to New York from Chicago, a few months before.

On direct examination, she said she had met Earl Carroll when she'd been employed by him as a model for a fashion show at the Hotel Astor.

As Carroll was paying her $20 for the night's work, he remarked, "Baby, you're pretty. How much would you charge to pose nude in a bathtub?"

"I told him it would cost him a helluva lot more than $20."

He then said, "What would you say to $1,000?"

"When I told him, 'That's more like it,' he said he was planning a little stunt for an after-theatre party the following night on the stage of his theatre. He told me the party would start after the regular performance and to get there about midnight."

Upon her arrival, she said, Carroll told her to go behind a curtain until the bathtub was made ready, and gave her a chemise to wear. While she was waiting, Chris Scaife, of Carroll's staff, had persuaded her to drink several glasses of wine, as she called it. She added piously that it was the first time she ever tasted champagne.

"What effect did the liquid have on you?" asked Mr. Buckner.

"It got me drunk," replied Miss Hawley. "Finally—I don't know how long it was—Mr. Carroll called, 'Baby, all right—come on out,' and led me to the tub. While Mr. Carroll held a coat in front of me, I took off what I had on—the chemise and my slippers. And then I got into the tub. Mr. Carroll picked up one of my slippers, dipped it in the champagne, and, holding it up, invited everyone to take some of 'this beautiful drink.' All of a sudden, about 15 or 20 men crowded around and they were dipping their glasses into the tub all around me. I was so embarrassed—and besides, the champagne was so cold. Then, I don't know what happened. The tub started to move."

"What did you do then?" Mr. Buckner asked.

"I dressed and came out and Mr. Carroll seemed very annoyed and said, 'Damn it, keep your head up or get off the floor.' He told me to tell reporters my name was Vera Hawley. Two days afterward, I saw Mr. Carroll at the theatre and reminded him I had been promised $1,000 to get into the tub. Then Mr. Carroll laughed and asked me whether I wanted the $1,000 or $20 in cash. I was crying and did not answer. I never received anything but $20 for the bathtub act. I went to a lawyer. I don't know whether a suit against Mr. Carroll was started or not. I have not seen Mr. Carroll since."

During cross-examination by Carroll's attorney, Joyce Hawley testified with tears and temper. In moments of irritation, she flared at her cross-examiner and tore to shreds a "Buddy Poppy"; at other times, she laboriously pulled on and off a white glove, then lowered her head and wiped tears from her eyes.

In answer to Mr. Smyth's opening questions, Miss Hawley testified she could neither sing nor dance, but had offered herself merely as a model and showgirl. She willingly admitted she had used various names. She said that in Chicago, where her parents live, she used any name she thought of, if she did not want a person to whom she was introduced to know who she was. She said she did not live with her parents in Chicago, but in various hotels there, including the Congress and the Morrison. She had been earning $1.50 to $2.50 an hour posing for artists in Chicago, and had paid $3.00 a day for her hotel room.

When Miss Hawley refused to give the address of her parents, the judge asked Mr. Smyth whether he thought it necessary to go into such matters. "I want to learn something about the young lady," said the attorney.

"I think you know enough now," snapped Miss Hawley.

The girl said she had also lived in the 44th Street Hotel in New York for four months, and was then living with a graduate nurse and her husband.

Asked how she had come to take the bathtub job, she replied: "I was broke and I thought I might as well do it as to let some other dame get the money for it."

Mr. Smyth pressed on, by asking Miss Hawley whether she had been "so drunk" that she could not recall details of what had happened the night of the party.

She answered: "I remember things, but I was feeling very good. I had to feel very good to do a thing like that."

She admitted she had been a brunette in the tub, and that she was wearing a "transformation" on the stand, but said that she was naturally a blonde. She denied she was bitter against Carroll, but said what he had done was "not a nice thing for him to do."

Mr. Smyth asked the witness whether she had told Jim Carroll she had a grand jury subpoena, and that she wanted $1,000 and a $4000 contract, and also whether she had told Scaife, Carroll's assistant, she would sue for $100,000 in damages. She denied she asked for $100,000 or for a $4,000 contract, but insisted she had wanted only the $1,000 promised her.

Then, Miss Hawley accused Scaife when she said, "I told Scaife I would drop my suit against Mr. Carroll for $500 and he told me he would give me $350 after the trial if I would deny everything."

Miss Hawley said she had first retained an attorney, Mortimer Abrahams, because she thought she would need a lawyer when she went before the grand jury, but later "gave him the air" because he would not proceed for her against Carroll.

Smyth then said, "Miss Hawley, you testified earlier that you tasted your first champagne at Mr. Carroll's party. Tell us, was that the *first* time you ever drank any kind of intoxicating liquor?"

Miss Hawley hesitated for a moment, then as she ripped the stem from her "Buddy Poppy," exclaimed, "Oh, you asked such damned foolish questions—you get me all balled up."

After the judge had pounded his gavel to stop the laughter and restore order in the court, Mr. Smyth continued: "Miss Hawley, isn't it true that you are now doing a bathtub act in a Broadway show?"

"Yes, I am working in the *Greenwich Village Follies.*"

"And aren't you posing in the nude for pictures and making more money than you ever did before?"

She went on to explain that before the show opened, the newspapers wanted to take nude pictures for publicity purposes, so she let them take them, but added, "I wasn't completely in the nude. I was wearing a chiffon scarf."

"Well, tell the court, aren't you billed 'The Queen of the Bath,' and don't the ads in the newspapers promise viewers a sensational 'Tub Tableau'?"

Impatiently she murmured, "Yeah, that's right."

Mr. Smyth then produced a brochure that was being sent to dance halls and theatres all over the country, which issued a scale of prices for her services:

Personal Interview:	$100.00
With Photograph:	$150.00
True Life Story &	
Inside Peeps Behind	
a Nudity Revue:	$1,000.00

For a girl who was only a hog-butcher's daughter from Chicago, still only a year away from the smell of the stockyards, the statuesque young model showed a highly professional business sense, when she also demanded a share of all syndication rights.

After Miss Hawley identified the document, Mr. Smyth offered it in evidence, and the court received it as an exhibit.

Jim Carroll was then called on the stand and testified that Miss Hawley had several times tried to see Carroll after the bathtub party, and had once asked him to telephone his brother, threatening; "You can tell Mr. Carroll that I have another appointment and that he will be sorry. He will soon be seeking me out. Tomorrow, I am going before the grand jury. This is his last chance."

He was followed by Chris Scaife, who quoted Miss Hawley as having said she would make "plenty of trouble" for Carroll if he did not come up with the money, but would give any testimony he wanted if she received the $1,000. He added that she later offered to "testify to anything" for $500.

Some bitterness characterized the summing up by Mr. Smyth and also that by United States Attorney Emory R. Buckner.

In a speech lasting an hour and a half, Mr. Smyth charged the government with conducting the trial "under the disguise of a sex case," whereas, he said, it was an attempt by a "pretty woman" to blackmail Carroll in order to "wreak her vengeance upon him." He told the jury it should disregard the testimony concerning the presence of a woman in the bathtub, as the grand jury inquiry had been conducted solely into possible violations of the Probition Law and the bathtub scene was not material.

"There is nothing more charming than a pretty woman, yet how often pretty women without consciences will go to any length to wreak their vengeance upon men."

Mr. Smyth then reviewed Miss Hawley's testimony, said she had deliberately fooled Mr. Buckner and had given him not her own name but that of a younger sister, knowing he would send for the birth certificate of the person whose name she gave. He pointed out that she had admitted living alone and being in Chicago hotels at the age of 14 and posing in the nude as a model.

"Her object here in court was obvious," Mr. Smyth continued. "It was to impress you gentlemen with her need for sympathy and protection. Even the learned judge admonished me, at one time when she was on the stand, and spoke of protecting a young girl, because he did not know what I knew. Sympathy! Why she, even now, is

Young Earl Carroll as a
Bible salesman in China

World War I doughboy bids
goodbye to Mama Elizabeth,
whom he adored

Marcelle Hontabat, French
showgirl of the Folies
Bergère, loved, married,
and then left him

Lieutenant Earl Carroll,
the 206th pilot in the world
to receive a F.A.I. pilot rating

The neophyte song writer

Lady of the Lamp
Carroll's first flop on Broadway

Bavu—another bomb, notable only
for introducing a young new
actor to the Broadway stage,
William Powell

"Me Tondeleyo"
White Cargo was Carroll's first hit

Peggy Hopkins Joyce
Sex to her was not a word;
it was a way of life

Earl Carroll
The female form
—always within reach

Peggy's hobby was collecting
diamonds, furs, expensive
automobiles—and millionaire
husbands

Dorothy Knapp

Her face and figure conformed
to all requirements of rare
beauty. In 1923, Carroll
proclaimed her "the most
beautiful girl in the world "

Kathryn Ray

In the second edition of the
Vanities the luscious Miss Ray
became Earl Carroll's paramour
on and off the stage

EARL CARROLL THEATRE

For displaying this "obscene" picture in the lobby of his theatre, Earl Carroll spent four days in the New York Tombs, 1925

A Familiar Scene in the Carroll Chronicle

Pretty Eileen Wenzel is the girl in the center looking at Earl Carroll. The tall brunette with the wide-brimmed hat at the right of the picture is Faith Bacon, the provocative fan dancer

NOTHING BUT THE TRUTH

NEW YORK EVENING GRAPHIC

THE WEATHER—Fair and Colder

COMPLETE EDITION

**The Phony *Graphic*
Picture that Sent Carroll
to the Federal Penitentiary**

Joyce Hawley in the bathtub full
of wine; a chemise-clad Dorothy
Knapp doing the Charleston;
comedian Frank Tinney and Harry
K. Thaw in the background
looking on; host Earl Carroll
at right; and Irvin S. Cobb,
shielding his face, at left

Convict #24909 on the
prison honor farm

**"For God's Sake,
Marcelle, Get Off My Back!"**

The Graphic had a field day
depicting Earl's problems with
his wife in the Greenville
City Hospital.

**Arriving in New York
after His Release from Prison**

"A wife's place is by her loving
husband's side in his hour of
need." The look on Carroll's
face showed that he didn't agree

The man responsible for Earl Carroll's successful comeback on Broadway—the inimitable and irascible—W. C. Fields

It was in this show, *Vanities of 1928*, that Beryl Wallace walked into the life of Earl Carroll

Vivacious singing star Lillian Roth had "a right to sing the blues," she didn't get along with Carroll

Even the "support" of the great
Fanny Brice, Leon Erroll, and
Lionel Atwill couldn't help Dorothy

Fioretta

Dorothy Knapp
Unsinging Prima Donna

When Earl Carroll tried to star
his sweetheart in an operetta
called *Fioretta*, it proved to be
one of the most costly flops
in Broadway history—it lost
$350,000

In 1935 Broadway looked like a
tawdry, decadent strumpet in
the rags of her outmoded finery

At the opening night party on
the stage of the Winter Garden
with the new heavyweight
champion of the world, James
J. Braddock, and my red-headed
friend, Jim Carroll

With his persuasive powers Earl Carroll was able to con three pretty good workmen to break ground for his new Hollywood theatre—
W. C. FIELDS • EDDIE CANTOR • JACK BENNY

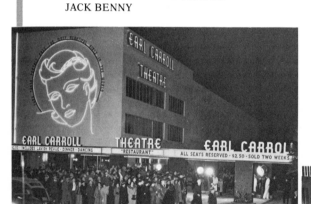

On the set, "A Night at Earl Carroll's"—Paramount

December 25, 1938 The opening of the new Earl Carroll Theatre Restaurant in Hollywood

Errol Flynn and Jimmy Durante go up on stage

Beryl Wallace and Milton Berle

Bob and Dolores Hope, Jerry Colonna, Bill and Philippa Goodwin, and Beverly Carroll

W. C. Fields and Jean Tighe

Beryl Wallace and Joe E. Brown

Robert Taylor and admirer

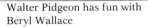

Walter Pidgeon has fun with Beryl Wallace

Gloria Lynn and Don Ameche

It soon became the playground of the stars

Not to be outdone by the
footprints in the forecourt of the
Chinese Theatre, Earl Carroll had
his own Wall of Fame in Hollywood,
and he had some pretty stylish
signatories, among them—
Ingrid Bergman

Earl Carroll's yacht, *Vanities*
panking along in a fresh breeze

In 1938, Earl Carroll gave a
party for his sweetheart Beryl,
celebrating the tenth anniversary
of their romance

The Earl Carroll mansion
at 1140 Schuyler Road,
Beverly Hills

At one of the masquerade parties, host Earl Carroll was costumed as John Barrymore in the *Merchant of Venice*. That's Elaine Barry, John's last wife, helping Earl adjust his mask

Judging a beauty contest
at the Ambassador Hotel

The winner, beautiful
sixteen-year-old Norma
Jean Baker

Marilyn Monroe had that
indefinable something that
made her a bit special; the
rare element that is such an
important part of the chemistry
that makes a great picture
personality

d
f

a
u

Stassen-Taft Deal

nightly duplicating her bathtub act and making more money than she ever did before."

There was a long pause, then Smyth turned to the jury and in a voice fraught with emotion proclaimed: "The author of the Volstead Act never had any idea, in his wildest imaginings, that it would be used to obtain a conviction based on a girl in a tub without clothing. Yet, that is the issue the government has been stressing here. If you try my client on that, you will go outside anything over which the government has jurisdiction. Mr. Buckner has often complained of the clogged wheels of justice. Yet, he has taken up a great deal of time, and part of the $70,000 a year he claims it requires to enforce Prohibition, to try this kind of case. If liquor was not in the bathtub, the incident was not material. The grand jury inquiry was under the national Prohibition Law."

His final words were: "Assuming the worst, that the government charges are true, I ask you jurors to keep in mind that if Mr. Carroll lied, he lied like a gentleman, to protect his guests."

Then Mr. Buckner arose and, before addressing the jury, caused a smile by taking a drink from a bottle of ginger ale.

After placing it back on the table, he characterized his opponent's summing up as the most "daring, brazen, and desperate" he had ever heard.

"For Mr. Smyth to say that Carroll lied like a gentleman is virtually a plea of guilty."

He described Carroll's party as a "publicity stunt from the very beginning" for the benefit of Carroll and the *Daily Mirror*. "This talk of Carroll protecting his guests is bunk," declared Mr. Buckner. "No guest violated the Prohibition law. It is no violation for a guest to drink when his or her host offers it."

The prosecutor paid only brief attention to Miss Hawley's part in the case, making practically no reply to Mr. Smyth's attack on her character.

"Miss Hawley is not mine," he shouted to the jury, "I didn't put her in the bathtub. She's Carroll's. I brought her here because she's the woman he put in the tub. Anytime Earl Carroll puts a better woman in one of his bathtubs on the stage of his theatre, then I'll bring a better woman to this courtroom."

Mr. Buckner, staring directly at Carroll, repeated slowly the oath Carroll took when testifying before the grand juries. He then turned to the 12 men in the docket and said: "Carroll lied to protect his bootlegger. On two occasions he took this oath, then spat on the Bible and lied deliberately to protect commercial bootlegging. He did it because he thinks he is above the law. But he is not! No man can say I have treated one person differently from another in my prosecutions or investigations upon complaints. Gentlemen, as the judge will instruct you, if you find that there was a woman in that bathtub, whether it contained wine or ginger ale, you *must* convict the defendant of perjury. This case has not so much to do with Prohibition, but with what is to become of God, of our oaths, our courts, and institutions if a man like Earl Carroll is to be permitted to boot the Bible out of this building, have his attorney apologize for him, and get away with it!"

At the conclusion of Mr. Buckner's oratory, Judge Goddard adjourned the trial for the day, saying that he would begin his charge to the jury at the next session.

WHEN THE COURT CONVENED the next morning, the judge began his charge to the jury by reading from the indictment the four counts the jury had to consider. Judge Goddard said: "Earl Carroll is being tried on a charge that while testifying before two grand juries, he committed perjury, in that he stated material matter which he did not believe to be true. The purpose of the grand jury inquiry was to determine whether any liquor was possessed or furnished to the guests at the party.

"Whether the party was public or private is immaterial. The defendant is not being tried for a violation of the Prohibition Law, and his guests needed no immunity for they were not violating any section of it. The only question before you is whether the defendant told the truth, or, if he lied, did he lie willfully and knowingly? The charge that there was a girl in the bathtub on the stage of the theatre during the party has not been contradicted at this trial, and the court has already ruled that the presence of Joyce Hawley in the bathtub was material to the grand jury's inquiry.

"Perjury," Judge Goddard charged, "is a kind of interference with the functions of a grand jury or trial jury that must not be tolerated if our courts and our system of justice are to operate effectively. If this defendant lied about a material matter before the grand jury, it matters not whether he 'lied like a gentleman,' as his counsel so adroitly put it, because the law makes no distinction between a gentleman or the commonplace sort of man, in a matter of this sort."

Commenting on testimony of the character witnesses for Carroll, Judge Goddard told the jury they had a right to weigh such testimony carefully. Then he pointed out that the possession of a good reputation by anyone did not make it impossible for that person to commit a crime, as he might have concealed his true character from those persons who believed it was good.

During a part of Judge Goddard's charge, a band in City Hall Park played so loudly that he had to raise his voice almost to a shout to make himself audible to the jury. The band played, "I Don't Believe You But Say It, Say It Again." Later it played a song that runs, "I Want To Go Where You Go, Stay Where You Stay."

After ordering the windows of the courtroom closed, Judge Goddard gave the jury the customary legal definition of a reasonable doubt and pointed out that Carroll's non-appearance as a witness in his own behalf was not to be taken by the jury as an evidence of his guilt, as he was merely standing on his constitutional rights.

"The questions and issue before you are simple enough. Did the defendant serve intoxicating liquor at his party? Did anyone get into a tub at his party? Did Carroll swear falsely in saying that no liquor was served and no one was in the bathtub? These are the issues for you to consider."

The jury then retired, and while they were out Carroll expressed confidence of acquittal and said he could "not afford" a conviction of any sort.

After deliberating an hour and five minutes, the jury announced its verdict, "Guilty" on the two counts that consisted of Carroll's testimony that no person had "stepped into, been pushed into, or otherwise entered a bathtub." They returned a verdict of "Not guilty" on two other counts in the perjury indictment that alleged Carroll had testified falsely when he said he neither possessed or served any intoxicating liquor at his party.

Though the jury also presented the court a petition recommending leniency, signed by 9 of the 12 jurors, when Carroll heard the verdict he paled perceptibly with the realization it was possible for the judge to sentence him to serve a maximum of 10 years in prison and pay a fine of $4,000 on the two counts. His attorney immediately tried to give him encouragement by pointing out that the sentence was not necessarily mandatory. He reminded him that the court could remit the fine entirely and sentence him to one day's imprisonment or even suspend sentence, or the fine could be imposed and the prison sentence suspended.

Carroll's wife, who sat near him with a trained nurse, seemed stunned and suddenly moaned, "Oh, God," and slumped to the floor in a dead faint. Her nurse and a court attendant administered aid to revive her.

Mr. Smyth demanded that the jury be polled, and moved for an arrest of judgment and also that the verdict be set aside, on the ground that it was "contrary to the law and the evidence." The motion was denied.

Judge Goddard doubled Carroll's bail, making it $5,000, and deferred sentence until the following Thursday.

Carroll furnished bail promptly, and hurriedly left the Federal Building.

Attorney Smyth announced that the case would be appealed promptly. "I feel confident that the law will be straightened out by a higher court."

The following Sunday, the sin-chasers were at it again. Headlines in the New York *Times* read:

DR. REISNER HAILS THE CARROLL VERDICT

In his sermon in the Chelsea Methodist Episcopal Church, 178th Street, west of Broadway, the Reverend Doctor Christian F. Reisner praised United States Attorney Emory R. Buckner for prosecuting Earl Carroll.

He said: "Emory Buckner deserves commendation from every decent citizen of America for prosecuting the Carroll case so successfully. Imagine the possibility of a man being able to get character witnesses when, after 'proving' that no liquor was served to dull his moral nature, he could, nevertheless, calmly put on such a heathen orgy. In spite of anti-Prohibition prejudice, a decent American jury still could not allow our fair city to be stigmatized by passing over such a crime. I find it surprising that in this great metropolis where the greatest editorials are written, there has been such silence about this disgusting case!"

In the week that followed, Broadway had to get in its licks, too.

Ziegfeld had already had his say, and another of Carroll's competitors, George White, the producer of the *Scandals*, was quoted in a dispatch from London as saying: "Look at the *Vanities*, for instance, and you'd better look quick. As things are going, it may be padlocked before you get across. New York won't stand that sort of revue much longer."

Carroll took particular offense at White's statement, and when asked for his reaction as he entered the Federal Building the day he was to be brought before the court for sentencing, he protested. "George White's tactless condemnation of my work in the theatre is the first public expression of those unseen hands which have been working so hard to remove me from the field of competition," he said. "Even if it were true, as Mr. White told the London correspondents for the New York *Times*, that the *Vanities* should be padlocked and that New York wouldn't stand that sort of revue much longer, surely it reveals a great lack of the human touch to broadcast such an opinion at a time when I need friends so badly."

Proceedings in the courtroom did not occupy much time, but long before Judge Goddard stepped up to the bench the room was filled to capacity. Many of those present were friends of the producer. They crowded about him with good wishes before the sentence.

Carroll had arrived in court alone, but was closely followed by his attorney, his brother Jim, and his wife, Marcelle. She was again accompanied by a trained nurse.

During the calling of the calendar, the defendant sat at the right of the counsel table. The clenching and unclenching of his hands gave evidence of his nervousness as he nodded his head in recognition of friendly greetings.

Just before the clerk called Carroll to the bar for sentencing, United States Attorney Emory R. Buckner came into court.

Before sentence was pronounced, Mr. Smyth moved to set aside the verdict. The motion was denied. Counsel then made a fervent plea to the court, asking for "any sentence that would not carry with it a term of imprisonment." He denied that Carroll had obstructed the grand jury.

"There is nobody more jealous of the integrity of the grand jury than I am," said Mr. Smyth. "Your Honor may be sure that I would not stand here pleading as I am doing if it were not for the fact that I do not believe Mr. Carroll intentionally, or otherwise, denied to the grand jury any information that was material to the subject of its investigation. For instance, although he denied that anyone had been in the bathtub, he knew that the grand jury had the name of the girl, Joyce Hawley, said to be wanted as a witness, before he made denial, for he had been asked whether he knew Joyce Hawley before he was questioned about the bath."

Mr. Smyth held that in view of the finding that no perjury was committed in the denial that alcoholic beverage was dispensed at the party, the question as to whether Miss Hawley got into the tub was not material to the subject of the inquiry.

"Carroll was not concealing anything pertinent to the investigation," Mr. Smyth continued. "No moral culpability was involved. No desire to obstruct justice. Under the circumstances, has not this man suffered sufficiently? He knows definitely now what his responsibility as a witness is, and that no one should ever think of concealing from the grand jury anything its members wish to know.

"In view of his value to the community and the fact that his continuance in business makes it possible for many people to earn a living, and that many of the best known and most respected people in the community have testified to his good character, I do not think it is too much to ask, Your Honor, that, though making the sentence severe otherwise, as you may, you refrain from depriving this man of his liberty."

There was quiet in the courtroom as Mr. Smyth made his plea, and it continued as Mr. Buckner arose to oppose leniency for "perjury defiantly, and repeatedly" committed.

The prosecutor said some unkind things about the theatrical producer. He pointed out that Carroll had been recalled by the grand jury, requestioned, and asked whether he desired to change any part of his previous testimony. Carroll, he said, had replied that he had no changes to make in what he had said.

Mr. Buckner also pointed out that, although there were more than 200 people at the Carroll party and they had all been obliged to sign so-called release cards, the host swore that he could remember the names of only a very few of his guests. As to the statement of Mr. Smyth, that the reputation of the defendant for truth and veracity had been unquestioned before the indictment, the prosecutor held that this only increased the degree of culpability that had become his through deliberate perjury.

"From him that hath, shall much be required," Mr. Buckner said. "The more people that this man knows, and is known by favorably, the more reprehensible was his conduct in defying the grand jury."

Judge Goddard began by saying, "Mr. Carroll has had a fair trial and he has been justly convicted. I have only one course to follow and that is to fix a just penalty."

He then pronounced sentence: *"A year and a day in Atlanta Prison* on each of two counts in the indictment. The sentences to run concurrently. And a fine of $1,000 on each of the two counts."

Sentence was pronounced in a low voice, and only those near the bench heard Judge Goddard as he spoke.

The hush in the courtroom was broken only by a loud anguished moan of "Oh, my God" from Mrs. Carroll, at the counsel table, who promptly fainted again. Carroll seemed visibly shaken, if not slightly frustrated, by the hysterical outburst.

The extra day was added to the sentence so that Carroll would be sent to the federal prison at Atlanta. If the sentence had been one year, he would have been sent to the county jail in Westchester; if for less than six months, to the Essex County, New Jersey, jail.

The conviction also deprived Carroll of his citizenship, which could be restored only by presidential pardon or by special legislation.

His friends gathered around to tell him of their regrets and to wish him success in his appeal. There was no demonstration by the spectators in the courtroom and the dramatic element was entirely absent.

Immediately after sentence was pronounced, Mr. Smyth moved that his client be admitted to bail pending argument on appeal before the United States Circuit Court of Appeals.

I N THE ENSUING WEEKS AND MONTHS while Carroll threw himself into work on the new edition of the *Vanities*, a headline in the paper told the untiring but futile efforts of his attorney, family, and friends to save the producer from going to prison:

CARROLL JAIL TERM UPHELD BY CIRCUIT COURT OF APPEALS. PRODUCER'S LAST CHANCE UNITED STATES SUPREME COURT.

Reporters, anxious to get Carroll's reaction to this new setback, found the impresario busily rehearsing in his theatre, the interior of which had been transformed for the new edition to represent a Spanish castle with high stone walls.

Carroll, wearing his usual attire of a tam and pale blue smock, was standing in the middle aisle; his secretary, Miss Ruth, beside him taking memos.

"I regret very much that the decision was not reversed," he told reporters. "I am truly sorry to know it came out like that. Of course, we have one more chance, but if the Supreme Court rules against us, I am ready to go to prison. I want the public to know that the proceeding out of which the case against me was made was not a publicity stunt. I feel I've already been punished to the limit by what I have gone through. Putting me in prison in no way benefits those who have prosecuted me, for I intend to be law abiding whether I go to prison or not. If this final appeal fails, it does seem hard that many innocent persons may have to suffer. There are many dependent for work on my productions, and I hope as many as possible will not be thrown out of employment."

He went on to say, as he took a swig out of a big bottle of Poland water, "Not only may this production have to be abandoned, but also a new musical comedy I'm working on will have to be put on the shelf if I'm sent to prison. And 100 or more of my principals and cast will have to seek work elsewhere."

But Earl Carroll's *Vanities of 1927* was not abandoned. It opened right on schedule, and Carroll, unable to resist the fruits of all the publicity (or notoriety, if you wish) that had been engendered, defiantly announced that the new record price for opening night seats would be $100 a ticket.

The previous record, the unheard-of price of $50 per ticket, was held by Florenz Ziegfeld for one of his *Follies*, which had starred Will Rogers, W. C. Fields, Fanny Brice, Bert Williams, Eddie Cantor, and Marilyn Miller. This had been accomplished by tying in with Mrs. William Randolph Hearst's charity, the Milk Fund for Children.

The *Vanities'* $100 price would apply only to the first rows of orchestra seats, one of which, Mr. Carroll announced, he would occupy.

On opening night of the *Vanities*, the rather gaudy tickets bore, in bold print, the spectacular legend, **"Golden Horseshoe—$100."**

Brooks Atkinson, in his review, remarked that "although many of the couples in those decadent rows might be at home with a $200 bank note, most of them looked rather like 30¢. Rumors in the lobby reported that 71 people had paid the established price. No matter how many tickets Mr. Carroll sold at that figure, he has at least had his grandiloquent gesture."

Mr. Atkinson also reported: "For the new edition, which was only about three quarters over at eleven o'clock, 'The theatre is decorated to represent a night in Spain,' the program explains, 'and you are supposed to be at a Spanish fiesta, a garden party, so enjoy yourselves. Accordingly, pretty gypsies will show you to your seats, pretty flower girls will give you boutonnieres, and pretty fortune tellers will tell you your past and your future.' "

But there was one man sitting in the $100 section, surrounded by the make-believe high stone walls of the theatre, who did not need a fortune-teller to predict his future—that was Earl Carroll.

Just that morning he had received word that the United States Supreme Court had denied his plea, and his attorney had informed him that now all avenues of appeal had been exhausted.

Early the next morning, reporters found Carroll busily cleaning out his desk and putting business affairs in order for his absence while in prison.

In the presence of the press and Dorothy Knapp, sitting languorously on the sofa, he was giving instructions to his brother Jim as to what should be done while he was away for a year and a day in Atlanta.

Jim anxiously told the newsmen, "The absence of Earl from his activities will have a serious effect on his theatrical productions, and all will suffer during his absence."

"We will attempt to carry on his work," interjected Miss Knapp, "however, Earl's personality is very important in making his productions successful."

Earl went on to express his gratitude to all his friends who had valiantly but unsuccessfully interceded on his behalf, trying to obtain a pardon from the Department of Justice.

He also mentioned, with a sardonic smile, that he was appreciative of the rumors that Miss Joyce Hawley had been trying to help.

It had been reported that a woman who said she was Joyce Hawley had telephoned the United States Attorney Charles Tuttle's office and tried to make an appointment with him. The woman said she wanted to speak to him on Carroll's behalf.

Mr. Tuttle told the woman that she should communicate with Emory R. Buckner, who had brought about Carroll's conviction. Mr. Buckner said he had received no message of any kind from Miss Hawley. Asked whether he would consent to intercede for Carroll if Miss Hawley asked him to do so, he replied:

"It would all depend on what she had to say. This was not Miss Hawley's prosecution, however, she was not a voluntary government witness. We had to hunt her out and subpoena her before the federal grand jury. It was the grand jury that indicted Carroll—it was not Miss Hawley."

All this, at a time when Miss Hawley was having problems of her own. After she had lost her job with the *Greenwich Village Follies*, some fast-buck operator had attempted to book her on a nationwide tour of dance halls doing her "Queen of the Bath" act.

Right from the start she ran into a storm of violent protest in Cincinnati, when Bishop Theodore Henderson, of the Methodist Episcopal Church, and the Reverend H. P. Atkins, secretary of the Federation of Churches, demanded that city officials rescind a permit granting her appearance. They were joined by a group of club women who told a police lieutenant that if the city officials did not prevent Miss Hawley's appearance, "the decent women of Cincinnati would."

The reaction was the same in North Hampton, Massachusetts, President Coolidge's home town, where Mayor William M. Welch refused to issue a permit for her appearance in a local dance hall, explaining:

"Any young woman who will jump into a bathtub nude before a crowd of men, as Miss Hawley is reported to have done at Mr. Carroll's party, is not the type of attraction we want in Northhampton. She certainly will not come here if I can prevent it."

Joyce Hawley finally gave up, abandoned her "career," and announced she was going home to mother. "I'm going to college," she said, "and I'm going to help my parents." After that, she escaped notoriety and drifted into oblivion.

Earl Carroll, on the eve of his departure for the federal penitentiary, went to pray at the grave of his mother in the Uniondale Cemetery in Pittsburgh. It was the sixth anniversary of her death, and he was accompanied by his two brothers, Jim and Norman, and his sister, Alice Schneider.

The visit was no eleventh-hour undertaking. Each April 10th since his mother died, he had visited her grave. Two years before, an airplane had brought him from Boston.

Carroll sought no company and had few words for anyone. A midnight train took him back to New York.

Earl Carroll's smile was wan as he waved in response to the crowd at the Federal Building where he surrendered to United States Marshal William C. Hecht on the morning of April 12th. He was accompanied by his brother Jim.

His love for publicity, which had obviously been responsible for his present predicament, was not in evidence as he walked up the steps. He refused to be interviewed.

When the prisoner's name was called in Federal Judge Augustus N. Hand's courtroom, his attorney answered for Carroll and explained that he was then in custody. Carroll was fingerprinted, a procedure that greatly depressed him.

During the morning, he had two female visitors in the marshal's prison room. One was his private secretary, Ruth Rosenblatt, and the other his long-time sweetheart, Dorothy Knapp, who was starring in his current *Vanities.*

Miss Knapp's attitude seemed to reflect indignation as she left the Federal Building deploring the fact that "Lieutenant Carroll of the Air Service," who had done such good work for his country during the war, had come to grief through "ill-advised efforts to protect his friends."

One reporter queried: "How does the lieutenant feel about losing his citizenship?"

Miss Knapp seemed visibly moved, and there was an edge to her voice as she snapped back: "I cannot recall any inquiry along that line when he volunteered as a private in the 71st National Guard during the war. Nor do I recall any such question arising when he voluntarily transferred to the Air Force, where he received a commission as a pilot lieutenant after training in Texas. Also, I have no recollection of any doubt being expressed when he suffered injuries from two crashes in the Air Service doing his bit during the war." Ending the interview she added, "And remember, he was born in Pittsburgh, Pennsylvania, and his father was a naturalized American citizen."

About 3:00 P.M., Carroll, followed by Jim, came out of the marshal's office. On his arm was a light topcoat, and his blue sack suit and boutonniere gave him a natty appearance. His head was up and he smiled at some of his newspaper acquaintances, but had no words for them.

A crowd had gathered in the corridors on the third floor outside the marshal's office, and as Carroll entered the elevator the spectators rushed for the stairs to get down and have another look at the convicted man on the street.

In the car, he waved goodbye to the friendly crowd on lower Broadway, some of whom were calling out to him.

He reached the Pennsylvania Station at 3:30 P.M., just 10 minutes before his train pulled out. Some 20 patrolmen had difficulty in keeping open a space through which Carroll and the 20 other handcuffed prisoners could walk. Sprinkled in the assemblage were a number of *Vanities* beauties, some carrying placards reading: "Don't Worry, Daddy Carroll—We're with You all the Way."

At the last moment, Mrs. Carroll rushed up and, with the permission of the guards, threw her arms around her husband. He kissed her goodbye on the cheek, whispered something in her ear, and boarded the train as the camera flashlights boomed and the air became thick with smoke.

Marshal Hecht was in charge of the prison Pullman attached to a Seaboard Airline train that was to travel over the Pennsylvania Railroad to Washington and thence by way of the Southern Railway to Atlanta. He had as aides in the car Deputy Marshal Joseph Mc-Court and the government's tallest peace officer, John Pinkley, who towered several inches over seven feet.

The prisoners were allowed $3 for the three meals served aboard the train, but could spend more money if they had it.

The train was due to arrive at Atlanta at five o'clock the next afternoon, and then railroad officials were to call up Warden John Snook and advise him when the special car was to be shunted onto the prison's special spur track.

At 6:30 the next morning, as the Crescent Limited sped on its way to Atlanta, Marshal Hecht got up from his berth in the drawing room located at the end of the prison car. He dressed hurriedly, as the prisoners had to be called for breakfast at seven.

As he attempted a quick shave—not an easy job with a straight razor on a swaying train—he couldn't help thinking of the nervous young man he had picked up at the Federal Building.

He had watched him closely all the way down the line, and it was apparent that the prisoner was decidedly dejected and didn't wish to talk to anyone. Hecht had tried to ease him into conversation by mentioning that only a couple of weeks before, he had taken his wife, Bessie, on their anniversary to see the *Vanities* in Carroll's beautiful theatre and thought Carroll would get a laugh out of his wife's remark that "it certainly didn't cost Mr. Carroll much for costumes!" But the prisoner had just nodded a weak smile and went back to the letter he was writing.

Hecht, a veteran of 20 years, had taken hundreds of prisoners down this route and had always made it a strict rule not to get emotionally involved in their problems, but this guy was different. He didn't belong in this prison car with a lot of burglars, cokies, and murderers. Hell! All he had done was to put a beautiful girl in a bathtub of ginger ale or champagne, or whatever it was. What's so bad about that, he thought. Hell! He'd have liked to have been at that party himself! And then he chuckled, "Bessie'd kill me if she heard me say that."

As the prisoners tumbled out of their berths at his call, Hecht noticed that the curtains on Earl Carroll's berth were still closed, and he called out, "Mr. Carroll, time to get up for breakfast." When there was no response, he pulled the curtains open and repeated his call, simultaneously shaking the prisoner's shoulder. Several moments elapsed before Hecht felt any concern. At first he merely thought that Carroll was sleeping more soundly than usual because of the exhausting day he had passed through. But, as further efforts to arouse him failed, Hecht noted that Carroll seemed to be in a stupor rather than a deep sleep. Alarmed, he shouted for his aides, McCourt and Pinkley, and they and some of the prisoners worked untiringly, employing resuscitation methods, to bring color and animation back to Carroll's ashen face.

William C. Amos, former New York assemblyman, one of the prisoners (he had been convicted of mail fraud), was among those who gave unstinted service. After more than five hours of effort had failed to revive Carroll, Marshal Hecht decided to remove him to a hospital for treatment as soon as possible. A wire was sent ahead to Greenville, South Carolina, and the train was met by an ambulance and physicians in that city.

Jim Carroll, who was on the same train in another car, accompanied his wan and pale brother, who had the appearance of a lifeless man, to the hospital. In the ambulance, he scoffed at the idea that someone might have slipped "dope" to his brother, expressing his opinion that a nervous collapse was responsible for the illness.

Earl Carroll lay unconscious throughout the day at the Greenville City Hospital. Dr. R. C. Bruce labored all the afternoon to revive him and to ascertain the cause of the coma, but he was at a loss to diagnose the case. Bruce and a white-capped nurse, Lillian Gilbert, who stood at the bedside, declared that Carroll, whose face was yellow and waxy, like a deathmask, was a very sick man. They could offer no idea as to when, if at all, he would again become conscious.

An analysis of the contents of Carroll's stomach was made, but this threw no light on the reason for his illness, the physician said.

The analysis did, however, dispel the possibility that a poison or an opiate of some kind had been taken. Not the slightest trace of any foreign substance was found, the examination showing that Carroll had taken little but water since boarding the train the day before.

He remained in acute collapse, and was still not able to speak. He swallowed constantly and with difficulty as though he were choking at times. Dr. Bruce, who lifted his eyelids, remarked that they remained open and did not drop back as is the case with a normal man.

After several hours passed without his brother being revived, Jim, who had remained at the bedside or just outside the room throughout the afternoon, sent a call to Atlanta for a specialist, Dr. C. O. Bates, who arrived at the hospital the next morning.

On the night of April 15th, Carroll entered the thirty-fourth hour of his coma, and for the first time since he was taken from the train a spokesman for the hospital issued an official statement declaring his condition had been diagnosed as a serious nervous breakdown.

"The patient is in an acute collapse or coma, and these attacks not infrequently occur in the type of illness from which he suffers," the statement said, adding that the illness resulted from the "severe mental strain under which he has been laboring for the last few weeks."

Marshal Hecht, who remained constantly in the room with the patient, having sent the other prisoners on to Atlanta in the charge of deputy marshals, ventured an opinion.

"I tell you, Doc. The way we left New York was enough to drive any man crazy," the marshal said. "There must have been 200,000 persons lining the streets and on top of the buildings. All wanted a look at Carroll. This unnerved and humiliated him."

Carroll's state of collapse persisting, Dr. Bates would offer no estimate as to how much time would likely elapse before he could be taken to Atlanta. Dr. Bates stated: "While not conscious yet, Carroll is regaining muscle control and is slightly improved. However, I cannot predict the duration of his illness. While it is my belief he will recover, under no circumstances should be moved before a week or ten days, and then only after careful medical consideration."

On the evening of the second day, Marcelle Carroll showed up at the Greenville City Hospital and demanded to see her husband.

Against the advice of Dr. Bates but with the permission of Marshal Hecht, she was allowed to enter the patient's room. When Carroll gave no sign of recognizing anyone, Marcelle became hysterical and had to be carried to another room in the hospital, where she was put to bed and given sedatives.

Although she was fully recovered the next morning, Dr. Bates protested that Mrs. Carroll's actions could be damaging to the health of his patient and demanded that she leave the hospital. Jim accompanied her to the station and Marcelle reluctantly returned to New York.

As Carroll's problems with his wife were common knowledge up and down Broadway, the *Evening Graphic* dutifully recorded Marcelle's visit to the Greenville Hospital with a phony composite picture. It depicted Carroll in his hospital bed, with Marcelle pleading at his side and the doctor, nurse, and Marshal Hecht looking on. Someone at the *Graphic* must have had a sense of humor, for Carroll, arms outstretched, a look of futile exasperation on his face, seemed to be saying, "For God's sake, Marcelle, will you get off my back?"

During the next few days, Carroll gradually began to respond to treatment. His breathing grew more normal and his pulse was regular, but his condition was still serious. He was able to take a little nourishment, and attendants said he was showing some strength, stirring frequently, and at times seemingly endeavoring to speak to those near him. Carroll muttered semiconsciously several times, conveying to attendants and physicians the impression that he believed himself in Atlanta prison. In some of his intervals of consciousness he recognized Jim.

In the weeks that followed, after watching their patient emerge periodically from his acute coma, Carroll's doctors announced there seemed to be no reason why the improvement should not continue steadily, and they indicated that he might be able to resume his journey to Atlanta before very long.

He spent most of his time propped up in bed. He began taking more nourishment and was able to converse coherently, even to the point of teasing his nurse, Miss Gilbert, about becoming a Carroll Girl.

On the morning of Friday, May 20th, dramatic news came over the radio that had not only everyone in the hospital but everyone in the whole world bubbling with excitement and expectancy. A young barnstorming pilot had taken off from New York, attempting to make the first nonstop flight across the Atlantic Ocean to Paris.

Jim, knowing his brother's enthusiasm for anything pertaining to aviation, rushed into Earl's room, exclaiming:

"Earl, you won't believe it! Some crazy kid named Lindbergh took off from Roosevelt Field this morning to fly to Paris—alone!"

Smiling weakly, Earl replied, "That certainly beats my stunt in Central Park, huh, Jim?"

With the doctor's permission, Earl was allowed to have a radio in his room for the first time since entering the hospital. He and Jim listened, at first half-doubting, then growing confident, to reports throughout the day of the "Lone Eagle" winging his way across the Atlantic.

Earl hadn't shown such keen interest in anything since his troubles began, and Jim was delighted when his brother asked for a pad and pencil. Inspired by Lindbergh's attempt to crown the record of American aviation, Carroll expressed the emotion he felt for this high drama by putting down the words of the first song he had written in years.

FLY HIGH, LONE EAGLE

Words & Music by
Earl Carroll

Verse

One day in New York Bay, the Statue of Liberty heard a roar
And saw a plane open the ocean's door—and said . . .

Chorus

Fly High, Lone Eagle, onward through the sky
Fly High, Lone Eagle, and let the clouds roll by
On through the ages heroes so true
Nearer to heaven, your path leading you
Fly High, Lone Eagle
You're the spirit of red, white, and blue.

(Optional last line:)
Fly High, Lone Eagle
America's proud of you.

There was great enthusiasm in the hospital room the next day when word came that Lindbergh had successfully completed his flight. Jim urged Earl to scratch out a music lead sheet of his song and he sent it to the same publishing company that Earl had worked for years before—Leo Feist—but it was too late. A few days later, Jim received a letter from Feist saying that they were sorry, but they were already publishing a Lindbergh song, "Lucky Lindy." It was written by a close friend of Earl's, L. Wolfe Gilbert.

(Years later, in 1933, when Charles Lindbergh and Earl Carroll were both guests at William Randolph Hearst's fabulous "ranch," San Simeon, Carroll had the opportunity to mention to the colonel the song he had written, and sat down at the piano in the beautiful Assembly Room and sang it for Lindbergh and his wife, Ann Morrow. When he finished, Colonel Lindbergh remarked that he regretted that Carroll's song had not been published first, adding that although he felt that "Lucky Lindy" unquestionably had merit, it had always disturbed him that the word *lucky* was so prominent in the lyrics. He stated emphatically that the most important part of that flight was *preparation*.)

A few weeks later, Carroll's recovery was to have a setback, when he learned that prison authorities were becoming impatient over the fact that he had not been turned over to them to begin serving his sentence. The ominous realization that he was not to escape the humiliation of spending time behind prison bars engulfed him. And when reports came that Attorney General Sargent had ordered a thorough physical and mental examination by government neurologists and psychiatrists, Carroll suffered a serious relapse. Physicians at the Greenville City Hospital became alarmed at the deterioration of his mental attitude. He seemed to slip into a semicoma, became listless, refused nourishment, and was confined to his bed 24 hours a day, being removed to a chair only when his bed was being made.

Dr. Bates said that his patient was steadily becoming worse. "Carroll's condition is worse at present than it was a week ago, and a week ago was worse than a week previous."

Asked whether Carroll's life was in danger, Dr. Bates replied that "death would be preferable to other consequences that might be involved in his incarceration."

Information in official circles in Washington was that President Coolidge might extend executive clemency if the physicians employed by the Department of Justice reported that Earl Carroll's confinement in prison would lead to fatal illness. In the event the report declared his confinement could be made in safety, after he had improved in the hospital in South Carolina, the belief existed that executive clemency would not be extended until at least three months of his term had been served. President Calvin Coolidge let it be known that the Department of Justice had not made any recommendations.

On June 8th, Attorney General Sargent ordered Earl Carroll to Atlanta to begin serving his sentence, declaring, "There is nothing the matter with him."

This, despite the conflicting reports of the two doctors who examined Carroll at the request of the government.

Dr. James S. Fouche, a Veterans' Bureau diagnostician stationed at Columbia, submitted a report with the following conclusions:

"From the above examination, my conclusions are that this patient's despondency and emotional state have interfered, and are interfering, with his nutrition and that his physical condition is entirely normal; that he shows no indications of a psychosis; and that there is nothing from a mental or physical standpoint at the present time, in my opinion, that makes it improper for him to be transferred to the federal prison in Atlanta. However, his confinement in the prison might increase his despondency and emotional state. I suggest that definite action be taken in his case, for I do not believe that prolonging his stay in the Greenville City Hospital will be of much benefit to the patient."

Dr. C. Fred Williams, superintendent of the South Carolina State Hospital for the Insane, a specialist in nervous diseases, reported:

"My examination revealed no positive evidence of mental disease and it is my belief that his mental and physical condition would not interfere with his being transported to the United States penitentiary at Atlanta, Georgia. However, I am of the opinion, in view of the extreme nervous condition of the patient, and evidence of an excitable, nervous makeup, that to confine him in the penitentiary would possibly bring about definite mental disorder."

Jim Carroll issued a statement to the press that the family believed the removal of Earl to the penitentiary meant sure death for him. "We are very bitter at the government for disregarding the diagnosis of Earl's condition by the five different specialists other than those employed by the government," Jim said. "By them, his present condition is regarded as most serious, and it is believed his incarceration will, in all probability, precipitate a most serious and lasting mental disorder that will terminate disastrously."

Earl Carroll appeared pale and thin as he was taken from the hospital in an ambulance and placed aboard a sleeping car of the train, and seemed to be in a coma or asleep. His physicians said, however, that he was awake and his condition was about the same as for the past few days.

After making public the doctors' reports, Attorney General Sargent stated that there was nothing in the Carroll case that would justify its being referred to President Coolidge for action on a petition for executive clemency.

Adding further to Carroll's discomfiture and anguish, a controversy arose over the question of whether he had been serving part of his sentence while in the hospital. Deputy Marshal Hecht said that in his opinion, Carroll's commitment papers specified that he began his sentence on April 12th. In Atlanta, Warden Snook agreed, and was quoted in news dispatches as saying a prisoner's term began when he was "started toward Atlanta in custody with proper commitment papers." But, in Washington, Attorney General Sargent firmly ruled that Carroll's sentence would date from the time he was admitted to the prison.

Few persons were on hand when Carroll's train reached the Atlanta station. Newspaper reporters and photographers made up most of the small group, which included his wife, Marcelle, who had arrived on an earlier train. Despite the repeated entreaties of Jim, that she "could be of no help," Marcelle proclaimed indignantly, "A wife's place is by her loving husband's side in his hour of need."

Stifling the sobs that shook her body, she hysterically tried to push her way to the stretcher as it was carried about 150 feet from the train to the waiting ambulance.

"It will kill him! It will kill him!" she screamed, and collapsed into the arms of Jim.

Earl Carroll, apparently in a semicomatose condition, gave no heed to the outburst except for a slight movement of one hand as he seemed to wave Marcelle away, and made a feeble attempt to say something a moment before he was put in the ambulance and driven through the gates of the penitentiary.

The formalities of registration were shortened because of his condition. He was assigned number 24,909 and taken to a private ward in the prison.

"He will get a rest, which is what he needs most," Warden Snook said, "until his physical condition is such that he can be assigned to a task."

As it is customary to assign prisoners to work for which they are best fitted, it appeared likely that Carroll would draw clerical duties.

The warden added that perhaps the greatest interest in Earl Carroll's arrival was felt by those prisoners who had some theatrical experience. "As you know, each year a show is given by the prisoners; first one for the men themselves, and then one to which the public is invited. I'm sure the other inmates are looking forward to Mr. Carroll's return to health, as he is the unanimous choice to direct the prison's annual Christmas show."

ACCORDING TO THE PRESS, Earl Carroll was supposed to have had a high old time in jail—living on the best food and liquor, entertaining girls, and building up his scrapbook. Reports were printed by the *Evening Graphic,* without any known authority for their truth, about his special privileges, which included sharing catered dinners with his fellow prisoners, and lists of famous guests he was alleged to entertain on visitor's day.

But actual information from the penitentiary tends to refute these allegations. Records show that convict number 24,909 was a model prisoner. For one thing, at the time of his incarceration *all* special privileges had been abolished as a result of a scandal during the regime of the preceding warden, Albert E. Sartain, who was then serving a term in the prison he once ruled.

In the first few weeks of his prison confinement, Earl Carroll seemed to have lost interest in all about him. He confided to Warden Snook, "My humiliation is complete. I don't care what happens now."

But in the quiet, well-ordered life of the Atlanta Federal Penitentiary, Carroll began steadily recovering his health.

In answer to queries, the warden said, "The prisoner's condition has improved so greatly that he is able to eat anything he wants.

He spends his time walking around the hospital or lounging in his room. He is still weak, but when Carroll is able to work, he will be assigned to some clerical position in the penitentiary."

Nearly a month after he entered prison, Carroll had his first contact with the outside world. On July 4th, Dorothy Knapp visited him. It was the fifth anniversary of their meeting, and she was still wearing on her ankle the inscribed gold bracelet that he had given her at that time.

Miss Knapp arrived early at night after visiting hours were over, but when her errand was explained, Warden Snook waived the rules and allowed her a long interview with the prisoner, the official being present all the time.

It is understood that the interview that night, and one that followed the next day, concerned her "contract" for the ensuing year.

Miss Knapp told reporters that she had found Mr. Carroll "in very much better health than had been reported. Thank God, Earl is rapidly recovering and returning to normal. He looks great, has recovered his appetite, and takes a keen interest in his surroundings."

Miss Knapp went on to say that she, his brother Jim, and other friends had been continually working "to get him out of this terrible place. And make no mistake about it, gentlemen—it's a prison, not a country club." She added that they were hoping he could be sent "to some place where he could get the proper treatment for his condition. If there's no such prison, we hope he can be released in the custody of members of his family so they can place him in a sanitarium where he will get the rest he needs most."

(This visit was to cause a congressional investigation more than a year later, on August 13, 1928. The *Atlanta Weekly* ran a story intimating that Dorothy Knapp had received special privileges from Warden Snook—that she had even been a guest in the warden's home that night. The warden denied this, and sought an indictment against the editor, Parkes Rusk. Warm admirers of the warden's in Atlanta declared he would welcome an investigation. They expressed complete confidence that any inquiry would show his administration to be clear of any irregularities. The whole investigation led to nought. The popular Warden Snook was shown to run a clean ship.)

On August 1st, Earl Carroll was transferred to the prison honor farm, two miles from the penitentiary, which was the goal of all the prisoners, for confinement there allowed them much freedom in the open air. It was a reward for good behavior and carried certain privileges that remained at the option of the Parole Board, which was to meet the following September 8th.

In a short time, Carroll looked the picture of health and was enjoying his farm duties. The *Evening Graphic* couldn't resist carrying a phony composite showing Carroll grinning like a Cheshire cat among the hollyhocks.

He occupied, together with several other prisoners, a neat white cottage. There were no bars and no locks. It was during this period that Carroll made some very valuable connections with a number of prominent leaders of the underworld who were also guests of the government, mostly on Prohibition raps. These contacts were to serve him in good stead a few years later, after the repeal of Prohibition, when liquor was no longer profitable and kidnapping for ransom had become a popular means by which hoodlums were extracting large sums from high-salaried actors and opulent Broadway characters. During the run of his *Sketchbook* in 1935, Carroll was tipped off that he was to be snatched, but a phone call to an underworld chieftain brought the assurance that he would not be bothered, and he wasn't. A few days later, the papers carried a story that a small-time hoodlum had taken a "bath in a cement overcoat" in the Hudson River.

It also may or may not be significant that while, at times, other producers were harrassed by union troubles, there is no record of any Earl Carroll show ever having been hit by a crippling strike.

One evening in the early part of September, Carroll was alone in the prison library, listening to the Guy Lombardo orchestra on the radio and finishing up his librarian duties for the day. Suddenly, the program was interrupted by the voice of Graham McNamee:

*This is a special news bulletin. This is a sad day for the Fourth Estate. One of the great newspapermen of all time, Philip Payne, managing editor of the New York **Daily Mirror** is dead. . . .*

Three months after Lindbergh made his historic flight to Paris, with the attendant glare of tremendous press coverage, Philip Payne, always alive with enthusiasm for the BIG story, had persuaded his boss, Hearst, to sponsor a transatlantic flight to Rome. As it was a distance greater than to Paris, the flight would be an aviation first.

Suiting action to words, he named the Fokker monoplane *Old Glory* and secured two British flyers, Lloyd Bertaud and James Hill, who were keen for the venture. Dramatically, he added that he would go along to cover the daring trip and become the first newspaperman to engage in such an exploit.

Despite bad weather prevailing over the whole Atlantic, at Payne's insistence *Old Glory* rose into the rough air from Old Orchard, Maine, on the cloudy morning of September 16, 1927.

The small craft soon disappeared somewhere in the churning Atlantic during a wild storm that was raging. The occupants were never seen again.

Ironically, Philip Payne's own death provided that big story that had eluded him throughout his lifetime.

What thoughts were running through Earl Carroll's mind as he turned off the radio that night, no one will ever know.

On October 15th, Carroll personally went before the Federal Parole Board in behalf of his application for parole. His appearance was brief, and the board asked questions about a few points on which the members wished more specific information than was contained in his parole papers.

Then the conditions for his release were laid down by the board for Carroll to agree to. Among them were "that he will not during the term of his parole frequent saloons or other places where intoxicating liquors or beverages are sold or furnished, and that he will not drink intoxicating beverages; that he will not during the term of his parole associate with persons of bad reputation; that he will not go outside the limits fixed in the certificate of parole without the written permission of the Parole Board or the president thereof."

Four days later, Warden Snook informed convict number 24,909 that he had received from Attorney General Sargent a formal order for his release, and the doors of freedom were opened for Earl Carroll on Friday, October 21, 1927.

He spent his last day at the penitentiary, where he had arrived early from the honor farm on a truck filled with vegetables for prison consumption, visiting the many friends he had made. The guards were more than lenient. The run of the building was given him and he went to the hospital ward, to the library, and to other departments of the institution, cheering other prisoners with expressions of hope that they soon would join him in freedom.

When the necessary papers finally arrived and his fine of $2,000 had been paid, he was called into the warden's office. There the conditions of his parole were formally stressed and he was given a suit of clothes and a ticket to New York with $5 for meals en route. Warden Snook praised him for his good conduct and expressed a wish for his happiness and prosperity.

Carroll reciprocated by inviting the warden to drop in and be his theatre guest whenever he visited New York City.

Carroll left his radio and a considerable sum of money—said to be more than $1,000—with the warden to aid prisoners in need of funds, and carried back with him to New York not only the best wishes of the officials and inmates but also messages for members of families of some of the men with whom he had been associated at the prison.

Jim Carroll was then notified, and he drove from the hotel to the prison. When he saw Earl in the warden's office, browned by the sun, alert and clear-eyed, Jim rushed over and threw his arms around his brother with hearty congratulations, and the two men embraced warmly.

Jim couldn't hide his enthusiasm for his brother's excellent physical appearance. Two months in the sun and fresh air at the honor farm had worked wonders with the man who had entered the prison on a stretcher, doomed to die.

Dr. Charles T. Nellans, who attended Earl at the prison, confided to Jim that more than anything else, Earl had suffered from a nervous reflex brought about by mortification at his plight, and once that attitude had been dissipated and he had been removed to the honor camp his recovery was rapid.

As they left the warden's office, Dr. Nellans told Jim confidentially: "Your brother is a healthy man, physically. Of course, we cannot say to what extent his mental strain has affected him. It's obvious he has always been a nervous, excitable type, and in my opinion the nervous breakdown he suffered would have occurred even if he had never been sent to prison."

Later, a press conference was arranged at the Henry Grady Hotel. After posing for pictures, Earl Carroll handed the newspapermen a prepared statement he had drawn up before leaving the federal penitentiary. It read:

For over six months I have been a prisoner. During every moment within this grim penitentiary—with its grey walls, armed guards, shrieking sirens, and long nights of ceaseless tossing—I have experienced a common heartache with a thousand other men in this sorry place. My constant companion has been a great shadow of humiliation, a heavy sense of moral degradation, and I find it most difficult to express my real emotions without having them misconstrued for self-pity. Those who felt that I should be severely punished for my "misguided" gesture of chivalry, may rest positively in the assurance that I have suffered, that I have undergone an irreparable loss of self-respect, a realization of unworthiness such as each and every man feels when a door of a prison clangs behind him. Being, perhaps, hypersensitive, I have endured the most acute mental agony at being fingerprinted for future identification, at being photographed for the rogue's gallery; and I never watched the red of each setting sun through the bars of my window without seeing written there in those iron shadows the loss of my priceless heritage, my American citizenship.

Earl Carroll's journey back to Broadway was broken the first night by an informal reception of ten minutes, in which 200 Greenville, South Carolina, citizens joined while his train made its customary stop there.

Among those in the crowd to whom Carroll expressed thanks for kindness to him during his confinement in the Greenville City Hospital was Miss Lillian Gilbert, who nursed him in his illness. Carroll put his arms around her and kissed her.

Drs. C. O. Bates and R. C. Bruce, who attended the producer, congratulated him on his release.

"I finally got my mental self settled by a process of relativity," Carroll said, "in the prison hospital. My night nurse was serving 20 years for murder. My day nurse, 20 for robbery. I saw their lot, compared it to mine, and it helped."

As his train sped northward, he received telegrams of good wishes and welcome from many close to New York's theatre life—among them, George M. Cohan, Al Jolson, Fanny Hurst, Ring Lardner, O. O. McIntyre, Irvin S. Cobb, and David Belasco, who wired: "The good news made us all happy, dear Earl Carroll, and you will be a welcome homecomer. Now you have only your future to think of and to take up your splendid, brilliant work where you left off. God bless you. We all love and admire you."

These messages cheered him as he was deeply concerned about whether Broadway's attitude would be censorious, or forgiving.

The Crescent Limited, the train that brought Earl Carroll back to New York, arrived at the Pennsylvania Station on Saturday, October 22nd, at 11:50 in the morning. Although there had been no definite plans for a celebration, several hundred had gathered to welcome the returned producer.

Still attired in the brand new suit the warden had given him, it was a subdued and chastened Earl Carroll who came out on the observation platform to talk to reporters. There were no shouts from the crowd. Everyone seemed to feel that such a demonstration would be inappropriate.

In a talk with newspapermen, Carroll admitted that he felt terribly disgraced—"I know I have dropped four or five pegs since I went to prison."

He expressed acute regret at the loss of his citizenship, and when asked whether he would apply for reinstatement he said, "I would give anything to get it back, but I don't know what I will be able to do."

There was only one minor interruption during the interview, when his wife, Marcelle, who was late, was rushed through the police lines to join her husband. A photograph in the newspaper the next day caught the look of irritation on Earl's face as his wife stood beside him on the back of the observation car.

As the reporters followed him up to the street, someone mentioned the name of Philip Payne, who was lost in the attempted transatlantic flight of the *Old Glory* and whose testimony did much to send Carroll to prison.

"I really and truly feel sad about Phil Payne," he said. "I have no feeling in my heart against him. He was just an actor in the drama that someone wanted played to the end, and he has proved that he was a brave man."

Before he got into his car, he said his plans for the future were unsettled. He planned to take up producing again, but when, and in what manner, he did not know. He said he would like to go to Allentown, Pennsylvania, the next night for the opening of a new play in which he was interested, but he wasn't certain if the government would permit him to leave the state.

"But right now, boys," he said laughingly, "I'm on my way to see whether my theatre is still there."

Being relieved of Marcelle by his brother Jim, he arrived alone at the imposing edifice bearing his name.

As he entered the lobby, a scrubwoman who had been in his employ for years dropped her mop and pail to kiss him. He embraced her and walked into the auditorium, where he found several hundred friends, associates, and employees, who, without invitation and formality, had gathered to welcome him home.

Standing on the stage of his own theatre where the bathtub party was held 20 months before, Carroll was host at another party. But this time it was not gay. There was no merriment among the guests.

He seemed emotionally moved as he spoke hesitantly and quietly to his well-wishers. "As you know, I have seen very few people in the last few months, other than my faithful brother Jim, and I have developed an almost uncontrollable fear of meeting people. So with this complex, I hesitantly step into the outside world today. My health is better, thanks to the humane interest of a truly remarkable executive—Warden Snook—and I believe my life was saved by the sympathetic understanding of Dr. Nellans, the prison physician.

"Today the book is finished and now I trust I may return peacefully to my work here in the theatre. I shall be forever indebted to all of you who toiled so untiringly for my release. The prison rules forbade my answering your letters and the countless hundreds of new and unknown friends who wrote such encouraging messages, but the Christ-like attitude that they expressed brings me back with an even firmer belief that what I did was the only thing I could do and that there are times when a man's honor is far more precious than liberty—and liberty more precious than life."

And with his familiar salutation, "I love you all," he left the auditorium and made his way up the private back stairs to his office.

He opened the door, and standing there in a black satin dress, on the brilliant red carpet of his luxurious office, was the girl that he proclaimed all his life was *truly* the most beautiful girl in the world—Dorothy Knapp.

Her eyes were luminous and filled with candid delight. She was beautiful and desirable.

With a wry smile, she said, "Welcome home, jail-bird," and suddenly she was in his arms so quickly, so inevitably, that they were unaware of which one had taken the first step toward the other.

He kissed her warm and appealing mouth, with the feeling that a wildly beautiful wave was breaking over him, claiming him by sheer magnificent force, and suddenly joy seemed to be singing in his blood again.

SEX HAD ALWAYS BEEN HIS FAVORITE therapy for whatever ailed him or didn't ail him. Those who were aware of Dorothy Knapp's enthusiastic welcome for Earl, sighed a sigh of relief. At any rate, all seemed well at first for Earl's return home. Everyone expected him to bounce back with renewed vigor. But this time, even Dorothy could not provide the cure. He soon lapsed into a state of acute depression.

The days that followed were bleak, lonely days. Earl moved into his sister's home on Park Avenue. It was to her, Alice, and to Jim, his brother that he turned in his darkest moments. He felt otherwise alone in this black recess.

The periods of self-blame and of guilt were long, and as each day went by they seemed to grow deeper. Alice and Jim tried all kinds of ways to break his despondency, even to bluntly accusing him of self-pity, but nothing really seemed to help or change him.

He could not accept the humiliation and degradation of his prison term and the feeling that somehow he may have closed the doors to any future in his life. When he did have a glimmer of hope that one day he might return to the theatre, he was obsessed with the fear that the public would not accept him. Once he saw himself as a man who could dare anything; now he could not even dare to face himself completely.

The situation with his wife, Marcelle, only tended to sharpen the dullness he felt within him. She had tried on several occasions to call him, but he had always refused to speak to her. Finally, one day after much persistence on her part, he did talk to her on the phone. Marcelle wanted one thing: to see him, to plead her love for him.

Earl coldly and bitterly replied, "There is no point in our getting together again. Once we had what I thought was a real love. I found out it was a phony dream. You made that clear enough and I think it is far wiser for us never to see each other again. The only reaction I have, is to end this silly charade. Marcelle, go back to France; there is nothing left for us."

Marcelle finally did give up and return to her homeland. And they never saw each other again. Earl could never be sure whether she had been truly in love with him. He just knew that he was not taking another chance.

The difficulties with Marcelle and his own lack of confidence in himself, his sense of defeat, plunged him deeper into depression.

Finally Jim said, "Earl, I think you had better see a psychiatrist."

"What for?" Earl retorted. "What can he do?"

"Maybe nothing, but what are you doing on your own—sitting indulging yourself in your own misery. Where is all the fight you used to have?"

Both Jim and Alice kept after Earl, and finally, in a moment of genuine desperation, he decided to accept psychiatric help.

The sessions were painful as the psychiatrist probed deeper and deeper in to the guts of Earl Carroll. He began to see himself for what he was. He began to get a much clearer conception of his own weaknesses.

He felt guilty about his treatment of Marcelle and began to wonder whether she sincerely wanted to start over again. He told the psychiatrist he had been unfair to her, and he continued to labor over that thought.

The psychiatrist listened for days on end about this, and finally he said, "Stop enjoying your guilt and indulging in it, for it's not realistic. In the first place, you will never be happy with any one woman. You have always poured out all your passion, tenderness, all you have to give, all your love, and vitality and libido, into the theatre. And why? Because it is an escape for you from the realities of life.

"All right, so you have made a mistake. You've got things in your life to be ashamed of, but so have we all. What makes you think you are so different from the rest of us? So what are you going to do? Give up and die, or fight? You can either continue to give in to this desperate defeat and guilt that you are wallowing in now, or look at yourself for what you really are. Unless you can do that, there is not much more we have to say to each other."

No one knows exactly what made Earl get on his feet and begin to fight back. But one day, he made the announcement that he was going to produce a new edition of the *Vanities*. He never told anyone what made the change in him, but there was much speculation. Some felt that one of the reasons might have been the fact that Flo Ziegfeld had not only a big new hit but a brand new theatre to play it in. The show was not a revue; it was Ziggy's first venture into musical comedy—*Rio Rita*. It was housed in the new Ziegfeld Theatre on 54th Street and Sixth Avenue (now the Avenue of the Americas). It was built by his old friend, William Randolph Hearst, especially for Flo, who had introduced the newspaper mogul to his "friend" and companion, Marion Davies, more than 10 years before, when she was a showgirl in the *Follies*.

Whatever the reason, the dark days were over. A new chance was ahead. But Earl Carroll astutely realized that to restore the name *Vanities* to its former degree of popularity, as well as ease himself into public acceptance, he would have to secure the services of a stellar luminary to head the cast—a big star like the very popular Beatrice Lillie or the great W. C. Fields, whom Ziegfeld had made so famous.

He started to make weekly pilgrimages to Chicago in an effort to sign Bea Lillie, who was appearing there in a show called *Oh, Please!* Those mornings in the Windy City that he did not visit her in person, he sent her flowers, merely a symbol of his presence. Because of international conditions, he was unable to gain the services of Lady Peel.

Learning that W. C. Fields was out on the coast making motion pictures, he invaded Hollywood with only a checkbook, and fought the movies with a language they spoke long before the talkies.

He checked into the Beverly Hills Hotel, and made a number of unsuccessful efforts to contact Fields at his home.

Finally, through his old comic employee, Dave Chasen, who had appeared in the 1924–25 *Vanities*, and who later became a very successful restauranteur in Hollywood, Earl learned that Fields spent a great deal of time playing golf at the Lakeside Golf Club. He made repeated calls to Fields at the club, which were never returned.

One day, a caddy ran out from the clubhouse to notify Fields that Mr. Earl Carroll wanted him on the phone.

"Tell him to go to hell!" said the comedian, and he chopped viciously at his ball, which was buried in a sand trap.

"But he said he wanted you to appear in his new *Vanities!*" exclaimed the caddy.

"Tell him to take the *Vanities* and stick it up his ass!"

As a star of the Ziegfeld *Follies*, Bill Fields felt he had gone as far as he could in theatrical importance. An Earl Carroll *Vanities* would be only a comedown.

Putting aside his disdain for agents, Carroll then called Billy Grady, who had handled Bill Fields' business for more than 14 years, and asked him to come over to the hotel.

"I went to see Carroll," Grady told me, "and I had to level with him. Bill Fields had always expressed his violent dislike not only for the man but for any Carroll operation. I felt it hopeless for Carroll to seek Bill Fields' talents and told him so. I also said that Fields' demands would be such that he could not afford him.

"But Carroll would not take 'no' for an answer. He insisted that I see Fields for a final decision. Bill's reaction was as I had anticipated: 'I wouldn't work for the sonofabitch if he gave me his theatre.' "

"Carroll wants you pretty bad, Bill."

"Oh, he does, does he?" snarled Fields, who was immediately put into a combative humor because Carroll thought well of him. "Well, he'll damn well pay for it," said Fields. He got a pencil and a piece of paper and figured out a list of penalties for Carroll's rash urge.

"Tell him," he said at length, "that if—and I repeat, if—I go to work for the bastard I'll want so much money he won't be able to afford me, and he'll forget it. You tell that guy I want $5,000 a week, and I must be paid $2,500 on Monday morning and the other $2,500 on Wednesday. I'll furnish four sketches for myself, and I want $150 royalty a week for each, plus substantial bonuses and percentage clauses."

Grady, in exasperation, then arose and said, "Okay, I'll do it, Bill, but it's the most outrageous demand I've ever heard of in all my years in show business."

Eyeing him carefully, Fields lit a cigar and, with a false ingratiating smile, said, "I never did like that guy's setup. He's a sensation and publicity seeker. All he knows is to put a lot of bare-assed dames on the stage and call them Carroll 'Beauties.' "

Grady went back to Carroll, presented the surrender terms, and returned to Fields in about an hour. "Believe it or not," he reported, "Carroll said he'll do it."

"Said he would, did he?" Fields gritted savagely. "Well, you trot right back and tell that jail-bird I've changed my mind." The comedian thought for a moment and slyly said, "There's a couple of other conditions. I want my $5,000 guaranteed for 30 weeks; I must have my name advertised in all publicity, and in lights *over* Earl Carroll's name and *over Vanities*. My name, at all times, must be in larger type."

Grady said, "Bill, he'll never go for that. Besides, he can't afford it."

"Then I don't work for Mr. Carroll," Fields said, picking up three balls and starting to juggle.

Grady left without comment, went back to Carroll's hotel, and delivered the shift in terms. "Frankly," he told Carroll, "it's disgraceful behavior. If I were you, I'd tell him where to go."

Carroll, always trying to convey the impression that he was a nice guy but the world was against him, put the tips of his long, bony fingers under his chin and seemed on the verge of tears.

"Billy," he said, "I am terribly disappointed."

"Earl, as I told you earlier, Fields does not want any part of the *Vanities*. I tried to help the situation, but those terms are the result. It looks like it is down to take it or leave it."

"Well," Carroll said, "naturally I am greatly disappointed, but under the circumstances, I guess I will have to say 'no' and forget Mr. Fields."

One morning a few days later, to his amazement, Grady told me, he read in *Variety* the announcement:

W. C. FIELDS TO STAR IN EARL CARROLL VANITIES.

Grady added bitterly, "Carroll, in his usual slimy manner, had somehow got to Fields, personally."

They had not only closed the deal that Grady had outlined, but Fields, after sarcastically questioning Carroll's solvency, had further demanded that the full amount of his salary for the whole 30 weeks be put up in a bank *in advance*. Finally, in desperation, Carroll had to agree, and later he took the comedian to the Irving Trust Company and segregated $150,000 of his personal balance in a separate account, out of which Fields was paid five thousand a week.

This much seems sure: W. C. Fields holds the distinction of being the only actor in show business who was ever paid by a bank.

The Fields mission accomplished, Carroll returned to New York and enthusiastically began selecting his 1928 beauties. He gave them as much thought and attention as he did to choosing his cast.

He sounded his call for chorus girls that summer where it had never been heard before.

Having been denied the medium of radio, instead of putting up the customary chorus call in the offices of Equity he inserted advertisements in all the daily newspapers for good-looking girls with stage aspirations—no experience necessary. To enable those who worked in shops and stores to come to the audition, he fixed the hour at six o'clock in the evening at the Earl Carroll Theatre. When he got there, more than 2,000 young hopefuls had jammed the sidewalk and street, and others were still coming. Several hundred mothers chaperoned their daughters. Traffic was at a standstill, and mounted police were holding back a huge crowd of delighted spectators shouting and whistling their admiration.

The girls were of every type imaginable, but were predominantly blondes. Those were the days when tankfuls of peroxide were being poured on feminine heads to turn brunette locks into various hues of gold, yellow, and platinum. With their long tresses snipped off, they twirled what was left of it into spit curls and imbedded their scalps in a helmet-like contraption known as the cloche hat. Their eyebrows were plucked and replaced with thin, pencilled lines that gave their faces a fixed expression of vacuous surprise.

Though it had been less than a year since Carroll's last audition, not only faces but figures and clothes had undergone a drastic transformation. Women had not only lost their waists; they were sitting on them. Everything female about them, including bust and hips, was either concealed or flattened out of all recognition. The only exception to this concealment was their legs, which poked obscenely from beneath their knee-length skirts, slit up the side and offering an even more intriguing view with an added note of vulgarity.

It required keen observation by Earl Carroll to distinguish, in the graceless attire, figures that would prove attractive in stage costumes, and to recognize nature's handiwork in faces mutilated by the mayhem of unskilled beauty operators. In judging beauty, his technique was much like that of wine tasters, who never drink of the liquid they are testing. They stay with it only a moment, because if they drink it, they are lost. Carroll once said, "I have seen as many as 5,000 girls in a day and must move along quickly as I examine their figures. Never do I stop in front of a girl. If I were to hesitate for a moment, I would be lost. If I look up and meet her eye I cannot go on, for then she is no longer just a thing of beauty I am judging; she becomes a woman to me."

That day, he broke his own rule. As he moved down the line, he glanced up and met the beautiful eyes of Beryl Heischuber.

The 16-year-old beauty, who had read the ad in the Brooklyn *Eagle*, was one of the first he picked. No one knew at that moment that this black-haired, bright-eyed, attractive girl was to play such an important part in the rest of his life. Carroll later changed her name to Beryl Wallace.

She enthusiastically joined the other girls in rehearsal clothes at the Earl Carroll Theatre the following night. His final selections comprised a chorus that held rare distinction for the number of girls who rose to fame from its ranks.

As the press agent for his comeback try, Carroll enlisted the services of the celebrated syndicated columnist and author Sidney Skolsky, who dutifully recorded Carroll's exhausting activities in putting on the new show, in the New York *Times:*

Tomorrow evening, Earl Carroll's latest collection of songs, dances, and witty sayings carefully tagged the Earl Carroll *Vanities*, opens at the maestro's own playhouse. Tomorrow, everything is in the hands of the dear public, the dear critics, and the very dear speculators. The rest will be history, but there were other days and nights.

There were the days when Earl Carroll started to assemble the girls. Then came nights of rehearsal. Carroll standing out in the orchestra in a lemon-colored smock watching Busby Berkeley put the girls through a dance routine until two in the morning.

Then more nights of rehearsal. Warm nights. Hot nights. Everybody sweating. Chorus girls and stars. Legs dancing; gags cracked without feeling funny. Carroll giving every girl a brand new silver dollar for learning a difficult routine.

Then came more days and nights of rehearsal, from eleven in the morning until five the next morning. Soon no one knows, and it doesn't matter, whether it is day or night. A final dress rehearsal and everything moves laboriously and seems to be wrong. A tryout in Atlantic City. This is merely a rehearsal with an audience looking on. After the audience goes, the players work on.

A week at Atlantic City and not one member of the *Vanities* was on the beach. Atlantic City. It's just another theatre. Days and nights and weeks of this, and then finally, the little item: Tomorrow evening at the Earl Carroll Theatre the seventh edition of the Earl Carroll *Vanities* starring W. C. Fields.

The next morning, the reviews proved that both Carroll and Fields were right. Carroll got his hit, and Fields' glowing notices justified his hard bargaining.

NEW YORK *TIMES*

Probably the chief accomplishment of Mr. Carroll's new revue, which stirred up considerable commotion in the vicinity of 50th Street last night, was to bring back to the more or less articulate stage, one W. C. Fields, who used to be a comic of great renown in these parts.

Considering Mr. Carroll's past achievements in the theatre and out, it is conceivably not too foolhardy a procedure to come out here with the unqualified statement that this is the best *Vanities* of them all.

NEW YORK *WORLD*

On the word of trusted envoys, one of the funniest single items in the show came last night as midnight approached and the presses panted. It is called, "At the Dentist's," and enlists the service of Mr. Fields. From beginning to end, this hilarious sketch was a study in frustration, of the general sort that this inimitable comic feels qualified, by long experience, to demonstrate with expert feeling. His humor derived almost completely from expression, attitudes, and the indolent, irresistible inflection in his speech. As he finishes, you have the notion that he has settled several old scores known only to himself.

Before that, Mr. Field's most laugh-provoking assignment had been the sketch called "Stolen Bonds," in which as Snavely, the prospector, he received at periodic intervals the brunt of an Alaskan snowstorm just over his prop moustache. Eyes screwed up in permanent mistrust, he exclaims in a creaking whine of a voice, "T'aint a fit night for man nor beast," as the door of the cabin slams in his face.

The performance of W. C. Fields will carry this edition of Earl Carroll *Vanities* very far with the canny boys who arrange ticket buys and otherwise help the poor producer fill his house.

To Fields should go such hurrahs as the fatigued Mr. Carroll can summon. It is he who provides a hilarious evening on the southeast corner of 50th Street and Seventh Avenue.

Although many people, audience and actors alike, had all but forgotten that Carroll was mixed up in the *Vanities*, the name of W. C. Fields having supplanted that of the producer in nearly all the important promotion, the comedian was not inflexibly austere. He granted Carroll frequent interviews, permitted him a decent but not exceptional return on his investment, and allowed him to come and go *unmolested* backstage.

One member of the cast who delighted in the treatment that Fields gave Carroll was pretty Lillian Roth, singing star of the show and later of *I'll Cry Tomorrow* fame. She had had a very unpleasant clash with the producer before the show opened. As with Fields, it was over a matter of billing, but unlike Fields she'd lost her case.

"As you know, Ken, I was 17 years old when I signed for Earl Carroll's *Vanities* for $400 a week," she said. "The afternoon of the opening, I came to rehearsal and found the marquee blazing with names. There they were: W. C. Fields, Ray Dooley, Joe Frisco, Dorothy Knapp the most beautiful girl in the world, Barto and Mann, and Vincent Lopez and his band. But the name Lillian Roth was nowhere to be seen.

"I read the marquee twice, to make sure. Then I walked into the theatre and stalked across the stage to where Earl Carroll stood talking to some others in the cast.

"Mr. Carroll," I said in a trembling voice, "I see the lights are going up. I'm one of the principals. You have everyone on that marquee outside but me and the man who sweeps the stage."

"Mr. Carroll focused his pale blue eyes on me.

" 'Who do you think you are?' he asked softly.

"I told him. 'I'm Lillian Roth, Broadway's youngest star. I was in the act called "Roth Kids." I was a star on B. F. Keith's Circuit. I replaced Winnie Lightner in the *Revels*. I was in Texas Guinan's *Padlocks*. I was a star at the Chateau Madrid. And, Mr. Carroll,' I went on, my voice rising as I reached a familiar line, 'you sent for me, I didn't send for you.' "

There was shocked silence, Lillian told me. Mr. Carroll looked at her thoughtfully, as if seeing her for the first time. She met his eyes defiantly. He stood there, a tall, thin, baldish man with long wispy hair, a worn gray artist's smock over his frail body. "There were two things he could do," she said. "He could take me over his knee and spank me, or he could kick me out of the show."

"Instead, he grabbed my arm and dragged me off the stage, through the stage door, and out into the alley into 50th Street, crowded with people. 'I'll show you how many people know you,' he muttered. When I caught my balance, he was buttonholing one passerby after another, demanding, 'Do you know Lillian Roth? Have you ever heard of Lillian Roth?'

"Some, taken aback by this startling apparition, halted for a moment and then hurried on. 'What are you talking about?' one man exclaimed, shaking himself loose. Another went along with what he thought was a gag. 'No, who is she?' But he didn't wait for an answer.

"Mr. Carroll wheeled on me. 'All right, young lady, now you know. Remember this: the people who went to see you in vaudeville did not pay $7.50, and the people who pay $7.50 to see my show don't know you.'

"I was undismayed. 'Well,' I retorted furiously, 'if you'd asked them whether they knew Winnie Lightner the way you asked them whether they knew me, they wouldn't know what you're talking about either. I'm leaving. Goodbye.'

"I was heartbroken, Ken. I cried all the way home. . . .

"Reality came quickly in an ultimatum from the theatre. If I wasn't back before the performance, injunctions would be brought against me by both Mr. Carroll and Actor's Equity. I'd never work a Broadway show again. . . . I was beaten. My contract had no provision for featured billing."

However, Lillian said, she wouldn't have missed the experience of working with W. C. Fields for anything in the world.

After the reviews came out, Fields' manner was assured, poised, and his confidence had ripened, even more, if that's possible. His occupancy of the number one dressing room was carried out with a kingly flourish that may never again be seen on the American stage. His deportment was in the rococo style of Caruso at Milan,

Bernhardt at the Comedie Française. The novice members of the cast tiptoed by his quarters, curtsied or saluted when they met him, and often applauded from the wings.

It was in this show that Fields acquired some reputation for being quick with the ad-libbed line.

"I'll never forget opening night," said Lillian. "I was singing a song in front of the New York skyline—they were really canvas cutouts on flats—and in my excitement as I took my bow, I backed up too far and bumped into the Empire State Building and it crashed to the floor. It was Fields' entrance, and as he walked on and glanced at the reasonable facsimile of the Empire State Building on the floor, he drolly remarked, 'They're not building them like they used to.'

"The audience howled," Lillian said.

BUT EARL CARROLL RECEIVED MORE than his share of accolades for that *Vanities of 1928*. And the one that pleased him most was the one that read:

A BOW TO EARL CARROLL

It strikes me that talent is extraordinary when it has the innate energy to declare itself in an atmosphere of utter stagnation. Earl Carroll has that sort of talent.

No one I know has been knocked around so much, and no one I know bobs up again so serenely for another swing from the ankle. In the language of the boulevard that spawned him, "He can take it!"

I cannot help but think of the formative days when as an obscure songwriter he lived in a tiny room over downtown Bustanoby's—four flights up and all the way back—"Ring O'Flaherty's bell!"

We used to prowl Broadway together, and with the unwinking brightness of the street itself, he would tell of the theatre he proposed to build that would bear his name. As he was at the time cutting his own hair and breakfasting now and then on a swiped bottle of milk from some neighbor's door, I was not tremendously impressed.

As everybody knows, he built that theatre.

It was no surprise to me—I've watched him too long. And now at a time when the theatre is reputedly gangrened with death, he brings us what I hear is his most extravagant revue.

Perhaps I am a doddering old softy, but in these blizzardly days of a world in chaos, it seems heartening that to Earl Carroll nothing is ever lost, that there is no such thing as defeat, and that life itself can be a perpetual triumph.

O. O. McIntyre

With all his fears and apprehensions dispelled about regaining his former prominence and public acceptance, as the momentous year of 1929 began, Carroll's seat on top of the little world that lay between 42nd and 59th Streets was soft. He had a hefty bank account from five successful shows in a row, and his current *Vanities of 1928*, thanks to the irascible Mr. Fields, was on its way to becoming the greatest box office success of them all.

But he was too young and too restless to loll in its comfort. Strange as it may sound to some ears, money making can become dull. Counting $60,000 from the sale of tickets during Christmas week was doubtless something to thank Santa Claus for, but the real fun in pocketing a buck is in the chase for it. He had a show that was good for a long run in New York and on the road. There was no need to prepare another immediately, but he was spoiling for some kind of action.

Carroll was a reckless man with money. He liked to gamble, and gambling was Times Square's second favorite indoor sport. However, his was never cards or dice—he always gambled on himself, though he did enjoy the races occasionally.

It was during this period that he found a new and more interesting game of chance. It resembled horse racing a bit, except that the steeds ran in both directions and you could bet on them to go either forward or backward. The track was in Wall Street, and millions of people in every walk of life all over the United States were crowding the betting windows that were handily situated everywhere. The stock-gambling germ had infected everybody. Instead of the usual backstage palaver, he began to hear in the conversations of his actors such names as Goldman-Sachs, Electric Bond and Share, Cities Service, and other words strange to actors' lips. Chorus girls began coming in excitedly with tips given them by gentlemen of distinction with whom they had just 'dined,' and he noticed his stagehands jotting down the names of the stocks. Even his barber would stop cutting his hair to grab the evening paper from the newsboy and hastily scan the financial page. The stock market was boiling and everybody was gleefully watching the bubbles.

A prominent financier appeared at Carroll's box office one evening with an urgent request for four seats for some friends from London. The house was sold out but the producer did a little maneuvering and got him what he wanted. He thanked Carroll profusely and whispered in his ear, "Buy yourself a few shares of Radio."

There was then no word so irritating to Carroll as *radio*. The medium had just emerged from the primitive crystal set and was blossoming out in costly and artistically carved wooden cabinets, and instead of going to the theatre, millions were staying home, listening to the music of the King of Jazz, Paul Whiteman, laughing at the hilarious antics of Sam and Henry, and a whole generation was swooning to the bleating of the first crooner, Rudy Vallée.

Carroll harbored a hearty detestation for the pitchmen who were giving away entertainment that those in show business were trying to sell. Nevertheless, the next day Carroll called up a broker and bought a thousand shares of Radio Corporation. Several days later, he sold them and laughingly pocketed a profit of several thousand dollars. He telephoned the financier to thank him, and his friend suggested Carroll buy another stock. He cashed in again. It wasn't long before Carroll was having his coffee in his starlight bungalow atop his theatre with the stock page of the morning newspaper in front of him. This was at noon, his rising hour, when the stocks were already halfway around the track. With the phone receiver to his ear, he played them into the home stretch. Starting with two or three entries, he was soon playing a dozen.

He began making thousands of dollars a day without even leaving his apartment. His acquaintances included brokers and bankers who seemed to attach much value to the little favors Carroll was able to do for them at the box office, and they reciprocated with advice on the market. In a surprisingly brief time, his accounts with brokers were running into the millions. It was exciting and flattering to his ego—gambling with the Morgans and Rockefellers.

On the morning of his thirty-sixth birthday, he was telling Jim over breakfast about his profits in the market. He remarked that counting his paper profits in Wall Street and real estate holdings, he estimated his wealth at more than $6,000,000.

"Remember on my tenth birthday, Jim," Carroll said, "when you gave me ten brand-new pennies for luck?"

"Yes, but don't forget, that was in cash," was his brother's shrewd rejoinder.

Jim had become increasingly alarmed about Earl's recklessness with money. Though he had tried to dissuade him, just a couple of weeks before he had reluctantly accompanied Earl when he had chartered a private railroad car and invited Dorothy Knapp and a large group of friends to be his guests at the Roney Plaza Hotel in Miami Beach, Florida.

He was even more disturbed by the petulance of his brother when Earl became irritated by a petty overcharge at the swanky hotel. He ordered all his guests to pack while he drove around Miami Beach with a real estate agent in quest of a house. An imposing newly built home, fronted by an expanse of green lawn and with white columns and a red-tiled roof glistening in the tropic sunlight, struck his fancy and he sent the agent to inquire about renting it. The realtor came back to say that the retired businessman and his mother who occupied the house the year 'round were not interested. Earl went to the door himself. The next day the whole gang moved in. Ten thousand dollars in cash proved too irresistible an inducement to the owners, who moved to a hotel.

Like other amateur millionaires, Carroll yielded to the urge to make a social splurge. He gave a party for more than 100 guests who included the theatre and motion picture notables wintering at the resort and several socially prominent New Yorkers who graciously accepted his invitation.

Two orchestras, one of them Rudy Vallée and his Connecticut Yankees, made music in the terraced garden, and a caterer provided the food and drinks the occasion called for. The whole trip was to cost close to $50,000.

It was at that party that he met the extremely wealthy Mrs. Anne Weightman Penfield, the matronly widow of Frederick Courtland Penfield, who had been ambassador to Austria-Hungary during the Wilson administration.

Carroll had no way of knowing it at the moment, but she was to persuade him to enter into an experience that was to be a theatrical nightmare within the next few months.

She had come as a guest of Will Edrington, who had been a close friend of her husband's, and they were having a late supper along with Earl, Dorothy, and Jim as the other guests were beginning to leave.

It was Edrington who brought up the subject. He said, "Earl, Mrs. Penfield has a special project that I think you'll be interested in."

Mrs. Penfield said, "Yes. Mr. Carroll, I'd like you to produce a show for me. I want it to be a book musical—really an operetta."

Full of enthusiasm, Edrington said, "And she doesn't want anybody but you, Earl. You must do this show! And it won't be too much work. She just wants you to write the book, and you don't have to worry about the music."

Mrs. Penfield's largesse was inspired by her interest in the musical careers of Romilly Johnson and George Bagby, nephews of an old and dear friend. The only stipulation was that they must write the score.

"You can't lose anything, Mr. Carroll," she added. "It won't cost you a cent. I insist upon putting up all the money."

"Sounds like an interesting idea, Earl," Jim chimed in, noting with delight the fact that it wouldn't be a strain on the Carroll coffer.

Dorothy said, "It's a wonderful idea. Here's your chance to beat Ziegfeld!"

Jim said, "She's right, Earl. You've proved yourself the world's greatest producer of revues. Look what happened to his last show."

Jim was referring to a recent Ziegfeld *Follies* that had been a disaster at its tryout in New Haven. It was so anemic that Ziggy changed the billing and brought the revue into New York under the title of *No Foolin*. It struggled along for a few weeks and finally gave up the ghost.

"You've got to do this show for Mrs. Penfield," said Edrington, who could make the simple statement, "It's a lovely morning," sound like a Patrick Henry oration. "Here's your chance to scale the heights of Olympus and rise to the apogee of your success as a producer of an operetta."

Carroll listened quietly, but his mind was spinning. Without knowing it, they had all brought the loud pedal down on a chord that had been softly vibrating inside him. He had never attempted a book musical, and he smarted at the fact that his arch rival, Ziegfeld, had two such recent hits, *Rio Rita* and *Showboat*.

He thanked Mrs. Penfield and told her he would seriously consider her proposition. After thinking it over, he decided it could be a wonderful starring vehicle for Dorothy in her first acting role, and to the delight of Jim he called Mrs. Penfield the next morning and said he would accept her offer.

On the trip back to New York he worked feverishly, and with the help of the delighted Dorothy he concocted a simple story: In Venice, once there was a duke who got the basic idea of the Atlantic City Beauty Pageant slightly mixed up with the annual Festival of the Ring. There was a beautiful maiden, Miss Knapp, who was loved by a count honorably, if that is possible, and by the Duke of Venice more illegally. The count is shot in the first act, and according to authentic tidings is restored to the human comedy of life in the second.

It was a naive plot but certainly no worse than the threads on which most musical comedies at that time were hung.

He decided to call his romantic operetta *Fioretta*, and it turned out to be the most expensive flop in the history of Broadway, costing the inexperienced Mrs. Penfield more than $350,000.

When Carroll took on the job of writing the book of *Fioretta* himself, in addition to producing the show and playing the stock market, he bit off more than he could chew.

Writing and producing a show with one eye on the script and the other on the ticker tape was not productive of satisfactory results. The impresario was more deeply involved in Wall Street than was good for him. The current *Vanities*, too, made demands on his time. Distribution of tickets among agencies, replacement of costumes, refurbishing of scenery, backstage frictions—there was always Fields!—and the tendency of performers to become lax and mechanical are among the worries that are concomitant with the long run of any successful show.

But the real difficulty came when Carroll attempted to outstrip his rivals in point of lavish recklessness.

Too practiced a showman to slight any of the familiar ingredients of musical entertainment, Carroll skipped nothing. His heart was in the display, and the display, heralded by fanfares, was set off against dazzling, bold-figured curtains. As embellishments for this simple little plot, most of the splendors of this and other worlds, and of this and other times, passed across the stage in a magnificent pageant of regal stuffs and gorgeous colors—harlequinades, high-church processionals, silver-tipped ballets, gowns of cloth of gold, ermine trains, iridescent coats for the high officials, a troupe of gondoliers, tossing feathers, burnished cuirasses, and state and church flags.

For the tryout at Ford's Theatre in Baltimore, it took seven railroad cars to transport the costumes and scenery, the 56 chorus girls, and the cast of 225 persons, counting stagehands, dressmakers, and special help—plus 15 mothers of chorus girls bringing up the rear in day coaches.

The critic on the Baltimore *Sun* was kind when he said:

> Leaving early, one tries dazedly to remember bits of the plot and fragments of the multiple embellishments, and carries away the impression of having seen two musical comedies, half of a revue, one-fourth of a romantic comedy, a two-ring circus, and part of a side show.

On the spot in Baltimore, Carroll realized that something was basically wrong with the show, and despite his feverish efforts all through the night, no amount of nutrition or medication could make the sickly infant strong and lusty.

Being a veteran of the Broadway wars, he was not surprised when the New York critics murdered the show, but he was hurt when they panned his star, Dorothy Knapp, particularly when they questioned the sanity of whoever was responsible for starring in an operetta a girl who couldn't sing. As leading woman of *Fioretta*, Miss Dorothy went through the entire show without singing one note, which fact caused considerable comment at the time of the premiere.

LeRoy Prinz, a very dear old friend of mine who was the choreographer for *Fioretta*, was there that night.

"Oh, God, Ken, that opening night was a disaster. Curtains wouldn't close, drops didn't come down, sets crashed during the dialogue, performers missed their cues, costumes didn't fit, chorus girls stumbled and fell. The biggest laughs from the audience were those occasioned by mishaps. The final curtain came down on the saddest-looking troupe ever seen," he said, shaking his head with a shudder.

"It was one of the most horrendous experiences I've ever gone through. If I live to be 100 I'll never forget it. God almighty, the show was beautiful—but no matter what happened it didn't have a chance.

"For one thing, this old gal out of Philadelphia—Mrs. Pen-something—in her sixties—she'd never been in show business be-fore—financed the show to further the careers of a couple of guys who wrote the music. She put up all this dough. God, it cost her a fortune! It must have been a half a million dollars!

"She wouldn't use any regular theatrical scenery. Everything had to be authentic—stuff that she'd brought over from Europe. Ken, you wouldn't believe it! All the drapes and tapestries were made of the most expensive velours, French satins, and silk brocades. And it was so sad closing night—we ran for only a short time—so many scissors came out of nowhere. They cut the drapes to pieces, the kids did, taking them home for blankets and bedspreads and making clothes out of them. And the old gal didn't say a word. She just stood there watching them with tears in her eyes.

"And the furs we used in the show—the minks, chinchillas, and Russian sables—all real. Not a phony thing in the show! We had one number where Dorothy Knapp came down the steps wearing a full-length ermine cape—and this wasn't just a full-length thing, it fanned out in a train the width of the stairs. Real ermine. That's what that old gal insisted on—she insisted on real ermine. It was the damnedest thing you ever saw in your life. And as Dorothy came down she was bedecked in jewels—diamonds, rubies, and emeralds—all real. God, that one number must have cost a fortune.

"Then she'd brought over from Europe all these suits of armor— the real, authentic heavy ones—and all the men, including the prin-cipals, had to wear them in the finale and do this dance in them, but they never had time to rehearse.

"Poor Leon Errol—he was in the show, you know, and he had to wear one of those suits and make a speech on top of a table. 'What is woman?' he shouted. His teetering legs collapsed and he fell off the table in a metal heap. Then he couldn't get up on account of the armor, and a couple of chorus boys had to pull him off the stage. God, it was funny. Pathetic—but funny.

"You know, Fanny Brice was in that show, too. Imagine! She was 'supporting' Dorothy Knapp. That Carroll could con anybody into doing anything!

"Poor Fanny—she was so miscast. Imagine, they had her playing an old Italian dowager—Dorothy Knapp's mother—quoting Shakespeare in a Venetian garden. This was supposed to lead in to her singing a beautiful straight ballad entitled 'The Wicked Old Village of Venice.'

"You know, she had a helluva voice. Remember how she belted out 'My Man' in the Ziegfeld *Follies?* Well, evidently Fanny said to herself 'The hell with this'—she could tell the show was a turkey—and for no reason at all she walked down to the footlights in this tremendously flounced gown, and with a broad leer, her wicked eyes crossed, and with shrugs and wanton gestures, she sang the song this way—'The Wicked Old *Willage of Wenice.'* It was a riot—nothing to do with the show, but the audience howled. And standing up in back of the theatre the two boys who wrote the song were screaming and pulling their hair.

"In all fairness, they'd really written a good score. Mrs. Penfield had no complaint about the music. But it burned her up when Carroll starred Dorothy Knapp at $1,000 a week. She was sheer decoration, didn't have a song in the show. An unsinging prima donna didn't make sense, but to pay her all that dough Mrs. Penfield considered downright insanity.

"She yelled at Carroll about it, and after four weeks he bounced Dorothy out of the show. But it *wasn't* on account of her not singing. The real reason was—look, Ken, I'm going to tell you something now that you won't believe. It was incredible.

"Dorothy Knapp and the leading man had a number near the end of the first act. It was a gorgeous set and she looked ravishing. She was a very sexy looking girl. To introduce the number I had 24 chorus boys lined up across the stage in one—you know, in front of the closed curtain. They were dressed as gondoliers and were lustily singing 'In my gondola let me make love to you. . . .' And doing a precision routine with huge double-high deck oars. At the finish they walked off the stage, pulling the curtains open, and there languishing in this gorgeous gondola was Dorothy Knapp and her leading man, who was supposed to be standing up like an Italian gondolier singing this love song—you know what I mean.

"Well, opening night, as the boys were singing this introduction number, Carroll, who was all over backstage in his blue smock checking on everything, took a last look to see if the principals were in place. And *how* they were! There was Dorothy with her beautiful dress pulled up and her leading man on top of her acting out the lyrics 'I'm a man, you're a woman, let me make love to you.' As

Carroll peeped through the curtain he incredulously saw them having a wild affair in the bottom of the gondola.

"Ken, I tell you, if that curtain had opened two minutes earlier Carroll would really have had a first on Broadway. They probably would have given him his old cell back in Atlanta!

"When Carroll saw them he was shocked beyond belief and rushed off the stage, and he was white—just white. I went back to his office with him and he became hysterical. He said, 'How could this happen to me? We've been together for five years. I'm going to commit suicide'—and he reached for a glass of Poland water.

"There had been rumors about Dorothy occasionally tearing one off with ushers in the balcony during rehearsals, but the stories had evidently never got back to Carroll, and if they had he would never have believed them. He had a peculiar set of ethics. It was all right what he did—he could lay every broad in the show—but when he picked out someone to be *his* girl he expected complete loyalty."

This was the end of the Carroll-Knapp idyll. The romance that had started in that baroque bed in Carroll's penthouse ended on the stage of the Earl Carroll Theatre in a gondola.

Shortly thereafter, adhering to Mrs. Penfield's wishes—she and her two music men had begged Carroll all during rehearsals to replace Miss Knapp and get a heroine who could sing, telling him it was a pity to spoil the show by using a chorus girl instead of a proper prima donna—Dorothy Knapp was dismissed from *Fioretta*.

She immediately filed suit for $250,000 against Mrs. Penfield, alleging she had agreed to back the Earl Carroll production only to further the composers; against George Bagby and Romilly Johnson for conspiring to deprive her of her employment by asserting that unless she was discharged they would stop the production; and against Earl Carroll and the *Vanities* production company for the balance due on her run-of-the-play contract. She contended that the amount sued for represented the damage to her theatrical reputation, and her mental and physical suffering.

Miss Knapp then entered St. Luke's Hospital suffering from what was described as nervous exhaustion. Then one thing happened after another.

A few days later Mrs. Penfield's protege, Romilly Johnson, committed suicide at the home of his father in Lynn, Massachusetts. He stabbed himself in the heart with a bread knife and his body was found by George Bagby, who had been his close companion for 22 years.

Ironically, before the trial began, the judge had dismissed the charges against not only the late Romilly Johnson but also his partner, George Bagby, and Mrs. Penfield.

The court expressed the opinion that evidently Miss Knapp "was not equal to singing the theme song or dancing as the heroine's part was originally cast." But the defendants, Justice Ernest Hammer held, were acting within their rights and did not "wrongfully cause an injury to the plaintiff."

The only issue that remained was whether Earl Carroll had paid Miss Knapp the balance due on her contract.

On the stand under cross-examination, tears streaming from her eyes, Dorothy Knapp denied she had received any pay after her dismissal. Her tears and her denials grew as three checks dated after her dismissal and endorsed with her name were shown to her by Moses Malevinsky, attorney for the defendant.

When she saw the three checks the tears continued to flow and she still denied that the endorsements were hers. When Mr. Malevinsky pointed out that the checks had been deposited to her account at the 49th Street branch of the Irving Trust Company, she repeated her denial.

"I know I didn't get paid for those three weeks," she said, beginning to wipe her eyes and looking rather beseechingly toward Justice Hammer.

"Look at the checks," the judge ordered.

Then Earl Carroll was put on the stand. He identified his former sweetheart's signature and icily stated he had given the checks to her personally.

Dorothy made an appealing yet curiously unconvincing witness when she returned to the stand. She finally admitted that she must have received the checks but said, looking defiantly at Carroll, "I have no recollection of them."

Before handing down his judgment, Justice Hammer surprised the spectators by paying Miss Knapp a compliment. He apparently had an eye for beauty, as he said, "Concedingly she is fair of face, form and figure. Although so advertised and exploited, plaintiff does not give an impression of sophistication or calculating worldliness, but that of education, culture, and refinement. . . ."

However his judicial integrity remained intact. He awarded Miss Knapp the sum of *six cents.*

"I am quite, quite through with him."

"I shall never in my life work for him again."

"I think my career would have been more advanced if I had never known him."

"I don't hate him but I'm putting him completely out of my life."

Those were the words of Dorothy Knapp to reporters as she left the courthouse.

Although she had named Earl Carroll in her breach of contract suit she added that she felt he had been "coerced" into dismissing her.

Dorothy went on to confess that she had been "very fond" of the temperamental producer for many years and also admitted that she had visited Carroll during his Atlanta imprisonment.

"My family wanted me to leave Mr. Carroll years ago," she said. "And I did. He said I would come back to him. And I did, after a year in the *Follies.*"

In answer to one reporter's query, "Any regrets, Dorothy?" she paused and reflectively said, "No, I don't regret any experience that I have had, but—I have learned that you can't mix business and pleasure."

While she remained for months in seclusion, Broadway speculated as to whether a broken heart, a fit of temper, or the sulks of professional jealousy followed the debacle of *Fioretta.*

Then Dorothy Knapp went into a mysterious retirement, and Broadway gossip concerned itself with who would be Earl Carroll's new love.

They didn't have to wait long. She wasn't very far away. She had been in his show for more than a year. Her name was Beryl Wallace.

LeRoy Prinz had some very nice things to say about Beryl. "She was a real knockout," he said, "well-stacked, not too much makeup, gorgeous hair, and lots of talent—tremendous dancer and a helluva singer. You know, I was with Earl when he picked her. I could see he was attracted to her right away. I'm sure she liked him and had heard plenty of stories from the other girls, but as long as he was tied up with Dorothy Knapp she wouldn't give him the time of day—not even go to lunch with him. She was really a sweet kid, Ken.

Got along with everybody."

And I can attest to that. I worked with her every night for eight months in *Sketch Book of 1935*. She was one of those upon whom Nature occasionally lavishes talent as well as beauty, in addition to which she was blessed with an affability and kindness that endeared her to everyone in the company.

So for the next show following *Fioretta*, Beryl Wallace replaced Dorothy Knapp as Carroll's number one star beauty on stage and off, and was in every show he produced thereafter for the rest of her life.

THERE IS NOTHING QUITE AS USELESS as an empty theatre. Other than perhaps renting it to a church or other organization for meetings, it becomes a tremendous liability if it is not used for the purpose for which it was built—housing a theatrical production.

With the sudden demise of *Fioretta*, Carroll was faced with the problem of losing $12,500 a month in rent; someting had to be done, and quickly.

Though he immediately received offers from movie companies—RKO, Warner Brothers— to lease the Earl Carroll Theatre, regarded as one of the most valuable houses in town for talking pictures because of its location at Seventh Avenue and 50th Street, across the street from the new Roxy, the thought of it being used for exhibition of the talkies was not only distasteful but abhorrent.

This new medium from Hollywood was like an ominous giant stalking across the continent, trampling down theatres venerable with tradition, and out of the ruins of their destruction was emerging a new world of entertainment.

The movie palace, with its full-length feature and stage show, was taking its toll of attendance at dramas and musicals.

In Los Angeles the enterprising Sid Grauman, who led the way by erecting the Million Dollar, Egyptian, and Chinese theatres, conceived the idea of preceding the motion picture with a stage show, which included a band, a line of chorus girls, and vaudeville acts. Its instantaneous success sent this new form of entertainment, with its low prices of admission, sweeping over the country. It was a body blow, mostly felt in the sticks—Times Square was still seething with crowds on the way to dramatic and musical shows. Nevertheless, there was an uneasiness at the tables in Sardi's, the Astor, and Dinty Moore's, where the guardians of the old established order gathered for luncheon. The portents of impending calamity were unmistakable. There was a hollow ring in the voices of the diehards, like Carroll, who tried to laugh it off.

Suiting action to the word, he hastily decided to produce a new show to fill the empty cavern on 49th Street and Seventh Avenue.

What prompted him to adopt the name *Sketch Book* for this show instead of his usual *Vanities* will never be known.

As was his wont, his first concern was the girls, and soon the stage of the Earl Carroll Theatre was ablaze with rehearsals of scantily clad dancing maidens reclining and rhythmically raising legs aloft; colored balls whirling and opening to pop young ladies onto the stage; and languorous females modestly hanging their heads and holding hands in a wistful daisy-chain effect.

But, as always, he wanted a big name that would attract attention. Much to the consternation of the Great Glorifier, he announced to the papers that Ziegfeld's big star, Eddie Cantor, was to appear in Earl Carroll's new *Sketch Book.*

The banjo-eyed comedian was then employed down the street under Mr. Ziegfeld's pennant in a show called *Whoopee*, and as by force of natural law and legal contract Mr. Cantor couldn't appear in two places at once, Carroll, for the first time in a Broadway legitimate theatre, presented a talking picture segment.

It showed Eddie Cantor on the screen, catching his rolling eyes and muffling his trebled speech in hot potato tones. He recited a vesper song entitled "Legs, Legs, Legs," whereupon the live show picked up the theme and shook a few.

Also, revealed in the program was the fact that Eddie Cantor wrote all the comedy sketches for the show, but unfortunately they didn't crackle with the familiar Cantor wit, and just what Mr. Cantor's services were in setting the literary tone of *Sketch Book* remained vexatiously obscure.

As one reviewer said:

> Surely no one would wantonly ascribe to Mr. Cantor the blackout jest
> about unfaithful wives and lovers in the closet, which for generations
> have served the stage in all their bespattered mirthlessness, or the hotel
> bedroom shockers, and/or the humor with bathroom proclivities which
> distinguishes the second act of the show. The humor of the *Sketch
> Book* sketches is either bankrupt or quagmire.

It was said that Mr. Carroll's audacious exploitation of Mr. Cantor's
services was remarked upon by Mr. Ziegfeld. At any rate, by way
of neighborly pleasantry, Carroll included a travesty of the famous
Godiva incident from Ziegfeld's *Whoopee* in his current show.

September 23, 1929, was notable for two happenings. It was the
opening of Earl Carroll's *Sketch Book*, and on the same day the
stock market reached its all-time high. Radio passed the 100 mark,
AT&T sold over 300, and U.S. Steel hit 260. At intermission the crowd
in the lobby was in gay spirits and not particularly concerned about
whether the show was good or bad. The talk was about the market,
not the actors or the music.

The critics' raps in the morning papers about the dirty material
didn't annoy Carroll too much. On the strength of the *Vanities* reputation the speculators had bought enough tickets to assure him of
good business for weeks to come. So, instead of keeping his eye
on the show, he kept it on the stock ticker.

Then came the first shock in Wall Street that halted the Big Spree.
The timid ones took their losses and fled. Others, like Carroll, put
up more margin and hung on. A few days later, when the market
started on the way up again, they had the laugh on those who quit.

Broadway was shocked and astonished when they then read in
the paper: "Earl Carroll To Build New Theatre." The story went
on to say that the daring entrepreneur was planning to demolish
his present theatre, opened in 1923, and erect a new one on the
site. Just that day he had acquired property adjoining the house
on 49th and 50th Streets at the aggregate rental of almost $1,000,000.
It was said that Mr. Carroll was extremely enthusiastic about the
new theatre, which would have a seating capacity of 3,000 and an
84-foot stage designed along new lines, and that the structure would
include studio apartments and stores as well as an additional exit
on 49th Street for the theatre.

Then there was another tremor, and this time Wall Street split wide open and stocks started tumbling into a bottomless pit. The panic was on. Those who weren't wiped out fumbled confusedly, as Carroll did, to salvage something, only to be dragged deeper into the hole. Carroll covered, bought, sold, and ran to the broker's office with the cash from his box office. On the day of the Big Crash a bewildered public despairingly dumped 13,000,000 shares—and most of Carroll's were among them. He joined the ranks of the many ex-millionaires. He wasn't exactly broke, but he drove his Rolls Royce into the garage and had it put up on jacks. It didn't match his mood.

The lights twinkled on Broadway but the sidewalks were deserted and the theatres were empty. Only the speakeasies were packed with mourners holding a wake over their stocks. The gloom was so thick that Mayor Jimmy Walker made a public request to movie theatre owners not to show pictures that might have a depressing effect on audiences and to keep the screen bright and gay with comedies. It was like asking for a funny story at a funeral.

Faced with a sagging box office, Carroll got the *Sketch Book* out of New York and sent it on the road, where it struggled through an unprofitable tour. He tried to recoup his losses by muddling along in the stock market, but whichever way he bet the stocks would go, they always went that-a-way. He was truly mad at the brokers now, and there's no sucker like one who loses his head. His pants are sure to follow.

He knew he was swimming in treacherous waters but he felt safe. There was a raft within easy reach that he could swim back to. He still owned his theatre.

With the gloom of the Depression deepening, he reluctantly was forced to accept an offer from Radio Pictures, a part of the Radio-Keith-Orpheum organization, to lease his theatre for a monthly rental of $12,750 and half the taxes. They were planning to use it for six new "road show" film productions. The first was to be the talkie version of his old arch-rival Ziegfeld's big hit *Rio Rita*.

Not without a note of defiance, Carroll immediately leased Zieg-feld's theatre, the New Amsterdam, and promptly announced that he was producing a new edition of the *Vanities*.

I T'S A STRANGE PHENOMENON. There is one industry that defies depression, unemployment, shortages, declining consumer buying power, and any other adverse conditions. That is the entertainment industry.

Although it may not be the only one to do so, it stands out because of the seeming contradiction: people enjoying themselves more under the worst of conditions.

Such was the case as the decade of the thirties began. Broadway began to bounce back and the lights were starting to blaze again for the musical revues. Though there were no Ziegfeld *Follies* or George White *Scandals* that year, there were *The New Yorkers, Simple Simon,* Lew Leslie's *International Revue, Wake Up and Dream, Three's a Crowd,* and, on July 1, 1930, the premiere of the Earl Carroll *Vanities* at the New Amsterdam Theatre.

Finding difficulty in casting the show—Hollywood had drained off all the stars that the New York producers needed, and Carroll, along with the others, was beginning to feel the effects of the migration to the west coast—there was nothing to do but fall back on his old standby: *sex.*

The new *Vanities* was heralded as "Meeting America's demand for sophisticated entertainment," and most of the reviewers emphasized its nudity and the low level of its comedy. "What passes for humor in it is generally degrading," one wrote.

Carroll had pulled out all stops in his efforts to provide New York with the sort of revue usually termed "Parisian." As always with the girls, he had generously gone the full distance in studying the anatomy rather scrupulously, particularly in Faith Bacon's fan dance. In it she waved two white feather fans, revealing her totally nude body. And on opening night, an unfortunate mishap occurred during Miss Bacon's pelvic gyrations. The top part of the 'pastie' covering her most strategic area came loose, and a long piece of tape dangled between her legs, causing the audience to gasp and leading them to wonder if it were indeed the real Faith Bacon or simply a careless female impersonator.

There was also a salacious comedy scene called "Modes—Window at Merl's," wherein five girls in evening dresses posed as wax fashion models and comedian Jimmy Savo stepped into the store window and completely undressed them. It was the strategic intricacies of his unfastening their garter belts and removing their long opera-length silk stockings that brought on the gendarmes.

After an uproar from press and clergy that Carroll had really over-stepped the bounds of decency this time, on the afternoon of the first matinee the show was raided by the police. It was like the rerun of an old Roaring Twenties movie.

About 4:30 P.M., while the matinee was still going on, three police sedans, with 12 patrolmen under Acting Captain James J. Coy, drove up to the stage entrance on West 41st Street, and word spread quickly that they were on the scene. A few minutes afterward a crowd of 1,500 had collected outside the main entrance to the theatre, and in the surrounding office buildings 500 others had gallery seats for the police show.

Captain Coy entered the theatre with warrants, but assured the stage manager that no action would be taken until the matinee was over.

The other patrolmen took up posts at the various entrances.

The word spread among the members of the chorus, many of whom went out on the 41st Street fire escape between scenes to boo or hiss at the police guards stationed at the entrances below.

The show went on and still the audience knew nothing of what was taking place behind the scenes. They were listening to Jack Benny, who was making his Broadway debut in this show and finding himself paddling steadily through the muck.

One opening night critic bemoaned: "Jack Benny hardly has a chance to show how subtle a comedian he can be when his patter is skillful."

When the show ended, seven warrants were served. Luckily "Old Blue Eyes" ran out of the money. The unlucky "winners" were Faith Bacon, Jimmy Savo, and the five girls in the "Window at Merl's" scene.

In the meantime the three police sedans drove from the stage door around to the lobby entrance on 42nd Street. The prisoners emerged, walking quickly through a lane in the noisy crowd, and entered the police cars to the booming of photographer's flashlights. They were whisked off to the West 30th Street Station where they were bundled into a rear room until Earl Carroll showed up and arranged for their bail.

At the trial, presided over by Magistrate Maurice H. Gotlieb, the jurors listened for an hour to police officials stating that "New York, with all its reputation for immodesty and badness, is not yet so bad that women can be permitted to appear on any theatre stage in a state of complete nudity," and blasting the whole show as "an obscene, indecent, immoral, and impure exhibition." Then, for another hour, they listened to Earl Carroll defending it as "art."

Playing his familiar role as the persecuted underdog, he said: "We have an artistic show, and if I have pleased the public I feel that I am successful. I knew nothing of any complaints and I believe the raid was totally unwarranted and ridiculous. It took 25 policemen to bring out one man and six ladies, where summonses would have been sufficient. If the police had come to us in the usual fashion we would certainly have taken their opinion into consideration. We do not wish to defy the city government."

After a few minutes of deliberation the jurors freed the defendants. When the cast heard the verdict they shook hands, kissed, laughed, commended the jurors, and also voiced gratitude for their "vindication."

Even the judge shook hands with Carroll for the photographers, saying, "I am not ashamed to grasp Mr. Carroll's hand. I was certainly not here to pillory or crucify him."

As Carroll left the court, he told reporters: "Somewhere there must be an ulterior motive. We have been successful, you know. It seems my career is just one thing like this after another—all unsolicited.

Somebody is trying to hurt us and I have my suspicions who it is."

The next day Flo Ziegfeld made a statement from his home in Hollywood.

In an exclusive interview for the New York *Times*, July 13, 1930, he expressed regret that "a show so bad that it had to be raided by the police had been placed in the New Amsterdam Theatre, of which I am one-third owner. I have been told that Mr. Carroll's show is one of the filthiest ever seen in New York."

Ziegfeld then emphatically emphasized, "I had nothing to do with its being booked at the New Amsterdam."

Reaction from Carroll was immediate. The *Times* printed his reply.

> I can only say that Mr. Ziegfeld's statement is an excellent example of poor sportsmanship. He is 3,000 miles away and takes it upon himself to adversely criticize a fellow producer and comment with more palpable venom than knowledge. Naturally Mr. Ziegfeld would not want a successful attraction of mine in a theatre in which he has a minor interest, and the box office receipts of the New Amsterdam Theatre, which were telegraphed to him nightly, were convincing proof that the *Vanities* had broken all box office records even *before* the raid. I was invited to produce the *Vanities* at the New Amsterdam Theatre because Mr. Ziegfeld, instead of producing one of his own revues to protect the theatre, had gone west to produce pictures. When he returns to New York and sees the beauties of the *Vanities* I modestly venture the opinion that he will start west again.
>
> He should be the last one to prate of purity on stage. His holier-than-thou attitude is ludicrous in view of the fact that he has openly boasted that he is the father of nudity in the American theatre. How well we all remember the glorified exhibition in the former *Follies*. We smile at Mr. Ziegfeld's lack of knowledge of the raid that was made. We suppose that he will be just as "surprised" when the facts are exposed that one of his best friends in New York was the instigator of the raid—a raid that was totally unwarranted and with but one object, to ruin my career.

Vanities of 1930 played to packed houses and chalked up a healthy run of 215 performances.

It was to be Earl Carroll's last hit on Broadway.

1931 WAS THE MOST DISMAL YEAR in the history of show business. Lightless marquees drooped in front of lifeless theatres. Through most of the year, Broadway was about 45 percent dark. During the summer there were only 12 shows on the boards. Muscials lost $2,000,000 on the season. Even popular Jolson's *Wonder Bar* could last only 76 performances.

Most Broadway producers of dramas and musical shows took a holiday. They had to. Shows that somehow got on the stage folded after a few weeks, and scenery and costumes were hauled away to Cain's warehouse while still practically new. Even the Shuberts went into bankruptcy.

Had Earl Carroll been more normally cautious and less self-confident—or, should we say, conceited—he would have "passed the dice," as most producers did, in 1931 when the whole world was on a losing streak.

But incongruously, that was the year he chose to *build* the new Earl Carroll Theatre on the same site as the old one.

"Angel dough" had vanished for most producers, but Carroll had his own private gold mine, Will Edrington, who put up $4,500,000 for the new theatre, a mecca that was to be fancier than the New Amsterdam, Music Box, and Winter Garden combined. It caused Broadway to buzz, and in the days and weeks that preceded the gala opening the press coverage was tremendous.

The New York *Times* wrote:

Because Broadway is, in spite of itself, sometimes dramatic, wiser citizens have long since learned to be surprised at nothing. Or, if they are, to give no tell-tale indication.

Among the recent reminders of the stage doldrums, for instance, none has been more pointed than the fact that not one new theatre has gone up in the last three years on Broadway, where a new theatre used to be unveiled every other evening if the weather permitted, or even if it didn't. Indeed, if Times Square could ever agree on anything, it was thought to have declared unanimously and ruefully that it had too many theatres already and would have no more for many a season. But a producer called Earl Carroll has changed all that, unmindful, it would appear, that a depression is reported to be abroad in this land. Nothing seems to daunt anyone nowadays.

Ed Sullivan probably summed it up best:

If you have walked along 49th or 50th Streets just east of Seventh Avenue, you have seen in skeleton form the temple that will house the Earl Carroll "wonder works" this coming season on the same site where the former Earl Carroll Theatre stood for nine years. The theatre is in the "strictly modern" style in the "straight and setback" lines of the new skyscrapers.

If you've happened to notice a man hurrying here and there in an old smock "riding the whole horse," watching the builders, experimenting with costumes and colors and listening to the boys from Tin Pan Alley as they chanted their melodies, it was the indefatigable Mr. Carroll. It is hard work but he can stand it because he "grew up in theatres."

In dwelling on the impending innovations, of this, his latest and greatest project, he said, "What I want to be remembered for are the changes I have made in the theatre, even if they are quickly forgotten."

A very canny showman is Mr. Carroll, and a student of the public. So he has thought it all out. He took time out to say, "All that is wrong with show business today is the prices that are charged." The way around high prices, he intimated, is by mass production, and "The form to which mass production best adapts itself is the big revue."

So Mr. Carroll, a logician for all his persistent elegance, will concentrate on big revues, and his new edifice will seat 3,000 people with a $3 top, even for opening night.

Next Thursday evening, therefore, Earl Carroll—who knows how to make an entrance—will submit that a new $4,500,000 theatre, bearing his name, will be opened and ready with the ninth *Vanities* to do business. It will be a milestone. One has Mr. Carroll's word for this.

On the night of August 27, 1931, the small world that was Broadway and the larger world that wasn't, turned out en masse to provide a capacity audience for the opening of the new Earl Carroll Theatre and the premiere of the ninth edition of the *Vanities*.

It was apparently the verdict of nearly 3,000 spectators, to whom Mr. Carroll kept his promise of $3 top for first-night seats, that the theatre reached a new peak in novelty and design as well as its size, which made it the largest of New York's legitimate playhouses.

As the audience headed for their pews, they passed five house treasurers, all handsome fellows, who sold them seats from behind a long counter in the inner lobby. (Like the new Lincoln Center years later—no box office.) Eighty-four attaches comprised the entire house staff, whose ushers and attendants were required to be at least six feet tall and capable of wheeling a chromium-plated water wagon down the aisle between acts. As a matter of fact, the chromium idea, together with an effect of gold, also played a part in the uniforms of these dashing smooth young men who were trained in the fine old military tradition that prevailed in the nearby Roxy Theatre. Three of them were sheer Mercury with a seat check.

The five doors opening into the orchestra aisles were of etched metal. Inside, first nighters saw lines of black metal streak the ceiling of the auditorium and follow down the side walls from a flat dome, with flame-shaded terra cotta to relieve the black and the metal. The carpets were in three tones of green. All the seats in the theatre were of coral color, and those in the orchestra were equipped with flashlights for the reading of programs when the houselights were dimmed (pre-Radio City Music Hall).

Among the mechanical innovations on the stage were two interchangeable elevator platforms—a little creation of the master's. Also, a duplicate counterweight system handled the machinery and hydraulic lifts, which enabled the orchestra to be heard after the musicians had descended into the basement and another platform had been raised and put into use.

Particular attention had been given to the acoustics in the theatre. Five thousand Berliner acoustical discs, it was said, had been imbedded in the walls, 6 loudspeakers installed in the auditorium for the general reinforcement of the performance on the stage, and 20 more in other parts of the theatre.

The theatre was equipped with four light circuits—red, blue, green, and white—the fixtures were, nevertheless, invisible. From the same hidden sources (this was all pretty mysterious) the lights turned on in whatever combinations the Earl Carroll estheticians chose to play them. The conductor of light (no longer a mere electrician) presided in a tuxedo at a controlling console in full view of the audience.

A lower-left box for occupancy by Mr. Carroll's notable guests had a telephone and a private entrance to the stage, guarded by a gay, sympathetic girl rather than a surly oldster.

Liberal with his splendors, Mr. Carroll saw fit to install them on both sides of the footlights. It was the first legitimate theatre on Broadway to have a cooling system both backstage and out front. The modernistic design went straight through, from one end of the house to the other, with individual variations backstage according to the temperament of the artiste. The dressing rooms for the chorus girls were finished in chromium, satin, and silk, and each girl had a complete dressing table with triple mirrors. The decor of the stars' dressing rooms was a sunset in another world. There were intercommunicating telephones; safe deposit vaults for valuables; a refrigerator for flowers; a gymnasium and shower bath; and a mirror room for the last-minute inspection of costumes.

It was an amazing theatre. It required 60 stagehands, whose salaries alone could float a war loan. Literally, it had two of everything, and was twice as big.

At the end of the first act, with the entire cast standing on stage—among them Lillian Roth, Mitchell and Durant, the Slate Brothers and Beryl Wallace—Mr. Carroll, clad in his faded working smock, was hailed from the orchestra pit to the stage by Will Mahoney and William Demarest. The producer, smiling his response to an ovation, offered his thanks to George Keister, the architect, and particularly to Joseph J. Babolnay, the interior designer. He expressed his thanks to his good friend and financial backer, William Edrington, who was sitting in the special guest box, and the wish that other similar attempts to inaugurate the popular-priced theatre would follow, both in New York and on the road.

A little over six months later, he was to make another speech. This time he sadly announced the loss of his "impossible dream." All of Broadway was shocked to hear that because of economic conditions, he was forced to give up his theatre.

What had seemed to Carroll a popular price, $3 (he'd been used to $10, $50, even $100 a seat), was far from popular with Depression-time theatregoers. The less expensive seats—50¢ and $1—filled the balcony, but there were big cavities downstairs in the higher-priced sections. Business was miserable.

For the most part, a nation worried about its meat and potatoes had to content itself with the free entertainment it got from the radio at home. It listened to the crooning of a collegian named Rudy Vallée, to a couple of small-time vaudevillians who started as Sam and Henry but now had leaped to fame and fortune as Amos 'n' Andy, and to the singing of Kate Smith, Morton Downey, and Bing Crosby, who were becoming household headliners via the air waves.

When people did go to the theatre, they went to the movies, where, tired of the dreary search for jobs, they could forget their troubles in the enjoyment of a motion picture and stage show for a small price of admission.

So, less than a year after the dedication ceremony, the Earl Carroll Realty Company was sued for $366,632.90 by the Seven Fifty-Five Corporation, owners of the property on which the theatre stood.

The sum asked for represented the amount allegedly unpaid by the realty corporation on the cost of erecting and equipping the theatre. The complaint set forth that on June 14, 1930, the plaintiff leased property to the Earl Carroll Realty Corporation, which agreed to build a theatre not later than September 1, 1931, and to pay the entire costs of building and equipping it.

The theatre was built, but the entire costs were not paid, and according to mechanics' liens, conditional bills of sale, and chattel mortages the amount unpaid was the sum mentioned above. In addition, the same plaintiff obtained a judgment for $64,952.20 for three months in back rent plus taxes and interest.

Carroll closed his show, and on the day he left he sadly commented that he was forced to relinquish possession of the theatre bearing his name because "the box office business is inadequate to meet the demands of those who are unalterably disposed to secure the theatre for their own gain."

When Earl Carroll lost his theatre at Seventh Avenue and 50th Street, Flo Ziegfeld took it over and had a wonderful time. With hammer and chisel he delightedly hacked off Carroll's name and rechristened the house the French Casino.

Ziegfeld's jealousy of Carroll's success was an active and silly hatred. In the lush theatre of the twenties there was room for both.

Actually, Ziegfeld's attitude was a tribute to Carroll's showmanship. Although Carroll's taste for comedy was occasionally in the gutter, nobody could touch him for pageantry. His *Vanities* was every bit as lavish as the *Follies*, and, what annoyed Ziegfeld even more, Carroll often did have prettier girls. Carroll ran to sex and youth, Ziegfeld to stateliness and beef.

The big illuminated billboards all over town—*"Earl Carroll Foremost Judge of American Beauty"*—had always been a source of irritation to Ziggy. They gnawed at his vitals. It was he, Ziegfeld, who "Glorified the American Girl," and here was this upstart claiming everything—and to plug Carroll, not a show.

So when Carroll moved out of his theatre, the "Rajah of Broadway" moved in with a revival of *Show Boat.* But even Captain Andy had trouble picking up customers, and the "Blossom Queen" soon ran out of steam.

Following several unsuccessful attempts to keep the theatre viable by renting it to other producers, it became a dud and was soon torn down. The theatre that was to be forever Earl Carroll's monument is today a Whelan Drug Store.

MARCH 16, 1932, WAS BLACK FRIDAY for Earl Carroll. A news story from Fort Worth, Texas, reported that William R. Edrington had filed a petition of *bankruptcy*, listing liabilities of $822,840.42 and assets of $312,489.76.

The paper noted that for more than 12 years Edrington, Texas oilman, had been Carroll's backer in the producer's ventures, including the operation of the new Earl Carroll Theatre at Seventh Avenue and 50th Street. The bulk of the liabilities were for notes he had endorsed for the Earl Carroll Realty Corporation.

How much money Edrington put into Carroll's enterprises through the years only they knew, but it had to be several million dollars. In the 1920s, he was Broadway's biggest angel, but all of his dough had not been lost. A number of Carroll's shows made money.

Edrington took an awful beating on the new theatre on Seventh Avenue, but it is doubtful that anyone could have made that showplace pay. It had to gross $65,000 a week to break even, and for a time that was the box office take.

As a matter of hard sense, it was an unnecessarily large investment. Each $500,000 put into a theatre adds $1,000 a week to its running expenses because of the excess insurance and the upkeep cost of the furnishings.

But Edrington, who had all the money in the world—at the time—didn't care. He loved to be a part of Carroll's pageantry and the wacky world of the theatre, though for the most part he stayed in the background.

An amusing story types him neatly. One night, shortly after the theatre opened, Carroll's new stage manager, Eddie Diamond, bumped into a silver-haired gentleman wandering aimlessly backstage.

"Are you looking for someone?" asked Eddie.

"No," said the man.

"Well, I'm sorry," said Eddie, "but you just can't walk around back here unless you have business. You'll have to leave the theatre."

"All right," said the old man, and he left.

The next day Carroll said to Eddie, "Did you toss an old guy out of here last night?"

"Yes," said Eddie. "He was wandering around to no purpose that I could see, and I told him to scram, in a nice way. Who was he?"

"Mr. Edrington," said Carroll. "He just owns the theatre." Carroll wasn't sore. He thought it was funny. So did Edrington.

He was a sweet old white-haired gentleman whom everybody adored, and he treated Carroll as a son.

Shortly thereafter, when Carroll received word that his dear old friend had died in Fort Worth at the age of 84, he couldn't have taken it harder if the "Colonel" had been a member of his own family. He had been not only a financial angel to Carroll; he had been a personal one as well. With great sorrow, Earl flew immediately to Fort Worth and assisted the family through the difficult time of their mutual grief.

Later in 1932, there was another news story that, although significant to Carroll, carried a far less emotional impact.

On July 22nd, Broadway was shocked to learn of the sudden, untimely death of the legendary Florenz Ziegfeld.

When asked for a comment, Earl Carroll said: "As everyone knows, Mr. Ziegfeld and I had many differences, but his contributions were many and the man and his work will be sorely missed in the theatre world."

The passing of The Great Glorifier seemed also to signal the end of the girlie revue era, which Carroll was regretfully to learn as he prepared his next show.

Tough as things looked and were, he couldn't sit by idly. Against the advice of everyone, including his brother Jim's warning—"You'll only get killed if you do a *Vanities* this year. Besides, you couldn't top what you've already done"—Carroll went ahead with plans to produce Earl Carroll's *Vanities of 1932.*

There was still some cash in the Carroll coffers—he had stopped playing the market and had so far avoided personal bankruptcy. And here was the chance to pin his knocker's ears back by putting over a hit under the most adverse conditions.

This one was going to be a *big one*—an *International* revue. He would bring artists not only from England but from all over the world to participate in this extravaganza. Why not? Foreign importations had been very popular on Broadway. "Look at *Charlot's Revue* with Beatrice Lillie and Gertrude Lawrence. That was a tremendous success."

So, in true Carroll style, he flamboyantly announced he was sailing on the *Ile de France* for a quick tour of European theatrical centers to obtain continental stars for his next production. He stated he would visit London, Paris, and Berlin and would be gone about four weeks.

He sailed amid a confusion of excited farewells, and an orchestra, which arrived late at the pier, attempted to run through its entire repertoire.

As Carroll did not have sufficient room in his cabin to welcome all his guests, numbering well over 100, the line placed the main salon at his disposal. The only disturbing note was when Carroll stood up on a chair to say goodbye to his friends. A process server, who had been mingling with the group, paused momentarily in front of him to slap a folded summons gently on his chest. The summons, Carroll lightly told the crowd, was just another irritant regarding the theatre he had recently lost.

Some further confusion was occasioned at sailing time when a troop of beautiful showgirls all kissed Mr. Carroll goodbye, a proceeding that resulted in a five-minute delay of the sailing of the liner.

Other passengers on board were Miss Sonja Henie, Norwegian figure-skating champion, with her parents, Mr. and Mrs. William Henie; playwright Moss Hart; and much to the ecstatic delight of Earl Carroll, Peggy Hopkins Joyce was also present. She was sailing to Europe this time to marry her fifth husband, Anthony Easton, an English engineer.

She told reporters at the dock: "Yes, I'm getting married again, and I hope this is the one. I hate notoriety. I am always heartbroken to see a marriage end. There is no pleasure for me in seeing a wonderful institution like marriage destroyed. All I want is to marry and have babies. At heart I'm a simple woman." As she said this, she was adjusting the 20-carat diamond and emerald bracelets that mounted up her arm, which she laconically referred to as "my service stripes."

In less than a month, Carroll returned on the S.S. *Champlain* of the French Line, escorting 35 European artists for his new revue. The ship was greeted by a large crowd waving flags and cheering, and by a broadcasting outfit sending musical numbers and recorded greetings across the river as the *Champlain* came up to West 15th Street. Heading the artists was Will Fyffe, a celebrated Scottish comedian who had given three command performances before the King and Queen of England. Carroll had prearranged for a band of pipers to strut up and down the pier-head playing Scottish tunes in a greeting to him.

After the ship docked, the group was accompanied to the theatre by the American contingency, headed by the hottest young comedian on Broadway at the moment, Milton Berle. Everyone left the pier in taxicabs covered in bunting and painted signs.

But the opening of Earl Carroll's "International Revue" was a disaster. The critics murdered the show. The reviews were brutal. Poor Uncle Milty took most of the brunt of their wrath.

Time magazine said:

> Mr. Carroll's shows have long held the record for borderline humor. In comedian Milton Berle is to be found the acme of hysterical vulgarity. While one part of the audience blushes and the other part guffaws, Comedian Berle proceeds to imitate a person of uncertain gender, quip about the showgirl's fundaments, shout depraved announcements into a loudspeaker. He seems to get a great deal of fun out of it.

"I'll never forget the morning I read that. I was really bugged," Milton Berle told me. "But it's funny, Ken, you know you can go out and kill the audience—then you read a newspaper and they'll say he shouldn't have worn the brown shoes. I guess they weren't ready for that stuff in those days—camping and dancing and clowning around.

"I had a scene in that show. The funniest scene I ever did on a stage. Believe me, they screamed opening night. I played a fag-like and I went to the doctor lisping, 'You've got to nip me in the bud.' You know the idea, with setting the guy in one chair and the disease goes into the other with the stammering. It was a burlesque on Conrad Veidt's picture, *The Cabinet of Dr. Caligari.* We called it "The Cabinet of Dr. X." Well, I played the queer in it. You know the scene, and I have it if you want it.

"But the guy was right about the girl angle. I used to do a lot of jokes about the girls, looking at their beautiful big bosoms, and I'd say, 'Honey, you'll never drown!' 'I can't wait until she hiccoughs!' 'Hitler should have them for tonsils!'—standard jokes at that time."

"But I suppose the legitmate critics who reviewed shows were not used to that nightclub style. They wanted more of the Clifton Webb, Libby Holman, Fred Allen—you know, like sophistication, *The Little Show.* They thought I was brash and flippant, aggressive and energetic—a wise guy.

"I'll never forget the opening night of *Vanities of 1932.* There were so many foul-ups, I was on 11 extra times. They'd say, 'Milton, run out here and stall.' Well, I had to run out and ad lib my own act, yours, Bob Hope's, anybody's jokes I could think of. I'd hit the back of the drop in pantomime and say 'Are you ready?' and the audience screamed. The next day, one of the critics—Percy Hammond or Kelsey Allen or somebody—came out and said the title of the show should be *'Berle's Earl Carroll Vanities.'* "

"But there was one thing that happened that opening night. I'll never forget it as long as I live. The 1932 *Vanities* had an international cast—there was Will Fyffe from Scotland, the Harry Lauder of his day, a French comedian named André Randall, and another guy from Paris called André Renaud, who played two pianos at the same time. Imagine what he could have done with *four* hands! Helen Broderick, Robert Cummings, Patsy Kelly, Harriet Hoctor, and I were the Americans, and the guy who represented England was an alleged comedian called Max Wall. He was an obnoxious bastard—we never got along.

"We had only one scene where we worked together. It was a takeoff on *Mourning Becomes Electra,* called 'Mourning Becomes Impossible,' and was supposedly based on the death of a big movie star like Rudy Valentino. People were waiting in line, and selling flags and everything, and making a picnic out of it. Took place in front of Campbell's Funeral Parlor. And Max Wall was selling flags and I waiting in line. At the end of the scene there was a fight—a pantomime fight—oh, hubba hubba—and as the lights went out, somebody gave me a terrific punch in the nose. I knew it was broken. When the lights went up, I'm full of blood and I got a handkerchief, but I didn't know who hit me. I finally found out, and it was who I thought it was—this cockney creep, Max Wall. Now I cut this out of my book, Ken *(Milton Berle, An Autobiography)*—I had it in, but it's out, so this is fresh for you. I was 23 and kind of rugged and didn't give a shit, and thank God, it was my old nose—you know what I mean. So I grabbed him and nearly killed him.

"When Mr. Carroll heard about it, he was terribly upset and rushed backstage. He abhorred unprofessionalism, and immediately threw the sonofabitch out of the show and sent him back to England.

"The first time I met Earl Carroll, I didn't like him. He was chilly and he was cold. But when I got to work with him, learned more about him I realized he was all business and was strictly thinking of what was to come theatrically.

"I think Carroll has taken a lot of bum raps. I've heard him dismissed as a guy who sold gals and giggles, tits and titters, cunts and comedy, but he was more than that—much more. Some people even intimated that because his handshake was like shaking hands with a flounder—a wet fish—it made him a homo. I never knew whether he was AC or DC—and I don't give a damn—but his coolness, his suavity, his mannerisms, his sophistication were unusual in show business. Earl Carroll was a gentleman.

"I had a lot of respect for him. I worked for him. I learned a lot from him. I thought he was a great showman. He was a perfectionist, very disciplined—a fine producer. He never let down his standards on his shows so long as there was one more performance to go.

"Earl Carroll was what we'd call, today, 'cool.' He very seldom lost his temper. If you argued about something, he would simply say, 'Now, look, we're going to do it my way.' And what I liked was, when you asked him a question, if he disagreed he would at least give you a reason for his answer.

"I'll never forget the first day of rehearsal. He made an announcement. He said, 'Ladies and gentlemen, in this opening scene, you understand you'll all be wearing evening dress; the ladies in formals and the gentlemen in white tie and tails.' And I said, 'Can I speak to you after the rehearsal, Mr. Carroll?' He said, 'Sure, Mr. Berle.' —You remember, Ken, everything was always 'Mr.' Carroll, 'Mr.' Berle, 'Mr.' Murray. I said, Mr. C., I've got to have a meeting. I don't work in tails.' He said, 'Why?' I said, 'Well, I work with my hat turned up a la Ted Healy. I work flippant, in street clothes.' He said, 'Yes, you do, Mr. Berle. But you do that in 60¢-vaudeville theatres. Here we're getting $6.60 a ticket. Let me tell you something, Mr. Berle. I don't think,' he said, 'funny clothes make a man funny.' I said, 'Yeah, but all my moves—where I open my coat and close it—' and he said, 'Well, you won't do that. In this show, the funny word is on the page, and if it's not on the page, it's not on the stage.' I don't know whether Carroll originated that or not, but it was the first time I ever heard it.

"Incidentally, in that show was Earl Carroll's very sweet girl friend whom I adored, Beryl Wallace. Nice girl—one of the greatest kicks of all time.

"You know, she came from a large Jewish family in Brooklyn, quite poor, and she helped to support them all her life. She was what we call in our faith a real 'hamisher' girl. She was gorgeous, and she was nice, and you know, Ken, she didn't remind you of a typical showgirl at all.

"She was terribly in love with Earl Carroll. I never bought the theory that she stood for Carroll's escapades just because it was good to get in with him, and to stay there and make money, not for herself but to take care of her whole family. She was not a conniving girl. She didn't have a motive.

"She had a lot of rich guys after her—and prominent ones. Rudy Vallée, Conrad Nagel the movie star, and listen to this, Ken. You know who was crazy about her and wanted to marry her during his bachelor days?—General Douglas MacArthur.

"But Beryl Wallace was always devoted and faithful to Earl Carroll. She was crazy about him all her life and I can understand why. He had a great way with women. When he picked out a girl to be *his* girl, he concentrated only on her. When he talked to her, lit her cigarette, opened a door for her, there would be a feeling of intimacy. He had the knack of making a woman feel like a woman. That's why he had a great attraction for the opposite sex.

"Whenever you'd see him and Beryl together—at the Stork Club, El Morocco, or wherever—he treated her as though she was the only woman in the room and he never paid any attention to any other woman. If a girl passed by and tried to get his attention, he would just nod hello and go right back to Beryl.

"And I sincerely believe that Earl Carroll loved Beryl Wallace as much as he could love any one woman. He was very jealous and possessive and had no sense of humor as far as she was concerned.

"I remember one time at rehearsal, she was standing talking to him. I walked over and put my arm around her and said, 'Gee, I just thought of something funny. If you and I got married, do you realize what your name would be?—Beryl Berle.' It wasn't even a lip curler. The daggers in his eyes scared the hell out of me.

"But I felt awfully sorry for Earl Carroll the way things turned out in that year of 1932. He was pounded at from all sides. Like the day Winchell printed an alleged conversation in his column.

> GEORGE S. KAUFMAN: What do you think of Earl
> Carroll's *Vanities?*
> GROUCHO MARX: I'd rather not say. I saw it at
> a disadvantage: the curtain was up.

"Carroll really took that hard, and the following night, at the Central Park Casino, he spotted Winchell sitting at a nearby table with a bunch of guests, among them Mayor Jimmy Walker.

"Carroll walked over, looked Winchell right in the eye, and said, 'We've been taking it from you for a long time. I wonder if you've got the guts to take it now.'

" 'Go ahead,' Winchell replied. 'It's okay with me.'

" 'I want you to know that you are not fit to associate with decent people,' Carroll said. 'You don't belong!' He turned and left.

"Winchell just sat there. The entire party was stunned. Later, Walter, who was never known to make a retraction, did confide privately to friends, 'Carroll was certainly entitled to his scolding of me. I've treated him pretty mean for many years.'

"It wasn't that bad a show, but between the critics and the Depression, business was miserable.

"Carroll tried everything to shake some life into that *Vanities*—even reached back to that old bromide of putting salacious pictures of his girls in the lobby, hoping to get the show raided. All he got out of it was a ride in a police paddy wagon with 10 of the girls. The grand jury failed to indict and the whole thing was ignored by the press. Times were changing, Ken. The public wan't going for those cheap gimmicks anymore.

"We ran only a few weeks [87 performances] and then the creditors swarmed down like a herd of locusts. Oh, it was awful. They grabbed the scenery, the costumes, the props, all the music. Carroll had to let them take over the show so he wouldn't go into bankruptcy. He finally persuaded them to keep it open by making an offer to personally work for *nothing*, pointing out that it might be sufficiently profitable to pay their claims. But I always felt the real reason he did it was so that a lot of actors and girls wouldn't be thrown out of work.

"To me, Earl Carroll was a helluva guy—I miss him."

BEFORE THE FULL EFFECT OF THE DEPRESSION was felt across the nation, most Americans knew poverty only by reputation. But, by 1933, a large part of the richest nation on earth learned what it meant to be poor; for 40,000,000 people, poverty became a way of life. But Boomtime or Depression, Earl Carroll decided "the show must go on."

Convinced that the big lavish Hollywood musicals were killing spectacles behind the footlights, he made up his mind to try an experiment—a show called *Murder at the Vanities*, a whodunit with music.

As he told the *Times* reporter: "Presentations on the screen have dwarfed the efforts on the stage and make its spectacles look like tabloid representations. People, after seeing a film in which hundreds of beautiful girls dance on vast sets that we can't duplicate on the stage, will not be impressed by spectacle on a smaller scale behind the footlights." The producer pointed out that although the elaborate scenes in many musical films were illogical and obviously impossible of achievement in a theatre where they were supposed to take place, the public did not seem to mind as long as they were *entertained*.

So the innovative Mr. Carroll decided to try something different; something that had never been attempted before. It was to be a mystery drama using as a background the girlie elements of a musical.

Only enthusiasm, born of sheer love, got *Murder at the Vanities* into production. With the Carroll piggy bank getting low, his persuasive powers still held him in good stead, and incredibly, he was able to get most of what the production needed on credit. But without opulent scenery and elevator pits and all the gewgaws of flamboyant showmanship, he still prepared the show with precise care.

Opening, as usual, in true Carroll style, there was a number cozily occupied by stately young women in yellow dresses whispering confidentially, "We're getting away with 'moider.' "

Then into the plot: Backstage during a performance of the eleventh edition of the *Vanities*, two murders have been committed and a third has been attempted. A beautiful show girl is found lifeless up in the theatre wings, and other crimes are linked up with the original slaying. Whereupon James Rennie, the star, with his commanding voice and insouciant manner, appeared as Inspector Ellory of the homicide squad. He proposed to solve the murder sometime between the finale of the Saturday matinee and the finale of that evening's performance. He succeeded at 11:30. The villain was none of those whom the audience suspected.

The solving of the crimes in view of the audience furnished the drama of the combination, which was interrupted at intervals with a rehearsal of the *Vanities*. There were repeated references to Mr. Carroll in person. (He made his first and only appearance on the stage as an actor in this show.) While Mr. Rennie was catching the culprit, with his right hand holding a cigarette and his left in a pocket of his jacket, thumb protruding, Carroll had abundant time to wander backstage at a *Vanities* production, and concluded the first act by rehearsing chorus girls in action with a maypole of neon light tubes. Then with the assistance of a revolving stage, he made a grand tour of backstage, including the quick-change room of the chorus.

In the second act, there was a typical Earl Carroll fan number with four rows of blonde chorus girls tossing uneasily to languorous rhythms on a strange edifice in the center of the stage. Involved in all this was a horror monster, Bela Lugosi, who was followed by a strange green light as he played the part of a man reasonably embittered because, as a child, someone had dipped him in acid. It was a peculiar exhibit as Lugosi, bathed in the green light, chased the scantily clad, haughty Carroll chorines off their turntables and into the audience.

It was like the current movies—illogical—but it was *entertaining*, and the opening-night crowd at the New Amsterdam Theatre loved the show and applauded long after the final curtain. I know—I was there—and I've always felt Carroll never received the proper recognition he deserved for this noble experiment.

But the professional fault-finders still had to get their licks in. With no excessive nudity or obscenity to jump on—there was *not one dirty line* in the show and the girls were provocatively but tastefully attired—they had to confine their mildly snide comments to:

"The combination of musical and mystery yields a desultory evening. . . ."

"What he has done this season is to combine a mediocre musical show with a mediocre crime play. . . ."

"Without unlimited resources in silks and bangles, Mr. Carroll is the wizard bereft of his magic. . . ."

Not completely—Earl Carroll's *Murder at the Vanities* was a *hit* and the customers came in goodly number. The theatre was crowded at every performance and it looked like his long shot had come in.

With the inauguration of Roosevelt, a wave of optimism began to spread. F.D.R. was leading the nation in singing "Happy Days Are Here Again" and the public started spending a little of the money it had been cautiously hanging on to. It looked as though Carroll was on his way to the top again. Suddenly, the ladder collapsed. President Roosevelt closed the banks. The line-up at the box office for tickets ended abruptly.

Murder at the Vanities was a hit at the wrong time. The Great Depression was spreading its mantle of gloom and Broadway was already well wrapped in it. The Depression finished the job that talking pictures had begun.

But ironically, these same talkies were to take Carroll out of the nose dive, at the same time enabling him to realize one of his old ambitions.

Just before the show was to close, he received an offer from Hollywood to make *Murder at the Vanities* into a big movie musical.

"It all began in New York in the midst of February slush, in 1934. Earl Carroll had sold screen rights to Paramount for *Murder at the*

Vanities and was trekking to Hollywood, by way of a special railroad car, with Beryl Wallace and 10 of his most beautiful showgirls. The girls were all to appear in the movie with Carl Brisson (that wonderful Danish star, father of Fred Brisson), Victor McLaglen, Jack Oakie, Kitty Carlisle, Gertrude Michael, Gail Patrick (she later produced Perry Mason TV), and cute Toby Wing. Carroll was to be consultant on the picture."

The man talking is Teet Carle, veteran studio publicist for more than four decades—Paramount, MGM, Warner Brothers. He was with Earl Carroll when the producer made his very first invasion of Hollywood.

"You know, Ken," he continued, "during my many years in motion picture studio publicity, I have met several celebrities who would have been premiere exploiters had they not chosen to be even bigger successes in other fields. David O. Selznick was a prime example, C. B. DeMille another, and so was Earl Carroll."

Teet said that what made that four months with Carroll unforgettable was a refreshing *twist* he gave to an old Hollywood story—the heartbroken girl who chose to try suicide when stardom (even extradom) refused to smile her way. She was from Sisterville, West Virginia, and her name was Julia Graham.

But here, let Teet, himself, tell you the story:

"Well, Ken, I knew the first time I met Carroll he was a publicist's dream. I had been assigned by the studio to publicize the picture *Murder at the Vanities*, and I was in Manhattan to see the Broadway musical.

"At our first meeting in his penthouse quarters at the Essex House, the New York boys told Carroll they needed a springboard for his departure at 9:00 A.M. the next morning. Carroll suggested they take over the coffee counter at Grand Central Station for a press breakfast. Naturally, the photogs lined up the 11 girls on one long counter and shot their little hearts out.

"I shall never forget that trip all across the country with the Carroll entourage. Carroll led the way, ideas bouncing off his mind like champagne bubbles. Every day we wired a story from one girl (each in turn) to a bright new newspaper columnist named Ed Sullivan, and I got an inside look at how Carroll handled his cuties. Every night before bedtime he would gather all the girls around him in a circle, like Campfire girls, and would give them pep talks and lectures on 'Go on, be a Hollywood playgirl and see what "Daddy" Carroll does to both your eyes.' He had them behave exactly as well-trained soldiers, and heaven knows they'd had enough 'Squads Right!' to know how.

"I think he tried to pass off a father image to the other girls when Beryl was around. She was his girl friend. She was a wonderful person. She really was. Everybody loved her. Fine performer, too.

"One night on the train we were sitting alone in the club car and I remember asking Carroll a very personal question. 'When are you and Beryl going to get married?'

"He said, 'Mr. Carle, I will never get married.'

"And I said, 'Oh?'

"And he said, 'No, I already have a wife.'

"I said, 'You do?'

"And he said, 'Yes, she's a French girl, but I haven't seen her in years and I wouldn't touch her with a 20-foot pole. But she has been very important in my life because there was never any chance of the girls hooking me. They all knew I was married and there was no chance. She is my protection.'

"When we got to Pittsburgh, we threw a big party for the press. Someone suggested that a certain beauty give the boys a toast. Nervous, but still game and not quite sure what it was all about, the girl raised her glass (only wine, mind you) and with a sweet smile said:

Roses are read, violets are blue,
Never drink your own bath water.

"All of which threw the reporters into a state of something not even normal, and resulted in all of them having to be led from the train.

"When we got out west, as we were going through the wastelands from Omaha to Salt Lake, Earl Carroll, always thinking, came to me with the wildest idea.

"He said, *'Let's get this whole private car lost out here in the desert!'*

" 'How can we do that?' I asked incredulously.

"He said, 'Well, look, here's the idea. We'll get the cooperation of the Santa Fe and have them sidetrack our private car in the desert someplace.'

"Carroll was really charged up. 'Man, can you imagine the head-lines of a complete private car getting lost?'

"And you know, Ken, he actually might have pulled it off if he'd come up with the idea earlier, but there wasn't enough time; we were just rolling into Salt Lake City.

"Once in Hollywood, Carroll scurried over to the production boys at the studio. But they were in need of no advice, even on a Carroll show. They didn't invite him in on anything. He thought he was going to be in on production and the whole works, but actually, they made him a figurehead just to do publicity.

"His contribution (read the contract) was serving as a symbol for the picture in merchandising the product through all those lovely media.

"But Carroll kept busy; he got into everything. I began to wonder whether there was anything he wouldn't do to garner publicity. Al-most every night I was with him for some appearance. It was the heyday of radio, and everywhere we went we had interviews. He was one of the fastest men on his feet that I ever knew—and always insisted upon ad-libbing.

"He would never talk to the interviewer before they went on the air. 'If I know what the question is, then I'm planning my reply. It won't be spontaneous and can't be as effective,' he said.

"He could answer anything that was thrown at him. I saw him stumped only once, and that was a horrible thing. It was a big net-work show and I think the news guy who was running it was a little pissed off because Carroll wouldn't talk over the show before air time. So I think he decided to get him.

"Just before the end of the show this silly bastard came out with *'Mr. Carroll, how did it feel to be a prisoner in a federal penitentiary?'*

"I never saw a man's face turn so white. He put his head down and tried to swallow. He couldn't say a word—he just froze. There was the longest stretch of dead air you ever heard.

"God, it was terrible. I never realized how really sensitive he was about that thing.

"His biggest Hollywood splash was in selecting 11 Hollywood all-American chorines to match his Broadway bevy in the movie. More than 800 females mobbed the forecourt of Grauman's Chinese Theatre, signed in, and walked in scanty peek-a-boo playsuits across a specially erected platform before the producer, who was attired for the occasion in his usual black tam and colorful smock."

"Is that where the suicide girl entered the story?" I inquired.

"Yes, it was the damnedest thing. It was a hot afternoon. These hundreds of girls were walking across the platform and Carroll was spotting them. We thought we'd pull a little gag on him so we asked one girl to walk across a second time.

"She thought it would be fun and readily agreed. After all, she was getting two chances to get picked. Nice kid—her name was Julia Graham—pretty and all that—like a girl you'd see on a farm.

"When she got up on the platform, the minute Carroll spotted her he said, 'Oh, you've been up here before.'

"Imagine, out of those hundreds of girls! He wasn't just going through the motions; he was really sizing them up. But he didn't take her—she was too tall to fit in with the other girls. He picked only seven.

"The next morning I was sitting in my office at Paramount and Carroll bounced in waving a newspaper.

" 'Isn't this one of the girls I saw yesterday?' He asked excitedly.

"He showed me a news photo of a young girl from West Virginia named Julia Graham who had taken a massive dose of barbiturates because she had found the gates of Hollywood locked against her. She couldn't bear to go back home defeated.

"The story said she was hovering near death.

" 'This kid needs help and I'd like to be the one to give it,' Carroll exclaimed.

"Though my stomach felt queasy—this was the oldest and sleaziest trick in show business, capitalizing on the misfortunes of the piti-ful—I got right on the phone. He said it couldn't wait.

"From a newspaper reporter we found exactly where Julia Graham was in County General Hospital. When we got there he said, 'Now, don't stop and ask questions.' There were lines on the floor and you had to follow the black line all the way up. He knew his way around anything—he never stopped. We walked right up and the first thing you know we were in a third-floor hospital room with the girl and an intern who explained that she would pull through but it would be many hours, possibly days, before she emerged from a coma.

"What a pitiful sight. An unconscious girl, hardly more than a kid, with her showgirl body connected to dozens of tubes and dan-gling bottles.

"Then another doctor came in and said, 'What's going on here?'

"Earl said, 'I'm Earl Carroll. I want to help this girl.'

"When it became obvious the great New York impresario was really going to follow through on this publicity gimmick, I wanted to puke!

"Carroll left the girl a note—a philosophical gem about no temporary failure possibly being worth the surrender of a life. If she really wanted to make it into the movies, she was to phone me, and I would tell Earl Carroll. He would lend that helping hand.

"I made a verbatim copy of the note and phoned Louella Parsons, at the *Examiner* who had helped us locate the girl, and gave her the story.

"Headlines! Letters from her frightened parents, a telegram from the mayor of Sisterville, West Virginia: 'Give the Graham girl a break. She's a good kid.' I remember every word today, a generation later.

"I was relieved when the girl didn't call. Carroll checked me daily. I started calling the doctor and he really got sore. He had been bawled out for allowing strangers into the intensive care ward. Our story had not made him happy.

"I knew she'd been dismissed, and I told him I needed her address.

"He said, 'I couldn't care less. Stay away from her—you and your God-damn publicity stunts. Why the hell don't you leave the poor girl alone.' And he banged down the phone.

"Then Miss Graham finally did call. She was living with relatives in a small apartment back of the Ambassador Hotel. Carroll and I went over to see her. She was in good shape.

"He said, 'I'm going to help you so that you can be an actress. I'm going to get you a job. We'll be back tomorrow and we will have some reporters with us.'

"He told her to act as though she had never seen us before. 'When we get here don't be bouncing around. Look like you're still sick,' he said. 'Have you got a bed jacket? Be sure you're lying on the couch when we come in.'

"It was like staging a show—the whole thing.

"So I called Parsons, Hedda Hopper, Jimmy Fidler, Jimmy Starr, Edwin Schallert, Erskine Johnson, Bill Kennedy, Harrison Carroll—all the press—everybody—and we all met at her place with photographers and we posed her for the pictures.

"The visit that followed was a dream event, sticky with sentiment. A road show version of *A Star Is Born*. The press must have had throat lumps when Carroll patted her arm and told her to come to see him at Paramount the moment she was well enough to be up and around. He would take her to the talent folks at the studio.

"The space that following morning on the Graham story was tremendous—and there were a lot of plugs for Carroll's *Murder at the Vanities.*

"Julia Graham showed up at my office the following afternoon. I alerted Carroll, who came in and smiled, took her arm, and said, 'Come, we will go to the talent department,' and led her away.

"So I sat alone and thought: now comes the time for the sun to sink slowly in the west. End of another publicity project. The big space had been garnered. The great showman soon would be off to Manhattan, and I would be left with Miss Graham. Maybe she wouldn't call for too many weeks before she gave up. She was alive and well and Sisterville was only a continent away.

"Picture of a young man breathing bitterness.

"Then, much to my delight, when they returned to my office, they were both beaming. 'Meet your new stock contract player,' the showman said. She was crying. Hell, I was choking up, too.

"Incredible? Sure! But Julia Graham *did* have a contract and Earl Carroll got it for her. And for six months she was kept busy playing small parts. Like the secretary who opens the door: 'There's a detective out here to see you, sir!'

"I used to see Julia Graham occasionally hurrying through the studio. We would wave.

"The press did interviews. The fan magazines revelled."

While he was waiting for the film to be completed, Earl, who had begun to be a California devotee, spent his weekends driving around Beverly Hills and other, nearby areas in a rented limousine complete with a chauffeur. The driver's name was Ronald Ramsey, and he and Earl struck up a kind of friendly relationship.

Driving around the Bel Air area, the chauffeur pointed out some of the beautiful homes of famous stars that dotted the rolling hills, As they passed one English Tudor mansion, Ramsey said, "There's William Powell's house."

Earl said smilingly to the chauffeur, "You know, Ron, he used to work for me. I gave him his first job on Broadway."

Earl's past and present merged together as his driver continued to spot palatial residences belonging to people who had passed through his life, those who had found his *Vanities* a stepping stone to fame and fortune—Jack Benny, Milton Berle, Shirley Booth, Busby Berkeley, Lillian Roth, and, of course, W. C. Fields.

"You know, Ron," Earl said one afternoon as they were driving home, "I'd like to come back to California to settle down. I like the pace, the relaxed, comfortable way of life. Do you happen to know of any place I could rent?"

Ronald paused a moment and then suddenly said, "Yeah, I know of a house. A mansion is a better word. It's one of those big jobs, not a cozy cottage. It belongs to a Mrs. Jessie Schuyler, and I worked for her at one time. She is a real great lady. She's got this estate, and as far as I know she isn't living in it. I never heard her say anything about renting it out. She's very rich, but you might look her up and see if she'd be willing. Right now she's living in an apartment at the Chateau Marmont." With an abrupt change in tone, Ronald added, "I feel very sorry for Mrs. Schuyler. Poor woman, she's had a rough time."

One might assume that a woman who was reputed to be one of the wealthiest women in the nation would have little knowledge of a rough time. Jessie Schuyler was something of a legend in Beverly Hills. She was born in Denver, the only child of a wealthy family. She graduated from Vassar and then came back to her home in Colorado to marry her childhood sweetheart, Walter Farnum Schuyler, who was a wealthy banker and realtor. They had a baby boy their first year of an idyllic marriage, but the child died at the age of one in a flu epidemic. The death was a crushing blow to both Jessie and Walter, so to try to help her forget it, and hoping that a change of scenery might help them both, her husband arranged to move to California, where he bought a good deal of property in an exclusive section of Beverly Hills. They built a large estate on the land, and so impressed were the citizens of Beverly Hills that they named the place Schuyler Road, which it has remained to this day.

The Schuylers were exceptionally devoted and lived very happily until Walter's sudden death in 1930 of a heart attack. Heartbroken, utterly despondent, Mrs. Schuyler buried him in a mausoleum in Forest Lawn, and a few months later brought the body of their baby boy to lie beside him.

Loneliness was a searing thing for her. The estate, the land, the luxury were all painful memories. She decided to leave her home and move to an apartment in the hope that she could escape from the pain she felt. However, she did keep the house staffed with housekeepers and gardeners so it would always be exactly as she remembered it when she lived there with Walter.

She then turned to travel in Europe—and she became a patron of art, music, literature. Her gifts to religious institutions and philanthropies were enormous. She was frequently honored by the Vatican and by foreign governments for her generous interest in various forms of war relief work. Even though she was active in various affairs, she remained still a person who lived within herself and her memories.

Carroll had tried on several occasions to contact her, but was unable to get past her secretary, Virginia Lear. Mrs. Schuyler was not aware of his calls until one day, by accident, she overheard her secretary in a conversation on the phone.

"No," Miss Lear was saying, "Mrs. Schuyler is not in the least interested in renting her estate." A pause. "Why? Well, she prefers to leave it as it is." Another pause. "No, it is really quite futile to pursue this coversation. I know how Mrs. Schuyler feels, I'm sorry, Mr. Carroll," she said as she hung up.

Mrs. Schuyler listened intently when she heard the name Carroll.

"Was that man named *Earl* Carroll you were talking to?" she asked when the coversation was over.

"Yes."

"Was that the same Mr. Carroll I read about who helped that poor girl who tried to commit suicide?"

"Yes, I believe so," Virginia replied.

After a pause, she said, "Do you have his number where I can call him back?"

"I think I have—somewhere. Oh yes, here it is. He says he wants to rent your estate. He is in the picture business, I think, or something like that."

"Well, call him," Mrs. Schuyler said, "and let him come by. I'd like to talk to him."

She had read in the papers of the help he had given Julia Graham. His compassion for this young chorus girl touched her deeply because it was close to her feelings for the underprivileged and unwanted.

When Earl Carroll arrived the next morning, she was pleasantly surprised to see this tall, slender, polite man, who in no way resembled a typical Broadway producer. He briefly told her that her former chauffeur, Mr. Ramsey, had driven him past her beautiful estate and he wondered whether she would ever consider leasing it.

"Well, Mr. Carroll, I had never thought of renting it to anyone. It's a very dear place to me."

Carroll quickly explained that it was not for the present—he had to return to New York—but perhaps sometime in the future.

"Well," Mrs. Schuyler said, "when you return, call me and I'll see how I feel then." With significant hesitancy, she added, "I'm sure you realize it's hard to open the doors to others to as many memories as that place has for me."

After he left, she walked thoughtfully out on the lanai of her penthouse overlooking Hollywood. It is strange how fate brings people together. Mrs. Schuyler was in almost all respects the opposite of Earl Carroll. She was a woman who avoided the spotlight, who lived a quiet life, who indulged in no ostentatious display. The loss of her husband and son drew her more deeply into herself, and only intensified her withdrawal from the glare of the world.

But this mild-mannered gentleman with the warm smile and soft voice—qualities that had always endeared her to her late husband—struck a responsive chord in this woman who basically needed someone to belong to—again—after so many years of loneliness.

Then it was May; the picture was finished and it was time for the last splurge of publicity for *Murder at the Vanities*. The idea was to preview the picture with Carroll in person in a number of cities across the country.

Teet Carle said it was the most exhausting experience he'd ever had. "Carroll dreamed up the idea to have 10 press previews in 10 different cities within 72 hours. We got Paul Mantz to pilot his Lockheed Vega cabin airplane with a big sign, reading *Murder at the Vanities*, painted all over the fuselage.

"Mantz was a little fellow—a very fine guy—one of the best pilots who ever lived. He and Earl became very good friends. Carroll was a nut about flying, as you know, and even before we made this trip. Paul would take him up and Carroll would fly the little plane over Beverly Hills, always making a tight circle over the Schuyler estate, pointing out to Mantz where he hoped to live someday.

"The studio had chartered Mantz's plane and we went up from here to San Francisco where we had the first preview, after midnight. The next morning, we flew to Salt Lake City, then to Denver that night. The following day, it was Kansas City at noon, St. Louis at dinner, and then another midnight showing in Chicago.

"The third whirlwind day found us in Detroit at breakfast time, and then a switch in plans—and an extra $75 for Mantz—took us to Cincinnati at lunchtime instead of Cleveland. Then we took off for Pittsburgh, and, would you believe it, got lost and started to follow the railroad. Finally, Mantz spotted a railroad station and began flying around in circles.

"I had no idea what was going on until Carroll quipped: 'The great Mantz doesn't know where the hell he is!'

"Mantz finally got a bead on directions to Pittsburgh, flying pretty low, only about 1,500 feet. I looked out the window and couldn't believe my eyes. There was the word *Sisterville*, painted on top of the railroad station. I exclaimed to Carroll, 'My God, there is Julia Graham's home town!' And the topper was, later Carroll got a big letter from the mayor of Sisterville, signed by every citizen in the town—1,542 people. Some of the folks had seen Earl Carroll's name painted on our plane and they all wanted to thank him for flying over and acknowledging Miss Graham's birthplace.

"We got into New York in time for a last midnight showing and bash, and then we went to Boston and back and that was the end of our tour.

"Carroll stayed in Boston and I flew back with Paul Mantz. That's the last time I ever saw Earl Carroll."

"What about Julia Graham?" I asked.

Teet's face sobered and he paused a long time before he answered.

"That was tragic. About a year after Paramount signed her, I was on vacation in Sequoia. One day I sat down beside a three-day old copy of the Los Angeles *Times*.

"In that paper, a two-column headline story wrote *finis* to a snatch of human drama. *Julia Graham had committed suicide.*

"But to his everlasting credit, Earl Carroll had certainly tried—he actually got her a movie contract—but he had only *lent* Julia Graham a life wish. The death wish returned.

"This time Julia Graham had made sure. She used a gun. . . .

"There's been much speculation as to what prompted Carroll to go to such great lengths to secure a job for Julia Graham. The obvious conclusion is he went into the whole thing with the thought of getting publicity for the picture, at the same time making a big man of himself, projecting a benevolent image, and actually never intended to do anything for the girl at all.

"There are those who suspect that as it built up he got more and more publicity, Carroll felt that he was compelled to make some sort of gallant gesture, and to his surprise and relief, it paid off.

Teet Carle said he disagreed, "Though my first impression of Earl Carroll was that he would do anything on God's green earth to get a publicity break and get his name in the paper, during the five months we spent together I witnessed many acts of unpublicized generosity.

"No, Ken, I don't buy that stuff that he was cold, calculating, and had no heart. I liked Earl Carroll," Teet Carle said. "I think behind it all he was a very compassionate man."

I had to agree with him. I was to see an indication of that when I worked with him the next year in Earl Carroll's *Sketch Book*.

One of the girls in the show—Eileen Wenzel—had been injured and badly scarred in an automobile accident. Carroll went down to court (voluntarily) and made an impassioned plea to Justice Ferdinand Pecora to help her win the case against the other driver.

"Before the crash," Carroll said, leaning forward in the witness stand, "Miss Wenzel had all the attributes of physcial perfection." And before the court could stop him, he proceeded to give a clinical analysis on the one subject on which he was an expert.

"She was the ideal showgirl—5 feet, 5 inches tall, weight 118 pounds, with a 12-inch neck, 36-inch bust, a waist of 24½ inches, hips 35 inches, thighs 21, ankle 8½, and wrist 6 inches. She had lustrous hair of fine texture, a forehead like a snow peak, a lovely throat, her lips were inviting and she had eyes that made men swoon—"

"Strike that out!" Justice Pecora ordered, and Carroll stopped gesturing. He was told to be more specific in his description.

However, it was a sincere effort and Carroll was visibly moved when Miss Wenzel won the case.

It also must have been a novel experience for the producer—the *only* time he ever appeared in a courtroom *not* as the defendant.

AFTER SIX MONTHS IN THE VIGOROUS freshness and colorful charm of Talkie Town, to Earl Carroll Broadway must have looked like a tawdry, decadent strumpet in the rags of her outmoded finery. Dignified old theatres were plastered with glaring billboards of movie grinds, and at night the sidewalks were jammed not with smartly dressed theatre-goers but with a shuffling throng not unlike the crowd at Coney Island.

The New Deal's public spending had not yet reached its full momentum and there was as yet no war boom to fill the pockets of small tradesmen and workingmen with enough money to pay $7.50 for a ticket at a legit box office. There was, as there always will be, a segment of the public that would accept no substitute for the living stage, but it was made up of intellectuals and sophisticates who wanted Shakespeare and Shaw and musicals with ballets and other "arty" trimmings. But, there was not one fast-moving, girlie-and-laugh-filled musical on Broadway for the cloak-and-suit buyer and the big butter-and-egg man. Evidently Earl Carroll thought the time was ripe for one.

But it has always been a source of wonder to me *why*, after the success of his book musical, *Murder at the Vanities*, he decided to put on a *straight* revue, the *Earl Carroll Sketch Book of 1935*, a long, elaborate, and surprisingly old-fashioned extravaganza.

It was a mistake, as one reviewer said the next day:

Once, in the young days of Broadway's sex life, the invariable pattern from which Mr. Carroll cuts his entertainments could horrify and charm. Now it is as out of date as a 1910 Easter bonnet. When it comes to presenting young ladies in beads, feathers, or G-strings, as the occasion requires, Mr. Carroll is the Rip Van Winkle of Times Square.

Another critic complained:

As he approaches maturity, Earl Carroll, who certainly knows a shapely calf when he sees one, seems to grow more and more doubtful of the appeal of the unclothed human (feminine) torso, which has been his forte in previous theatrical endeavors.

And the critic was right. For some reason, for the first and *only* time in his life, he almost seemed to have lost his touch in displaying feminine pulchritude. He didn't have the enthusiasm—that sexy touch—that zing.

As I watched the first rehearsal with Carroll, what surprised me were the different types, sizes, and measurements of the girls under the banner of Carroll Beauties. By necessity, of course, chorus girls are always a blend of all classes of American society, partly blue-blood and partly wrong-side-of-the-tracks; you'll always find waitresses, art models, secretaries, runaways from convents and finishing schools. But in our show, in addition to stray debutantes, there was a sprinkling of overblown beauties, always picked up at the stage door by big black armored limousines, who were the properties of some of the biggest underworld figures of the day. Backstage at the *Sketch Book* figured to be a feast for bachelors, but you had to be careful because an awful lot of the stagedoor Johns packed rods.

Looking over this sea of misfits that day, I was surprised to hear Carroll sardonically observe: "You know, Ken—beauties run in schools, like *fish*. At times, the fishing is fine and a lot of beauties are caught. And at other times, the only thing a man can do is get a couple of finnan-haddies and hope for the best."

From that moment on, backstage seemed more like a health club as Carroll, with the enthusiasm of the "Galloping Gourmet" fileting a flounder, proceeded to turn the raw material into the finished product. Those who were underweight had to be brought up to normal, and the fatties had to be brought down. And all this, mind you, done under the guidance of a physician. (What a life some doctors lead!)

Carroll always had a motto painted over their dressing room door—**"I would rather you were less talented than less loyal."**

This time he got his wish. This group was completely unfettered by the slavery of talent, as John Anderson reported in the New York *Evening Journal:*

> The girls stand behind curtains and then come out in front of them; or vice versa. They wear feathers and they don't wear feathers; they put on costumes and take them off, sit on the edge of the stage and throw their garters at the audience. The girls can sit, stand, dance, lie down, and move their arms and legs. And they can do it all with or without mirrors. They probably can say "Mama" and "Papa" but Mr. Carroll didn't demonstrate that. Mr. Carroll possibly is not interested in such intellectual efforts at the moment.
>
> In one of the numbers, a chorus girl fainted and another fell over her, though neither, I was told on inquiry, was seriously injured. But the audience laughed, which just goes to prove that people ought to put things into revues that the audience *can* laugh at.

For a comedian, a big girlie show is no way to make his debut on Broadway, especially if the producer has no sense of humor. I learned very quickly, during rehearsal, that Carroll regarded his comedians as time-killers before Les Girls came on, and the opinions of the critics confirmed my apprehension.

Robert Garland of the New York *World Telegram* said:

> Mr. Carroll's latest skin tournament and peek-a-boo contest opened at the Winter Garden last night when the *Sketch Book* came to town. It is large, opulent, glittering, and as amusing as it is naked. Which is to say, *not quite.* A cockeyed chronicle of the making of America, a hashed-up history of these United States as it might be told by a dulcy of a chorus girl.
>
> This notion leads Mr. Carroll into such intricate and embarrassing numbers as the one in which an actor made up to libel Abraham Lincoln (with an Irish brogue) paces the Potomac followed by 56 young ladies in cellophane hoopskirts, or another in which the father of our

country with his wife, Martha, who sounded like Eleanor, takes part in a radio program broadcasting dirty jokes. There is a great deal of this sort of thing and it seems uniformly painful.

Ken Murray carried most of the comedy—no light burden, God knows. He works like a Trojan from overture to exit music. His assignments last night included everything from Noah Webster to Buffalo Bill to P. T. Barnum interviewing Papa Dionne, father of the quintuplets.

BARNUM: Tell me, Mr. Dionne, how did you
happen to be the father of five
children?

PAPA DIONNE: I guess I just fell asleep
and left my motor running.

I don't know what the hell this had to do with American history. Mr. Dionne was a *Canadian.*

In another scene, I played Justice Oliver Wendell Homes. As the curtains opened we saw the judge sitting on the bench. A burly policeman escorted three gaudily dressed, unmistakable prostitutes before the bar.

The judge asked the first one, "What is your business?"

The first girl said, "I'm a dressmaker."

The judge, scowling at the attendant policeman, snapped, "Take this girl away. Case dismissed!"

As the second girl stepped up to the bar, the judge again inquired, "What is you business?"

The second girl replied even more demurely, "Your honor, I'm a dressmaker."

The judge, getting more irritated by the moment, then shouted at the policeman, "Why do you waste my time? Case dismissed!"

He turned to the third girl, played by platinum-haired, shapely Marlyn Stuart, and again inquired very sternly, "Young lady, what is your business?"

Without a moment's hesitation she snapped back, "I'm a *whore!*"

The judge looked down and quickly said, "Well, how's business?"

The girl retorted, "It would be all right if it wasn't for *those God-damned dressmakers!*"   (BLACKOUT)

But it was the distinguished Brooks Atkinson who really got the work done when he wrote in the New York *Times* the next morning, June 5, 1935:

Although Mr. Carroll is inventive on the surface, he lacks originality. He cannot let go of a show formula that has gone stale. What he lacks most, however, is a sense of humor. Being humorless, he likes to put commonplace turns into a historical setting and sees nothing incongruous in staging a dance routine against the Louisiana Purchase or letting the careworn figure of Lincoln serve as a song cue.

Being humorless, Mr. Carroll traffics in filthy jesting. The bodily processes seem funny to him. Occasionally, Murray introduces humor into the *Sketch Book* by a trick of timing or by personal exuberance. But the joke book Mr. Carroll fingers is for circulation undercover among the court jesters of the backroom of the grocery store where the sniggering cannot be heard. They like 'em fairly slimy. Probably that is the element that throws the whole *Sketch Book* into disrepute. Even the most beautiful girls in the world begin to look a little slatternly when they are spattered by muck in the comedy numbers.

But wait a minute, Mr. Atkinson—I'm not going to take the rap for that one! Put the blame where it belongs—on the *cow* that Mr. Carroll hired for the traveling salesman scene.

When a sketch in an Earl Carroll show called for a cow, you got a real *live* one—not two men inside a reasonable facsimile. And this was the biggest damn bovine I ever saw.

In the scene, I play a traveling salesman and Beryl Wallace portrays the farmer's pretty daughter. I'm discovered walking along an old dirt road in front of a farmhouse. Behind the white picket fence, Beryl, dressed in a gingham pinafore, is standing holding this big brown Jersey cow by the halter.

I approached her, tipped my hat, and said: "How do you do? I'm a traveling salesman."

Beryl, very demurely, "Well, I'm a farmer's daughter."

I continued, "I wonder if you would like to take a little stroll in the woods and—"

At that moment, the apprehensive mother of the girl dashed out on the porch and shouted, "Daughter, you stop talking to that man and come into this house right now!"

And, as an after-thought, raising her voice, she exclaimed, *"And bring the cow in with you!"*   (BLACKOUT)

Though this always got a gut-roar, it was sometimes *topped* by the cow herself, who, we found out at rehearsals, had weak kidneys.

When I registered a complaint, I was reassured by one of Carroll's writers, Eugene Conrad, "Don't worry, Ken, if that ever occurs, just flick your cigar, look out at the audience, and say, '*Well, there goes our liquor license!*' "

Opening night, I must say, the cow was a perfect lady all through the scene—held her water all the way *until* the punch line. Then, I don't know whether it was the sudden blare of music from the orchestra denoting the end of the scene or the sudden dousing of the lights for the blackout, *but something scared the shit out of the cow and all hell broke loose.*

Humor like this reviewed at the present time seems quaint and dated, but the unsophisticated audiences of that period loved it.

But Carroll took no chances at the end of this "historic" extravaganza. He really went all out for the patriotic finale and threw his best ball.

After a tableau in which the ride of Paul Revere was represented by a costumed man riding a white horse on a treadmill, the figures of George Washington and Abraham Lincoln appeared. Then a troop of maidens in costumes more artistic than historic, drilled with true military precision before a painted eagle that fairly screamed, and a spotlight caught a frock-coated actor representing F. D. R. reviewing them, as the orchestra played the "Star Spangled Banner" and over the heads of the standing audience a huge American flag that canopied the auditorium was unfolded. Then a scenic tableau, that by an optical illusion showed a fleet of our battleships steaming through the night right up to the very breakwater at the footlights, growing in size with their approach, ended the spectacle.

It was only fitting and proper that General Douglas MacArthur, who was out front that opening night, was a guest at the party on the stage after the show.

It was a typical Carroll shindig—full of interesting and provocative people. I was particularly intrigued by the wide variety of guests who were invited. Among them was young, handsome Howard Hughes, the original collector of girls, who occasionally appeared in public in those days. Then, there was Lucky Luciano, whose abilities did not lie so much in show business as in the actual manipulation of machine guns and gangsters. He dropped by to pick up his beautiful girl friend, Gay Orlova, who was in the show.

Jim Carroll, who was a big sports fan, pulled me over and insisted that we take a picture with the new heavyweight champion, James

J. Braddock, who had won the title from Max Baer just a couple of weeks before.

Earl Carroll spent most of his time entertaining General MacArthur, and I noticed that MacArthur was particularly attentive to Beryl Wallace. Jim explained that Earl and the general had been very close friends since World War I, and he and Beryl had visited the general many times when MacArthur was superintendent of West Point, and every year they were his guests at the Army-Navy game.

He also confided that the general was infatuated with Beryl since they first met, and added that he thought that if the two men hadn't been such good friends, MacArthur would have stolen her away and made her the "general's lady."

In spite of the murderous reviews, Earl Carroll's *Sketch Book of 1935* ran for eight months, from June to January, but unfortunately, my association with Earl Carroll ended on a sour note.

I'd heard of the unethical practices of Carroll—never believed them—put them down as malicious rumors—but in an unpleasant incident that occurred before *Sketch Book* closed I was to experience another facet of Carroll's mercurial personality.

The show had been running for about six months, when one night Carroll dropped by my dressing room and ceremoniously informed me that he was going to have to close the show unless he could get my cooperation. I was a bit surprised. Business had seemed uniformly good. Of course, it could have been thanks to the cut-rate tickets at LeBlangs in the basement of Gray's Drug Store on 42nd.

Carroll's request was not an unusual one during a long run of a Broadway show, and considering that, as the star, I was receiving the largest salary—$1,500 a week—I immediately indicated to Carroll that under the circumstances I would be agreeable to making an adjustment. I then inquired what he felt would be fair.

His whole demeanor changed and his soft voice became brittle as he told me that he felt I should work for *nothing*—no pay at all—to help the situation.

He interrupted my protest with the inference that the reponsibility was all mine. He said, "All right, if you want to throw 100 people out of work—60 girls, many of whom have to take care of sick mothers...." He wound up with the devastating phrase, "Go ahead, Ken, it's up to you, if you want to close the show."

I've always been a sucker for good histrionics, and his performance that night was so effective that I agreed to go along for awhile and work without any compensation. Immediately, the old con man reappeared and with an ingratiating smile assured me it would just be for a couple of weeks.

He profusely thanked me over and over, telling me how much all the girls would appreciate my cooperative gesture.

By the time he left, I felt a surge of personal pride and accomplishment such as I'm sure Neil Armstrong must have experienced when he stepped on the moon years later.

As far as I could observe, business seemed to remain the same. The two weeks spread into four, then six, and all the while I was entreated by Carroll to "have a little patience." When a catastrophic slump failed to materialize by the end of two months, I'd had it.

I stormed into the front office and gave Carroll my two week's notice. He pleaded with me again to help him stick it out for two more weeks. The lush Christmas and New Year's season was coming. He predicted we would do capacity business (which we did). He assured me that not only would he pay me in full for the last two week's work, but was confident he could reimburse me for many of those delinquent weeks.

The Christmas season sped by rapidly, and in no time came the night the show was officially closing.

I wasn't disturbed when he failed to pay me at the end of the first week. I felt there was so much money involved, he was preparing to give it to me all in one lump.

At the end of the last performance, I hurriedly dressed, packed, and rushed out to the front office to see Carroll and pick up my check, but he was nowhere in sight. I asked for Jim, who was just leaving, whether Earl had left an envelope for me.

He expressed genuine surprise that I hadn't been paid and regretfully added that the treasurer who handled all the money had already left. Jim was also no help in informing me where I might locate Earl—Sardi's, Reuben's, et cetera? He said as far as he knew, he vaguely remembered his brother saying something about attending a party on Park Avenue, but he didn't have any idea where it was or when he'd get home. I felt a little sorry for Jim. He was always the hatchet man, facing the unpleasant situations his brother was forever dodging.

I grabbed a bite and later, when I got home, I started calling Carroll's apartment. I called to the wee hours of the morning. No answer. I called the next day and tried for days afterward with no luck. It slowly started to dawn on me—I'd been had.

There's an old saying in show business: you can steal an actor's money, burn his house down, run off with his wife—but one thing, don't *embarrass* him. And I was not only embarrassed, but so damned sore that a few days later I went over to Actor's Equity and filed a formal complaint against Earl Carroll for the $15,000 in back pay that he owed me.

The officials there received my complaint and politely informed me that they would investigate the matter and get back to me as soon as possible.

On the Monday of the following week, I received a call from Frank Gilmore asking me to come to the Equity office at eleven o'clock the next day. When I arrived, Gilmore was there with two or three other officials, who reluctantly informed me that my request for the back pay had been denied.

They said they had had a meeting with Mr. Carroll and he had brought up a very important point. He asked the question: wasn't it true that when Mr. Murray had waived that *first* week's salary without notifying Equity and getting its permission, he broke a union rule and forfeited the union's jurisdiction?

Mr. Gilmore said that after careful deliberation under the circumstances they were forced to agree to the validity of Mr. Carroll's argument, and therefore felt no obligation to require him to pay my back salary.

I felt quite bitter about being rooked out of the 15 grand, but I began to understand Carroll's problems a little better when I read a few months later, October 9, 1936, that for the first and only time in his life, Earl Carroll was forced to file for bankruptcy.

After *Sketch Book* closed, he had started to plunge again, betting his own money, and what he could borrow, that he could successfully produce shows *without* beautiful girls, music, and dancing—and lost more than $900,000.

Carroll's liabilities were more than double his assets, which amounted to $410,646.85 according to the schedules filed with his petition. A major part of the latter was salaries and other emoluments alleged due him for several years from his own corporation.

I felt even more distressed that I had contributed to the pressure when all his plays, songs, and stocks in various enterprises had to be auctioned off by Bankruptcy Referee Robert P. Stephenson, in the United States Courthouse on Foley Square.

It seemed incomprehensible when I learned that all his interests in the plays *White Cargo, Mary's Other Husband, So Long Letty, Canary Cottage,* and others, and all the royalties of his songs from A.S.C.A.P., of which he was one of the founders, including "Dreams of Long Ago," "Adorable," "Going to Town," and "All of Me" were sold to an attorney, Jacob L. Steisel, for the incredibly paltry sum of $600.25.

WITH THE BROADWAY WISEACRES dooming him to obscurity—
"That's the end of Carroll!"—but undaunted, he packed his
belongings and, following the advice attributed to Horace Greeley,
went west—all the way to Hollywood—where he confounded his critics by gaining a place for himself in the almost inaccessible world
of the movies.

Darryl Zanuck, trying to help his old friend, engaged him as a
producer at 20th Century–Fox. Jessie Schuyler, knowing of his
present financial difficulties, offered to "rent" him her estate for
a nominal sum, graciously insisting on continuing to bear the ex-
pense of the gardeners and household staff. Thus the beleaguered
entrepreneur was able to take his place in the Hollywood firmament
in true Carroll style.

It was the talk of the town, this strange combination. Mrs. Schuyler
was, in all respects, a singularly alien candidate for an alliance with
Earl Carroll. He was the direct antithesis of all she represented. Yet
it was to be this woman who would become one of his greatest
admirers and staunchest supporters, and from then on would guide
him through his financial morass and provide the monetary aid that
returned Earl Carroll to great prominence and made him a millionaire during the last years of his life.

Carroll's tenure at Fox was not a happy one. He produced a couple
of pictures—*Love Is News* with Loretta Young and Tyrone Power,

and, of all things, a picture called *Stowaway* with Shirley Temple. That combination was really the first "Odd Couple!"

But Carroll found it impossible to operate within the confines of a big film factory, and his association with the studio was terminated. Besides, he had become impregnated with a new idea.

Sensing the need for a combination theatre and restaurant in Hollywood, he started the project with the help of his dear friend, Mrs. Schuyler. He promised Jessie it was to be the most modern theatre in America. "It will make Broadway look provincial," he predicted.

And he was right. The legendary Carroll Theatre had the first *double* revolving stages ever constructed, 90 feet in circumference—the largest in the world. There was also a floating stage for montage effects. It was the first with auxiliary stages in the auditorium walls and the first with florescent illumination on the ceiling. Every seat had to be reserved. It had an acre and a half of parking space; the main dining auditorium seated 1,000. The design of this unusual theatre was created by architect Gordon B. Kaufmann.

For the show he planned another innovation. Instead of following his and Ziegfeld's tried and true pattern of always using stellar names developed by other people as the attraction, he planned to use as his *stars* for the show, *Broadway to Hollywood*, 60 of the most beautiful and talented girls in the world.

As Hedda Hopper said in an interview with Carroll (Los Angeles *Times*, December 10, 1938):

> When Earl Carroll's new theatre restaurant opens Christmas night, don't expect Al Jolson, Fanny Brice, or Eddie Cantor to walk out on the stage. The stars of his new show are to be the Earl Carroll Beauties. Perhaps Carroll's flair for girls finds him wary about engaging name players, which may or may not be the wrong idea.

It was the *right* idea. With a cast headed by Beryl Wallace and 60 gorgeous girls, the show proved a brilliant hit with the first-night audience.

The most dazzling event ever in the night life of Hollywood was the opening of Earl Carroll's Hollywood Theatre Restaurant on December 26, 1938. The audacious producer had announced that a lifetime cover charge of $1,000 would admit patrons to a private room padded with patent leather. Aglow with celebrities, it was a mingling of social and professional leaders who attended the colorful premiere and several thousand sightseers gathered outside the theatre to behold the stars as they drove up to the entranceway, where a chosen few of the spectators had procured the choice points of vantage to view the arrival of the film luminaries and others. Traffic was slowed for several blocks in either direction of the front entrance.

The beginning of the truly resplendent pageant was signalized by the advent of Marlene Dietrich, Dolores Del Rio, the Jack L. Warners, Richard Barthelmess, Louis B. Mayer, Clark Gable and Carole Lombard, and Tyrone Power and Sonja Henie. Shortly afterward, Edgar Bergen appeared on the scene, but without Charlie McCarthy. He didn't even carry a suitcase. He escorted Kay St. Germaine in a party that included Bob and Dolores Hope, Jackie Coogan and Betty Grable, Jack Benny and Mary Livingstone, and Phil Harris.

Others in large parties were Robert Taylor, Claudette Colbert, Constance Bennett, William Gargan, Conrad Nagel, Mary Brian, Darryl Zanuck, David O. Selznick, and two of the most eligible bachelors in town—Franchot Tone and Errol Flynn. It was that night that the beautiful 16-year-old Jean Wallace caught the eye of Franchot Tone, whom she was later to marry—and Flynn glaumed the adorable teenage Peggy Satterlee, who was later to make headlines as the underage girl in Errol Flynn's famed statutory rape case in 1942.

Backstage, before the curtain went up, Earl Carroll was displaying another facet of his character, according to testimony given later by officials of the Screen Actors' Guild.

He reminded his showgirls that with L. B. Mayer, Jack Warner, and Darryl Zanuck out front, "This is opportunity night. I can make you famous and rich. Sign a contract giving me 50 percent of your earnings above $40 a week, for a period of one year."

Some of the contracts were signed, but later recalled. Carroll was right in one respect; it was opportunity night. As he had promised, the girls were the stars.

The girls opened the show with a number entitled "Talent Is What the Public Wants," in which they ribbed the audience for wanting what is generally expected of chorines. They finished by all coming down to the footlights and in rhymed patter humorously chided the audience for coming late and missing the opening chorus. The delighted crowd enjoyed the new experience of being intimately kidded by the Carroll Beauties.

Interspersed between clever specialties was as fresh an assortment of slim young lady nudists as had previously been revealed in Tinseltown. The stage proved to be an ideal setting when the girls ascended more than 100 treads of stairs to be 135 feet in the air.

Beryl Wallace was the principal star and served as spark plug for the whole production, and worked in many of the comedy sketches. In one, the comedian, brandishing a large pair of scissors, chases a girl dressed in a flimsy negligee across the stage. A few seconds later the two reappear. This time the girl is garbed in a hula skirt and the comic pushes a lawnmower. For their third and final visitation the young lady is revealed in an outfit of tin pants while the comedian, ever in pursuit, follows her armed with a blowtorch. Even the sophisticated opening night audience had to sit up and take notice when the fleeing young lady—her youth, brunette hair, and figure designed to entice whistles—was played by the ravishing Beryl.

In the finale the girls did everything that the principals had done—equally well, and in some cases better. The principals stood by while the chorus girls impersonated them and the audience howled.

The big surprise of the evening was when Beryl Wallace revealed a hidden singing talent and with the assistance of Ray Noble and his orchestra had the first-nighters cheering.

Hedda Hopper reported the next morning:

> As an active member of "We-Want-Earl Carroll-To-Have-a-Success-Club," I'm pleased to proclaim the Earl Carroll Revue an unqualified hit! Carroll is not one to give up looking for novelties, and he came up with a great one this time. Traditionally chorus girls are expected only to dance a little, sing a little, and display a lot—but Carroll lets his girls take over from beginning to end with their clever patter, and there are several scenes of exquisite beauty in which dozens of the most beautiful girls ever assembled take part. Needless for this reporter to add that some of their costumes can easily be packed into an ordinary-sized envelope.
>
> Carroll's lovely girl friend, Beryl Wallace, and the Earl Carroll Beauties are the major drawing card, and deservedly so. They have an "audience participation" where they pull some of the patrons onto the stage. Just to see Bob Hope, Jack Benny, Jimmy Durante, Errol Flynn, Milton Berle, Joe E. Brown, Walter Pidgeon, Don Ameche, Robert Taylor, and the great W. C. Fields all on the stage at the same time doing a patty-cake number with the girls was worth the price of admission.
>
> It was a great night!

Flushed with the success of his new theatre restaurant, Earl Carroll was riding high. He was on the top of the heap again. From then on, things started to happen fast.

On September 8, 1939, he obtained an order approving his discharge from bankruptcy. Two weeks later, Mrs. Schuyler "sold" him her beautiful mansion on Schuyler Road in Beverly Hills and Carroll started tossing a series of wild, lavish parties unequalled since the days of Fatty Arbuckle. There is no indication that Jessie Schuyler ever attended any of these soirees.

It was also from this same mansion at 1140 Schuyler Road that Earl Carroll, returning home from the theatre late one night, was indeed *kidnaped*.

The prowler, hiding in the entranceway, surprised Carroll and his chauffeur, and held them at gunpoint while he herded them into the showman's car. Covering them with a revolver and a shotgun from the back seat, the kidnapper forced his prisoners to drive to Western Avenue and Santa Monica Boulevard, where he dumped them out after emptying their pockets of $341.

Carroll immediately phoned the police, but the gendarmes, suspecting it was another of Carroll's publicity stunts, started to "spike" the report until the producer excitedly informed them that his abductor had stolen his custom-built car and was heading east.

Less than two hours later, the kidnapper was apprehended as he raced through the streets of San Bernardino. Officers John Trout and H. C. Mufflin had to fire four shots in the air before he surrendered.

In court, fifteen days later, the prisoner pleaded guilty and Superior Court Judge Clement D. Nye sentenced him to five years to life in San Quentin. *(It would seem that now, over three decades later, no useful purpose would be served in actually specifying the reckless young man's name.)*

In 1940, Carroll produced a picture at Paramount called *A Night at Earl Carroll's*. It was photographed entirely in his new showplace and Carroll appeared as himself in the movie. I was signed to play the lead, and the first day on the set I ran into Beryl Wallace who, naturally, had a prominent part in the production.

I hadn't seen Beryl since we worked together in *Sketch Book*, but we were good friends. That day she was bubbling with excitement. She told me she had just brought her family out from Brooklyn, bought a house at 6263 Leland Way in Hollywood, just in back of the Earl Carroll Theatre, and at long last the entire Heischuber clan was back together again.

I was delighted to see her so happy. Everything was going famously for her. She had been signed by Universal and appeared in such films as *Air Devils* and *The Rage of Paris*, and really did a superior acting job as one of the women in the life of Nazi Paul Joseph Goebbels in *Enemy of Women*.

I admired Beryl tremendously for her dedication to her career. Being an outstanding beauty, with a hit stage show, she could have comfortably coasted along now that she was established, but she continually took singing lessons, studied dancing and performed an array of exercises designed to improve her diction.

The star of a successful stage show going into its third year in Hollywood, she was naturally very popular and had many suitors. Considering that one of the most persistent was handsome movie star Conrad Nagel, I always marveled at her steadfast devotion and loyalty to her tall, slim, fiftyish, perennial Don Juan, Earl Carroll.

When I mentioned his name, her face lit up as she exclaimed, "Oh, Ken, you wouldn't know him any more. He's completely changed his life-style—home every night—and can you imagine, he's even taken up yachting." And though she smiled and talked with animation, I felt all the while that a beautiful *mask* was speaking.

I thought: Earl Carroll has changed his life-style? That I gotta see!

Later in the day, I received a call from Carroll inviting me to meet him the next morning at the Beverly Hills Hotel. He said we could have breakfast and discuss the scenes we were to do together that day.

I arrived bright and early at the Polo Lounge, and after inquiring for Carroll's table, I was informed by the maitre d' that Mr. Carroll had left a message for me to come over to bungalow 5C.

I knocked on the door. Receiving no answer and finding the door unlocked, I walked into the empty living room of the suite. Hearing some noise in the bedroom, I rapped softly and said, "If you're not up yet, Earl, I'll see you later on the set." Carroll's voice answered, "No, Ken, come on in."

As I entered, there was Carroll and a beautiful, voluptuous red-haired girl whom I recognized as one of a pair of luscious twins who had auditioned for the picture. With a sheet covering them only from the waist down, they were hugging, kissing, and fondling each other.

Embarrassed (sex has never been my favorite spectator sport), I turned to leave, and Carroll gasped between moans and groans of happy pleasure, "Don't go, Ken, I'll only be a few minutes."

I quickly left and closed the door, but not before I discovered where the other twin was—under the sheet at the foot of the bed, her deep throat adding to the boss's ecstasy.

Someone once asked Beryl Wallace how she could stand by and suffer his humiliating transgressions. With her beautiful brown eyes glistening, she smiled weakly, "Don't worry, he'll wind up with *me* in the end."

And he did. They were sitting side by side when their plane crashed in Mt. Carmel, Pennsylvania, on June 17, 1948.

The ironic part is, *it didn't have to happen.* A flip of a coin *literally* decided the fate of Earl Carroll and his beautiful sweetheart.

Beginning of the End

22

I N THE YEAR 1948, EARL CARROLL was at the absolute zenith of his career. But not satisfied with having produced nine major revues in his enormously successful theatre restaurant, Carroll, who could never hold still with just one interest (or woman), was planning *another* new project of Hippodrome proportions. Actually, it represented a partial desertion of the arts, or rather a linking of them with big business.

He decided to build in Hollywood the *world's largest theatre* with a seating capacity of 7,000, costing approximately $15,000,000. The structure, which would top New York's Radio City Music Hall, was to be built on the south side of Sunset Boulevard, a half block east of his existing theatre.

Indicating the theatre's magnitude, the proscenium opening was to be 130 feet. The theatre was to have three revolving stages, each 75 by 100 feet; one with wood flooring for stage productions, another, an ice rink for skating numbers, and the third, a huge water tank for aquatic routines.

Other "biggest and best" features were a modern motion picture theatre, a complete television studio (he was the first local impresario to broadcast on TV daily from his existing site), a cabaret-restaurant, and a high-rise executive office building, on top of which would be a heliport. Six motor lanes would lead under the building, which would have parking facilities for more than 1,000 cars.

Final plans were being drawn by architect Gordon Kaufman and ground breaking was planned for March, with construction requiring a year.

Carroll claimed the theatre alone would gross at least $100,000 a week, and he would use about 110 beautiful girls.

It was in this expansive mood that he gave his last New Year's Eve party at the Schuyler mansion. There are those who still say that it was also the last of the great Hollywood parties—and probably the best. He was celebrating the anniversary of his Hollywood theatre restaurant and had invited all the celebrities who had attended the premiere that night almost 10 years before, the night that had set him firmly on his comeback trail. From my vantage point, sitting on the terraced rocks overlooking the pool, it looked like they had all accepted.

Everything was geared for the plush, the lush, from the moment the guests drove up the long beautiful tree-lined road leading to the Schuyler estate, with big signs on every other tree saying "BE-WARE OF THE THING." To those in the know, these were allusions to the particular prowess of the host, Earl Carroll.

As if that was not enough to titillate the expectant guests, further evidence of the ecstatic abandon in store that night was the provocative sight of girls, au naturel, swimming around in the large pool, which was surrounded by terraces and waterfalls. Fortunately for them and for some of the others who were later to dunk themselves in the clear water in one stage or another of collapse, that winter night happened to be on the warm side.

There were several hundred guests in the huge manor-type house, and the bar and playroom were filled and doing excellent business. The entire picture was not so much one of reality but rather a kind of dramatization of something you might read about in an F. Scott Fitzgerald novel.

Beryl Wallace, looking radiantly beautiful, of course was the hostess, moving around, making sure that all were enjoying themselves.

Earl, poolside, was busily engaged talking to Errol Flynn. He had an affinity for this wild, romantic Irishman who lived life to the fullest with the attitude of "to hell with tomorrow."

Standing nearby, listening, was a young magazine writer named Jack Holland. It was probably an unlikely moment to break into a spirited conversation, but Holland decided to take the leap and corner Earl for an interview. He had written stories on just about every major star in the business, including the dashing Errol, who at that moment spotted a curvaceous number he wanted to initiate into the Flynn flimflams and disappeared into the noisy crowd.

Some celebrities were coy about interviews and issued generous doses of platitudes, but Holland found Earl to be loquacious, exuberant, and blissfully cooperative as he asked him:

"How do you rank this party in comparison with such memorable social delights as the famous champagne bathtub one of several years ago?"

Earl paused and then, with just a trace of a smile, answered, "There will be no bathtubs at this one. But you know, Mr. Holland, you might have something there. If I had thought of it I could have filled the swimming pool with champagne. After all, it's legal now. We've got the cast," he said, gazing out toward the pool where the naked nymphs were frolicing. "But it just never occurred to me," he concluded a little acidly.

Holland, sensing that he had touched a sensitive point, quickly switched to a more palatable subject, asking pointedly:

"Tell me, Mr. Carroll, in your opinion, what is beauty to you?"

"Well, let's face it—beauty is beauty. It is not changed by era or time. But the attitudes about beauty have changed as the years have gone on," Earl commented. "For instance, Lillian Russell was considered a great beauty in her day. I was fortunately able to judge Lillian Russell personally. You know, I started as a program boy in 1905 in a theatre in Pittsburgh, and at that time she had the beauty of the moment. The very popular hourglass figure.

"Looking back on it," Earl continued, "I can't say Lillian or her contemporaries were truly beautiful. Beauty is a relative thing. I believe that appreciation of beauty is hereditary. We all like regular features, the hair to be full and a compliment to the face, and features to be well set. In the days of Lillian Russell, the women who played in the extravaganzas were voluptuous. They were ample-bosomed, heavy-thighed, and hefty women. Moreover, being so thoroughly covered with clothing, they had no incentive to watch their food, so they overate and became overweight.

"But this is what the young dandies like Diamond Jim Brady liked in those days," Carroll pointed out. "This is what the men of that period desired. Men were responsible for the great restrictions that were placed upon women, which, in turn, had considerable influence on the dress. Until recently men have enslaved women. They want a woman for their very own, and they are constantly building walls around them. For example, veils worn by Mohammedans, the breaking of Chinese women's feet, the billowy all-covering skirts of the Victorian era, and perhaps the corsets were something confining to enslave her to him even more. You go into the Louvre in Paris and see Venus. She is oversized but she has curves and is well proportioned for her size. Reduce her and we have our hereditary ideas on beauty."

"Mr. Carroll, you have worked with and been associated with some of the world's most ravishing women. Of all of the beauties who have surrounded you, whom do you consider the most beautiful girl in the world—the most beautiful girl you've ever seen?"

"Well, Mr. Holland, I'd have to say there were two—Dorothy Knapp and Beryl Wallace. They both were endowed with exquisite beauty— symmetrical bodies, regular features, clear complexions, and inward loveliness. But Beryl has something Dorothy didn't have—intelligence— and brains help in the long-range plan of happiness."

As Earl said this, I was standing nearby and looked over at Beryl Wallace and was glad that she was close enough to hear the conversation.

"Give a man power and he is happy," Earl said. "Give a woman beauty and she is happy because beauty is power—but brains have an enduring quality that can't be overlooked."

Beryl listened intently; a happy smile lit up her beautiful face. She turned to me and said, "That's perhaps the greatest compliment he's ever paid me. I never realized he thought of me in terms of intelligence."

As Holland was leaving he said, "By the way, whatever happened to Dorothy Knapp?"

Acting somewhat coyly, Earl parried the answer with: "I've always felt sorry about that. Poor girl, she took it pretty hard when we broke up. The last I heard of her she had gone to France and entered a convent." Then he added resignedly, "And I suppose she's still there."

At that Beryl just shrugged amusedly as if she were used to Earl's bragging about his conquests.

Just then Art Linkletter came by and said, "Beryl, I forgot to ask you, what did Earl give you for Christmas?"

She said, "Would you really like to see?" She took him by the arm and said, "Come on, boys, I'll show you."

I trailed along, figuring that at the least I was going to see an expensive diamond bracelet or a fabulous fur coat.

But she took us upstairs to her bathroom and, gesturing with one arm outstretched, said triumphantly, "Just what I've always wanted—a *mink toilet seat!*"

I said, "Beryl, what did you give him—one of those little sable belly-button dusters?"

"Or a roll of toilet paper made out of $100 bills?" Art asked.

"No—I gave him something he really needed—a parking meter for his john!" she laughingly said as she left.

Art immediately sat down and said, "Man, now I can say I've really lived."

Later, in the playroom, amid the bedlam of clinking glasses, loud laughter, and general mayhem, I had a chance to ask Beryl, "What did you really give Earl for Christmas?"

Her eyes brightened as she said, "Oh, Ken, I gave him a beautiful watch—you know, one of those new LeCoultres that gives not only the time but the day and date and month." And she said, as she took a sip of champagne, teasingly peering over the rim of the glass, "There's a very interesting story that goes with buying that watch." She knew I was anxious to hear more as she continued.

"I bought it down at Magnin's in Beverly Hills. The nicest saleslady waited on me. She was really charming. Beautiful face, with just a trace of gray in her lovely brown hair. After I picked out the watch, I told her whom it was for and said I wanted to have it inscribed, but not just the usual trite 'I love you.' The lady paused, smiled sweetly, and said, 'May I make a suggestion? Why don't you just put *Forever Yours?*' I thanked her, and as I was leaving the store I couldn't help mentioning to the manager how nice the saleswoman had been to me. 'I'm surprised you don't know her,' he said to me. 'She used to be in show business.' "

Beryl looked me straight in the eye and hesitatingly said, "Ken, do you know who it was?—*Dorothy Knapp.*"

Before I could ask the obvious question, she said, "No, I didn't say anything to Earl. I wouldn't spoil his little dream story for anything in the world."

It was 4:00 A.M. before the party finally began breaking up. Nude bodies climbed out of the pool. Couples who had been engaged in various stages of love making wearily began untangling themselves.

One of the last to leave was Errol Flynn. He was always one of the last to leave. His car was filled with chorus girls he had chivalrously offered to take home. It was a beautiful new Fiat he had just gotten for Christmas, and as he was leaving with the gaily chatting and laughing girls—fully expecting the utmost with the gay cavalier—Earl asked him, "How do you like your Fiat?" Flynn replied with his usual nonchalance and flair, "I like everything that starts with f—fishing, females, and fucking."

There is no doubt about it, Errol Flynn was one of the last of the great free-wheeling romanticists.

I didn't see Earl again until a few months later when we were both judges for a beauty contest at the Ambassador Hotel. I could never forget it because the winner was a beautiful little 16-year-old girl named Norma Jean Baker. Neither of us hired her. Earl couldn't, because there was a new ordinance prohibiting using any girls under 18 in his theatre restaurant (he sold liquor); and I didn't, because I was on the lookout for an understudy for Marie Wilson and she couldn't fit Marie's costumes. It was a simple matter of mathematics: Norma Jean (Marilyn Monroe) was 36-24-35 and Marie was a very generous 39-21-36.

As we were driving back to Hollywood, we got on the subject of the difference between the eastern showgirls and the western variety, and Carroll said, "As you're well aware, Ken, the difference is, the New York girls are taller and closer to what I feel are perfect physical requirements, but the Hollywood girls have something that the ones from Broadway don't have—a natural, healthy beauty, like that little Baker girl we saw today. Of course, she had everything. I'm sorry she's so young. I would have signed her in a minute."

During dinner at the Brown Derby before we had to go to our respective theatres—I had the *Blackouts* just up the street—he was terribly excited about the fact that the government had restored his citizenship. His face beaming, he said, "Ken, just think, I'm going to be able to vote for a president for the first time in over twenty years." And he added that he hoped it could be for his very good friend, General MacArthur. He said he and Beryl were flying to New York the next day and then on to Philadelphia to attend the Republican convention.

I knew that shortly before, he had made several air trips to Japan in connection with a documentary he was planning to produce on the Nipponese people, and while in Tokyo he and Beryl had been the general's houseguests.

As we were leaving the Derby, I remarked casually, "You love to fly, don't you, Earl?" marveling at this brave aviator. At that time I was still of the "sweaty-hand" variety of air passenger.

Carroll said, "Yes, there is nothing like this plane travel. It's made the whole world a weekend away." And we parted.

That was the last time I ever saw Earl Carroll.

Since being a flyer in the first World War, he'd never lost his enthusiasm for flying—rarely ever traveled any other way—but, oddly enough, he *always* bought large sums of accident insurance.

Many times Earl prophesied that he would die in a plane. In fact, he once confided to an intimate that he had commissioned Will Pogany, the noted artist, to draw sketches and plans for a memorial to be erected on a resting place he believed Beryl would share with him after both died. It was later revealed that he had already purchased a plot at Forest Lawn Memorial Park.

On the morning of their departure, Maxie Rosenbloom, the former pugilist, who was scheduled to appear in Carroll's next edition, called Carroll from Detroit and pleaded:

"Look, Earl, why don't you and Beryl stop over here for a few hours and we'll get straightened out on the show for next fall. Then you can go on to New York and Philadelphia."

In Hollywood, Carroll turned from the phone questioningly to Beryl. She smiled and took a coin from her purse.

Carroll spoke to Rosenbloom: "We're tossing a coin, Maxie. If it's heads, we stop in Detroit. If it's tails, we fly straight through to New York. It's spinning now—and it came up *tails*. So we'll see you in Manhattan."

It was a final, fatal gamble for Earl Carroll.

The United Airlines DC6, flight #624, originated in San Diego and would make stops in Los Angeles and Chicago, on its 12-hour flight to New York. Piloted by George Warner, Jr., of Westmont, Illinois, the flight was a new one, only four days old.

The DC6 luxury airliners had been grounded after a series of mishaps some months before—on October 24th of the previous year there had been a crash in Bryce Canyon, Utah, and on November 1st, an emergency landing at Gallup, New Mexico. The liners had been restored to service after modifications had been made to correct the hazards.

However, after continuing their investigations, the CAA and the Air Transport Association of America sent telegrams to the airline on June 10th, informing it that a condition involving carbon dioxide fumes seeping into pilots' cabins from fire extinguishers could seriously affect a pilot's respiratory reactions, and on June 16th a flight bulletin went out to all crew members warning them of the danger and advising them to wear oxygen masks.

Unfortunately, as the order was not issued in sufficient time before the fatal flight took off, Captain George Warner *never received the bulletin.*

Just before Earl Carroll and Beryl Wallace boarded the New York–bound plane, Mrs. Schuyler's secretary, Virginia Lear, handed him a note. It read:

> Dear Earl, Just talked to Jessie and she asked me to put in a little note from her to tell you she will go to the Springs the middle of the week, but will wire you the dates. Also that she appreciates so much your telegrams and phone calls, and if you possibly can to please, please stay out of airplanes because we are all a little jittery here over the recent tragedy.　　　　V.L.

Approximately 10 hours later, flight #624 was winging its way over the anthracite coal fields of eastern Pennsylvania, near Pittsburgh, not too far from where Earl Carroll was born. At 1:23 P.M., DST, Captain Warner made a routine report to the CAA at Philipsburg, Pennsylvania, saying he was flying at 17,000 feet; it made no mention of trouble.

The CAA acknowledged his report and gave him clearance to the next CAA control point at Allentown, Pennsylvania, approximately

50 miles to the east, at an altitude of 11,000 feet. This was a routine descent in preparation for a landing at LaGuardia.

The sun was shining through partly cloudy skies, the ceiling was 5,500 feet, and the visibility was 8 miles, the CAA reported.

The next message from the plane came a few minutes later, when the pilot radioed, "New York, New York, this is an emergency descent."

One person who heard that frantic message was Captain Earl Bach of United flight #132. He was bound for Philadelphia in a twin-engine DC3, following the big DC6 but at a much lower altitude, 9,000 feet. He said that when he heard Captain Warner's voice over the radio announcing that the plane was making an emergency descent, "I could tell from the pilot's voice that they were in bad trouble."

Tragically, another listener was the pilot's wife, Mrs. George Warner, Jr., who always tuned in on the airliner's wavelength to hear her husband's radio chatter as he piloted planes from coast to coast. Horrified, that day she heard him say, "I'm going down." Then there was silence.

In that period the plane descended rapidly from about three miles until it was skimming ridges in the rough terrain studded with strip coal mines.

One eyewitness, George Bolich, who was operating a mine locomotive for the Midvalley Colliery at the time, said: "I suddenly saw this plane coming down very low through the valley. It was losing altitude fast. It was coming right at me between two rows of trees, scarcely 30 feet above ground. The motors were wide open and sounded strong and synchronized. It scared the hell out of me when it flew over my head. It just missed me and damn near hit a coal breaker of the Hazelbrook Coal Company—there were about 90 guys working there—then I heard a big explosion as the plane crashed into a 60,000-volt transformer, and suddenly there was a mass of flames. It sounded as though the end of the world was coming."

Another stunned eyewitness, Harry Stibitz, said he was standing about 50 feet from the power line when the plane struck it. "I turned to look up," he said, "and it looked like a big torch. I saw a mass of fire, explosions, plane wreckage and bodies hurling through the air. The whole scene looked like a living hell."

High in the sky, Captain Bach, in the DC3, also witnessed the crash. He said, "The big silver plane was going so fast its momentum shot it half a mile up the mountainside, shooting flames 90 feet up."

An alarm was sent for fire apparatus, and engines responded from Mt. Carmel and Ashland. The Mt. Carmel Fire Department was handicapped by the fact that all but one of its engines were attending a fire convention and parade in Sunberry, 30 miles away. The alarm was relayed there and a number of the fire companies taking part left hastily for the scene of the crash.

After the flames were extinguished, state police, aeronautics officials, Red Cross workers, and members of the Civil Air Patrol combed the strewn wreckage.

There was no sign of life. A number of the bodies, along with many of the cockpit instruments, seat belts, and personal property of the crew and passengers were thrown nearly to the crest of the rise, 450 feet from where the plane first touched the ground.

Scattered bits of torn and twisted wreckage, charred fragments of bodies and luggage were scattered over the hillside for 600 feet on each side of the crash—eloquent testimony of the swift tragedy that snuffed out the lives of all on the transcontinental plane.

Among the wreckage and debris the searchers found baggage and personal items of the passengers, much of it in such well-preserved condition that it was easy to trace the owners. For instance, there was a briefcase of Earl Carroll's containing plans for his new Hollywood project. Also a half-burned script of the TV show Beryl Wallace had appeared on the night before. Ironically, the show's title was *The Sky's the Limit.*

One searcher found a wallet containing Carroll's name and $1024 in cash. Close by was a new baby's purse. It contained one cent. And above, as a bleak and savage ensign of destruction, a tattered steamer robe fluttered from a burning tree.

Although the identification of many of the victims was extremely difficult, Miss Wallace's body, which had been thrown clear of the plane at impact, was easily identified. Earl Carroll had to be identified by his fingerprints.

Reconstructing the fatal accident, the testimony of Dr. Ludwig G. Lederer, Civic Aeronautics Administration consultant, was generally accepted as giving the true facts precipitating the disaster.

Dr. Lederer testified that there was a dangerous condition in the plane's fire-fighting equipment, *which allowed carbon dioxide fumes to seep into the pilot's cabin* from fire extinguishers.

He discussed recordings, found in the wreckage, of the last radio messages from the stricken plane.

"The first calls from Captain George Warner, a veteran of 20 years, were made in an agitated voice, almost a normal yell," he testified. "Then transmissions came in a gasping voice typical of respiratory trouble. The term *fumes in pit* was forcibly sounded with great effort."

In simple words, Earl Carroll and Beryl Wallace were killed in the most unusual plane crash in the history of aviation—the only one of its kind ever recorded.

With the entire crew asphyxiated, the United Airlines DC6 tore into a steep rocky hillside with all four engines running at high power, *with a captain and crew dead in the cockpit before the fiery crash.*

It sometimes seems as if the fates reserve the harshest ironies for those they have initially blessed.

Epilogue

Earl Carroll's fortunes were on the upswing when he died. Unlike Flo Ziegfeld, who was close to bankruptcy at the time of his death, Carroll left an estate of more than a million dollars. Although, like Ziegfeld, his theatrical projects had many times brought him debts and litigation, Carroll's various real estate properties, thanks to Mrs. Schuyler, had made him financially sound.

Even after his death, the two women who had done most to assist him in fulfilling the promise of Earl Carroll's life were the objects of his last wishes.

Earl Carroll's will, dated October 31, 1947, bequeathed one half of his fortune to his "life-long" friend, Mrs. Jessie Schuyler, and the remaining half to his "beloved friend," Beryl Wallace. The testament named them as joint executors.

A codicil added six months before the plane tragedy contained clauses that indicated a premonition of impending "accident or disaster" resulting in simultaneous deaths of the showman and his leading lady.

"It is my wish that after I and my beloved friend, Beryl Wallace, have departed this life, our remains shall be placed together in the final resting place which I have selected...."

In the event that the beautiful showgirl died at the same time, $50,000 of her share should be used to erect the memorial in Forest Lawn. The balance of her share, he wrote, was to be turned over to the University of Southern California for the research of cancer in women.

(The Earl Carroll Memorial Clinic was established as a mobile unit, and to this day fulfills a much-needed service at no cost to women patients in poor and middle-class rural areas where hospital facilities are inaccessible.)

In his will Earl Carroll said that this was his way of thanking all the women who had given him fame and fortune.

Mrs. Schuyler, in accordance with Carroll's last wishes, started arrangements for a tomb to be erected on the $6,000 site Carroll himself had chosen at Forest Lawn Memorial Park. Made of marble and granite, the tomb was to contain the ashes of both Carroll and his leading lady, Beryl Wallace, and also the remains of his devoted brother Jim, who had died in 1941.

A central feature, being designed by Will Pogany, was to be placed over the top of the crypt. It was to be a large replica of Carroll's own hands holding a beautiful life-sized figure symbolizing the lovely Miss Wallace. Carroll also requested that the entire gravesite be surrounded by winged nude forms of showgirls. Special municipal permission had to be obtained to carry out the showman's wishes.

In discussing the funeral, on August 23, 1948, *Life* magazine said:

> The scene of Carroll's funeral . . . is said to be the subject of Evelyn Waugh's best-selling novel, *The Loved One*. In as brutal a satire as has been written in modern times, Waugh excoriates the fatuousness, combined with cold commercialism, which produced this 300-acre graveyard where no mention of death is allowed and the deceased is unctuously referred to as "the loved one." Earl Carroll, another loved one, would have thought his funeral a wonderful production.

Some months before Carroll's death, a writer for another magazine, *Family Circle*, was interviewing him for an article prophetically entitled "Your Last Day on Earth." He asked him the question: What would you do if you knew you were to die tomorrow?

Earl Carroll's answer was:

> If someone with some sort of psychic power were to tell me today that I had only 24 hours to live, I think I know exactly what I should want to do.

My very first thought would be to call together all of my most trusted friends and associates. I would confide in them all that I have learned in my 30 years in the theatre and ask them to carry on what I have tried to build.

Because I know this one thing is true: if a man's work is important to him, it will be important to the world. For every man is an integral part of the progress of the universe. It would be not only pointless but it would ultimately lead to a return to savagery if a man worked ceaselessly for one goal all of his life, only to have the work in his field revert to its beginnings at the time of his death. No matter what our work is, we should try to be part of the whole pattern of living, and our contribution—great or small—should be part of the building of a better world.

It has been my lifework to stage and produce shows built around beautiful girls. And I would feel I had accomplished a lot if other showmen would carry on my policy of presenting beautiful girls as a source of artistic pleasure. If the public could be educated away from thinking of a stageful of beautiful girls as a leg-show display and come to recognize the body as the most beautiful thing on earth, it would be a great stride forward. It is my earnest belief that the stage show, designed to enhance the beauty of our girls, is an intrinsic part of the American theatre, and if I were to die tomorrow, I should like to know that someone would carry on this essentially American institution with dignity and sincerity.

To many people this work of mine may seem insignificant; I deal in beauty, it's true. But we are all starved and hungry for beauty; there is too little of it in the world. I would like to think someone else would go on with my work of three decades—the presentation of lovely girls as a work of art. A hundred years from now I hope the parade of young American girls will still be walking under the sign of my theatre in Hollywood which reads: "THROUGH THESE PORTALS PASS THE MOST BEAUTIFUL GIRLS IN THE WORLD."

She was an Earl Carroll Beauty

At the turn of the century America
was uptight about nudity

In the early 1920s sex
reared its ugly head

Marie Macdonald died of an overdose of drugs

Lois Andrews died of lung cancer

Peggy Shannon was found dead in the kitchen of her modest apartment in North Hollywood with a half-burned cigarette in her hand

Dorothy Abbott committed suicide

Jeanette Gray Mack took her own life with an overdose of barbiturates at twenty-two

Jean Spangler disappeared and no trace of her body has been found. Like the "Black Dahlia," the case remains unsolved in the Los Angeles police files

for others, tragedy

Whatever happened to the most beautiful girls in the world?

For over a quarter of a century, to be chosen as an Earl Carroll beauty was the top echelon for the glamour girl. For many it held the key to film contracts, successful marriages, newsworthy escorts, and, for some, tragedy.

Although not one ever achieved superstar status, Sheree North, Yvonne De Carlo, Marie MacDonald, and Jean Wallace came closest.

Exotic Yvonne De Carlo was a strange candidate for a Carroll cutie, as evidenced in her early films, where she exemplified a hardboiled, no-nonsense approach to sex. Born Peggy Middleton on September 1, 1922, in Vancouver, Canada, she made her first try at Hollywood in 1937, studying dancing with Fanchon & Marco. She went on to become Miss Venice Beach, at a contest in which Carroll was a judge. While she was under contract to him she was signed by Paramount as a starlet rival for Dorothy Lamour (*Rainbow Island*), but in 1945 she became a full-fledged star in Universal's *Salome, Where She Danced*. In 1971, Yvonne made her Broadway bow in a show called *Follies* (not Ziegfeld's) at the Winter Garden Theatre and had a show-stopping number, "I'm Still Here," which appropriately was a parody of her own life.

When studios kept trying to duplicate the Monroe image, Sheree North was first known as a sex-symbol, later as a dramatic actress. She was born Dawn Bethel in Hollywood on January 17, 1933. At 10, she danced in USO shows, at 13 she was part of the Greek Theatre chorus in musicals, *Two Hearts in Three-Quarter Time, Firefly, New Moon, The Wizard of Oz, Bittersweet,* and *Anything Goes*. An early teenage marriage to Fred Bessire caused her to leave Hollywood High at 15. Choreographer Bob Alton first saw Sheree dancing at Earl Carroll's and secured chorus work for her in films such as *Excuse My Dust* and *Here Come the Girls*. Alton was instrumental in her winning the part of "Whitey" in the Broadway musical *Hazel Flagg*, based on the 1937 film *Nothing Sacred*. Paramount bought the show as a vehicle for Martin and Lewis, and because of Sheree's notices had her do a jitterbug number with Jerry Lewis. Fox acquired her services next. As a platinum blonde carbon-copy of Marilyn Monroe, she inherited Marilyn's role in *How To Be Very, Very Popular,* co-starring Betty Grable. In *No Down Payment, The Way of the Gold,* and *In Love and War,* she proved her dramatic abilities. In 1962 Sheree returned to Broadway for producer David Merrick in *I Can Get It for You Wholesale,* which featured newcomer Barbra

Streisand, at the Shubert Theatre. She told the press, "Here I am, a blonde broad again." Now considered an extremely capable actress, her most recent work was in the prestigious Dino De Laurentiis production, *The Shootist*, with John Wayne.

Carroll first glimpsed Jean Wallace in a Chicago restaurant in 1938. Because of her pert young face and provocative body, he immediately offered her a contract. Born Jean Walasek on October 12, 1923, her first film was *A Night at Earl Carroll's* (1940). While at Carroll's she was frequently mentioned in gossip columns as the teenage girl friend of Franchot Tone. Jean was one of MGM's *Ziegfeld Girl* chorines. She then signed a Paramount contract, and while appearing in *Louisiana Purchase*, she married Tone and retired to have two sons. Important roles in *Blaze of Noon* and *Native Son* brought her back to the screen. Divorcing Tone upon the completion of *The Man on the Eiffel Tower*, she later wed star-producer Cornel Wilde, with whom she has continued to have a happy marital and professional relationship. Jean has proved herself to be an exceptionally good dramatic actress in husband Wilde's films *The Devil's Hairpin, Maracaibo, Lancelot and Guinevere,* and *No Blade of Grass.*

Basic-blonde Marie MacDonald, who changed her hair coloring almost as often as she changed her men, had the magic but unfortunately was better known for her troubles than for her talents. A favorite GI pin-up girl, her appeal was primarily ornamental. Born Cora Marie Frye on July 6, 1923, she was the daughter of a former Ziegfeld girl. Starting in 1939, she progressed from Miss New York City to singing with Tommy Dorsey's band, and then to become a Carroll Beauty. Another Carroll Girl, Evelyn Moriarty, roomed with Marie and recalls that Marie would tell people she was star Beryl Wallace's understudy. This not being the case, Beryl was none too happy when she accidentally came early to a rehearsal and found Marie singing her numbers. Carroll dismissed her when, during the radio show that emanated nightly from his club, Marie told orchestra leader Manny Strand that Carroll had given his permission for her to sing with the band, which was not true. Later, signed by Paramount to compete with peekaboo-tressed Veronica Lake, an enterprising press agent dubbed Marie MacDonald "The Body."

When wed to Vic Orsatti, a prominent agent, in 1947 she co-starred with Gene Kelly in the long-forgotten MGM picture *Living in a Big Way*. Marie, who had a sardonic sense of humor, was quoted as saying, "Nobody saw that pic except my mother."

Marie's wit was the talk of the town after she returned from her honeymoon with Vic in Hawaii. When asked how she liked the romantic atmosphere of the tropical isles in the blue Pacific, she replied, "Lousy—there's nothing to do at night."

Finally free of Orsatti and MGM, she embarked on her stormy marriage to Harry Karl. From then on, her career seemed dominated more by scandal than by cinematic achievement. A kidnapping (suspected of being a hoax—the alleged abductor turned out to be an old boyfriend) was highlighted in the press with her explicit testimony that she "had to hide her jewels [ring and bracelet] to prevent being robbed." *Where* she hid them and how they stayed up there amazed everybody in town, including her gynecologist.

On October 21, 1965, Marie MacDonald died from an overdose of drugs.

Fun-loving Lois Andrews followed in the true tradition of the *Lolita* myth. Born Lorraine Gourley on March 24, 1924, she was a likeable Huntington Park kid who paraded at Earl Carroll's after classes at Hollywood High. At her "sweet sixteen" birthday party she announced her engagement to George Jessel, forty-four, and married him three weeks later in Detroit while appearing in vaudeville with "Jessel and His Hollywood Stars" (the others were Jean Parker, Rochelle Hudson, Isabel Jewell, Lya Lys, and Steffi Duna). Her lush curves and photogenic face made her a favorite with the news media. She landed a 20th Century–Fox contract and the title role in *Dixie Dugan* (1942). A Betty Grable vehicle, *Meet Me After the Show* (1951), produced by ex-husband Jessel, was her last picture. At the time of her death from lung cancer on March 4, 1968, she was married to her fourth husband, army officer Leonard Kleckner.

There were others whose lives ended in tragedy: leggy Elinor Troy, after her Carroll stint, went into *The Harvey Girls* at MGM. It was during the filming of this picture that she first took ill; she was bedridden for four years and died of tuberculosis. . . . Dorothy Abbott worked at Paramount, was a Columbia *Petty Girl* and then Jack Webb's girl friend on the *Dragnet* TV series. She committed suicide in 1968. . . . Jeanette Gray Mack took her life with an overdose of barbituates at only 22 in 1946. . . . The mysterious disappearance of pretty Jean Spangler was first noted when she failed to report for work at Carroll's. No trace of her body has ever been found, and the case, like that of the famous Black Dahlia, remains unsolved in the Los Angeles police files. . . .

There were, of course, innumerable other beauties during the Earl Carroll reign: statuesque and raven-haired girls such as Marilyn Watts, who liked Corday perfume, became Mara Corday. She had secondary roles at Universal as in *Foxfire*, but the studio never developed her Ava Gardner quality. Widowed by actor Richard Long, she's now resuming her career. . . .

Wanda Perry and Anya Taranda were among the 11 showgirls Carroll took to Hollywood to appear in *Murder at the Vanities*. Wanda did bits at MGM and Fox; Anya became a Goldwyn Girl, an MGM *Ziegfeld Girl*, the wife of eminent composer Harold Arlen. . . . Carole Matthews, born Jean Francis, came from Montgomery, Illinois, was signed by Columbia and featured mostly in westerns, and is now in real estate. . . .

Platinum Diane Mumby signed with Paramount, later became a Goldwyn Girl (*Up In Arms*). She was an interior decorator when she died in 1974. . . . Vivian Coe was handmaiden to Maria Montez in Universal Pictures as Vivian Austin. She later changed her name to Terry Austin, married, and is now living in Palm Springs. . . . Peggy Pryer stayed at Earl Carroll's through many house changes; she is now divorced from actor Paul Burke. . . .

Delightful Evelyn Moriarty was George Cukor's protege, groomed by famed drama coach Gertrude Vogeler at MGM. At Cukor's, she met Garson Kanin and Ruth Gordon, who were charmed by her wacky sense of humor. Evelyn is considered by many to be the prototype for the ex-showgirl Billie Dawn character from their *Born Yesterday*. Sent to New York on a publicity tour for Earl Carroll's, she met Walter Winchell. At the time, Winchell and Carroll were feuding. She sent Carroll a wire: "Dear Boss, Here I am sitting at the Stork Club with Walter Winchell—That's more than you can do." During her stint at Carroll's, Evelyn was a publicity man's dream. She was then Marilyn Monroe's stand-in and now works for Ann-Margaret. . . .

Pretty June Nicholson used to bring her young brother—a fat Irish kid—backstage for rehearsals. At the time he was a mail boy in the cartoon department of MGM making $30 a week. In the year 1976, the same Jack Nicholson won the coveted Oscar for his brilliant performance in *One Flew Over The Cuckoo's Nest*. . . . Myrna Dell, whose real name was Marilyn Dunlap, was signed by RKO. They had big plans for her, but when the Hughes regime took over she was dropped, even after giving a credible performance in *Nocturne*. Myrna's mother was silent-film actress Carol Price.

Yolanda Donlan had great success on the British stage in *Born Yesterday*, settled in England, and married director Val Guest. . . . Beverly Carroll, niece of Carroll, wed Academy Award–winning composer Lionel Newman, now head of 20th Century–Fox music dept. . . . Virginia Cruzon, a girl who resembled Hedy Lamarr, transferred from Carroll's to the *Blackouts*, was a Goldwyn Girl (*Up In Arms*), and now lives in San Francisco. . . . Peggy Satterlee, in addition to gaining notoriety in the Flynn case, was a harem girl in *Arabian Nights*. . . .

A Carroll favorite, Sandy Donlan, became Laura Elliott, one of Paramount's Golden Circle. She co-starred in *The Denver and the Rio Grande* and had the plum role of Miriam in Hitchcock's *Strangers On a Train* (1951). As Kasey Rogers, she appeared as Barbara Parkins's mother on TV's *Peyton Place*, and later was a regular on *Bewitched*. . . . Kerry Vaughn was a "Salome" girl at Universal in *Salome, Where She Danced*. At Carroll's she used the name of Carol West, and later she danced in many MGM musicals. . . .

Marilyn Buford pulled a switch; she left Earl Carroll's and went on to become Miss America of 1946. A brief MGM contract followed, then Europe and starring roles in *The Wayward Wife* and *Adorable Creatures*. Jan Harrison had a successful modeling career, co-starred with Ben Johnson in *Fort Bowie* (1958), and is now in real estate. . . . Helen O'Hara and Dorothy Ford became two of the "Glamazons," tall showgirls featured by MGM in *Bathing Beauty* (1944). Helen was the daughter of artist Henry Clive. Dorothy was romanced by Mickey Rooney in *Love Laughs at Andy Hardy* (1946), later had roles in *On Our Merry Way*, *Three Godfathers*, *The Seven Year Itch*, and others. . . . Sandra Jolly was the first wife of Forrest Tucker, and was wed to Jack Carson at the time of his death in 1963. . . . Pokie Noonan is the widow of Tommy Noonan. . . .

Doris Houck and Patti McCarty were pacted by Columbia. Doris became Doris Colleen; she had the second lead in *Cigarette Girl*. Patti was in *Blondie Goes To College*, *Isle of Forgotten Sins*, and *Bluebeard;* later she became Martha Raye's secretary. . . . Virginia Maples had a stock 20th pact, and now has a boutique in Fort Lauderdale, Florida. . . . Fun-loving Alta Mae Stone built a reputation as a Mexico City playgirl. . . . Exotic Beverly Thompson made headlines when she refused to marry 11-times wed Tommy Manville. And with all of them Carroll never missed a bet for publicity. When Judith Woodbury married restaurant owner Jack Dennison, Carroll arranged for the wedding on stage during a performance. But the applause didn't last. Dennison went on to marry Dorothy Dandridge and Judith is now happily married. . . .

Others who caught the brass ring: Pretty Gloria Lynn married to Carroll's official lensman, Gene Lester, who is still one of Hollywood's most successful photographers and film producers; Barbara MacDonald married to James Fleming, chairman of the board of Mars Candy; Marie Cubitt to the district attorney of Sparks, Nevada; her sister Florence Cubitt to a Mexico City industrialist; Marie Allyson to jazz great Buddy Rich; June Ealey to Bob Wiener of the Bob's Big Boy chain; Caprice Capron, first wed to writer Philip Yordon, is now wed to Andre Badrutt, the owner of the Palace Hotel in St. Moritz, Switzerland; Joy Barlow to restaurant owner Bill Story; Wanda Barbour to Warner Brothers casting executive Hoyt Bowers; Dardy Moffett to showman Harold Minsky, and her sister Barbara Moffett to millionaire toymaker Louis Marx—both are the younger sisters of famed Lili St. Cyr.

Claire James won the title Miss California in 1938, but failed to become Miss America that year. Carroll, as one of the judges, vehemently disagreed; at a well-publicized press conference in New York he declared her the people's choice and crowned Claire James the real Miss America. Busby Berkeley chose her as the girl Tony Martin sang "You Stepped Out of a Dream" to in MGM's *Ziegfeld Girl* (1941). Berkeley and Claire married the same year. At Warner Brothers, she replaced Alexis Smith as one of the Navy Blues Sextette Girls when Miss Smith was assigned to *Dive Bomber* opposite Errol Flynn. Producer Mark Hellinger directed her test at Fox, where she remained under contract for six years. She was recently in Columbia's *The Black Bird*. . . .

They were all among the hundreds of beauties who passed through those famous portals.

But with the spectacular career of Earl Carroll brought to a dramatic and tragic climax, in the final years of the 1950s the historic club closed. The plush, lush days of the past were gone forever. The decline of the nightclub business ended simultaneously with the fall of the star system.

Today it is difficult to comprehend the girls' popularity, if only because looks no longer mark a beginning, but at one period the prestige of being an Earl Carroll Beauty opened many doors.

Although the press have long neglected the girls, they, like "Daddy" Carroll, were most certainly a part of an incredible era of theatrical history.

Index

ABOUT THE AUTHOR

Ken Murray, a six-foot-one bundle of restless energy and theatrical hoopla, is one of those rare men whose vigor and talent have brought him success in a variety of fields.

Probably his most cherished recognition was in 1947 when he received the coveted Oscar from the Academy of Motion Picture Arts and Sciences for producing the first feature-length all-bird picture, "Bill and Coo."

His voluminous collection of personal movies—candid snapshots of the stars—has provided material for several TV specials and a film on San Simeon now being shown to the 1,000,000 tourists who visit this world-famed estate each year.

Drawing from this priceless film library, Ken Murray's newest venture is a full-length feature picture for movie theatres called "Great Time To Be Alive." It will tell the intimate story of Movietown's greatest era, from the advent of talking pictures to the threat of the television age.

Throughout his career, Ken Murray has received many awards: among them, in 1951, the first Freedom Foundation Award ever given a TV program; in 1963, the Will Rogers Memorial Award as Entertainer of the Year; in 1973, the Edwin Booth Award, the highest honor bestowed by the Salvation Army. In 1971, he was selected by the United States Information Agency to join such illustrious personages as Dr. Michael DeBakey and Neil Armstrong in their special "One Man" series, which was translated into 37 different languages and will play to three billion people within the next ten years.

Ken Murray first gained fame as one of the great comedy stars of vaudeville and gave it a memorable shot in the arm in June, 1942 when he opened his Hollywood "Blackouts" at the El Capitan Theatre. The show ran for seven and a half years and holds the world's record as the longest-playing production in the legitimate theatre, 3844 performances.

Previously, he had moved interchangeably through every facet of show business—radio, television, motion pictures, the Las Vegas scene, including starring at the Winter Garden on Broadway in Earl Carroll's Sketch Book *of 1935. His experiences working with the notorious and colorful Mr. Earl Carroll prompted Murray to gather material through the years for this book,* The Body Merchant.

Born in New York City, Ken Murray has lived in Beverly Hills for the last 40 years. He has two sons, Ken, Jr. and Cort. He and his wife, Bette Lou, have two daughters. Their youngest, Janie, just graduated from Occidental College and is following in her father's footsteps, currently a member of the Tyrone Guthrie Repertory Company in Minneapolis. Their married daughter, Pam, recently blessed them with their first granddaughter, Kelli Ann.

He is the author of two previous best-selling books, Life On A Pogo Stick *and* The Golden Days of San Simeon.